HOW TO READ AND WRITE IN COLLEGE

Reading / Writing / Editing

SECOND SERIES
Form 2

Richard H. Dodge

Santa Monica College

Sponsoring Editor: Phillip Leininger
Project Editor: Donna DeBenedictis
Text Design: Betty L. Sokol
Cover Design: Karen Salsgiver
Production: Delia Tedoff
Compositor: ComCom Division of Haddon Craftsmen, Inc.
Printed and bound by Malloy Lithographing, Inc.

HOW TO READ AND WRITE IN COLLEGE:
Reading/Writing/Editing,
Second Series, Form 2

Library of Congress Cataloging-in-Publication Data
Dodge, Richard H.
How to read and write in college.

Includes index.
1. English language—Grammar—1950- . 2. College readers. I. Title.
PE1112.D6 1986 808'.0427 85-17637
ISBN 0-06-041665-3

94 9 8

ACKNOWLEDGMENTS

I gratefully acknowledge the following authors and publishers for allowing us to reprint their materials.

p. 4: "Dad" by Andrew H. Malcolm, *The New York Times Magazine* (About Men), January 8, 1984. Copyright © 1984 by the New York Times Company. Reprinted by permission.

p. 7: "Competition" by Nancy Friday. Excerpted from the book MY MOTHER/MY SELF by Nancy Friday. Copyright © 1977 by Nancy Friday. Reprinted by permission of DELACORTE PRESS.

p. 12: "Doc Marlowe" by James Thurber. Copyright © 1937 by James Thurber. Copyright © 1965 by Helen W. Thurber and Rosemary T. Sauers. From LET YOUR MIND ALONE, published by Harper & Row.

p. 17: "The Teacher as Dragon" by Anna Tuttle Villegas, *California Living Magazine,* January 23, 1983. Reprinted with permission from *California Living Magazine* of the *San Francisco Sunday Examiner and Chronicle.* Copyright 1983, *San Francisco Examiner.*

p. 22: "Loving County, Texas" by Larry L. King. Excerpt from "The Last Frontier" from THE OLD MAN AND LESSER MORTALS by Larry King. Copyright © 1972 by Larry King. Reprinted by permission of Viking Penguin, Inc.

p. 25: "The Crooked Wood" by Edward Abbey. From THE JOURNEY HOME, copyright © 1977 by Edward Abbey. Reprinted by permission of the publisher, E. P. Dutton, Inc.

p. 28: "In the Neighborhood" by Joseph Epstein. From *Familiar Territory: Observations on American Life* by Joseph Epstein. Copyright © 1979 by Joseph Epstein. Reprinted by permission of Oxford University Press, Inc.

p. 32: "The Use of Sidewalks" by Jane Jacobs. From THE DEATH AND LIFE OF GREAT AMERICAN CITIES, by Jane Jacobs. Copyright © 1961 by Jane Jacobs. Reprinted by permission of Random House, Inc.

p. 38: "Living with Jellinek's Disease" by Kathleen Whalen FitzGerald, *Newsweek,* October 17, 1983 (My Turn). Copyright 1983, by Newsweek, Inc. All rights reserved. Reprinted by permission.

p. 41: "Grant and Lee: A Study in Contrasts" by Bruce Catton, from *The American Story,* Earl Schenck Miers, editor. © 1956 by Broadcast Music, Inc. Reprinted by permission.

p. 45: "On Being a Mess" by Elizabeth Ames, *Newsweek,* July 7, 1980. Copyright 1980, by Newsweek, Inc. All rights reserved. Reprinted by permission.

p. 48: "The Plot Against People" by Russell Baker. Copyright © 1968 by The New York Times Company. Reprinted by permission.

p. 52: "Coon Hunt" by E. B. White. Pp. 267–273 from ONE MAN'S MEAT: A New and Enlarged Edition by E. B. White. Copyright 1943 by E. B. White. Reprinted by permission of Harper & Row, Publishers, Inc.

p. 57: "Champion of the World" by Maya Angelou. From I KNOW WHY THE CAGED BIRD SINGS, by Maya Angelou. Copyright © 1969 by Maya Angelou. Reprinted by permission of Random House, Inc.

p. 60: "Duel at Red River" by Marquis James. From THE LIFE OF ANDREW JACKSON, copyright © 1938, by Marquis James, used with permission of the publisher, The Bobbs-Merrill Company, Inc.

p. 64: "38 Who Saw Murder Didn't Call the Police" by Martin Gansberg, *The New York Times,* March 17, 1964. Copyright © 1964 by The New York Times Company. Reprinted by permission.

p. 69: "Massachusetts Drivers: Heels on Wheels" by Caskie Stinnett, *The Atlantic Monthly,* October 1978. Copyright © 1978 by Caskie Stinnett. Reprinted by permission of the author.

p. 73: "Driving for Dear Life" by Robert C. Wurmstedt. Copyright 1980 Time Inc. All rights reserved. Reprinted by permission from TIME.

p. 77: "On-the-Job Training" by Harvey J. Fields, *The New York Times Magazine* (About Men), January 1, 1984. Copyright © 1984 by The New York Times Company. Reprinted by permission.

p. 81: "It's Getting Hard to Ride the Gravy Boat" by Enid Nemy, *The New York Times Magazine,* January 8, 1984. Copyright © 1984 by The New York Times Company. Reprinted by permission.

p. 85: "Farewell to Fitness" by Mike Royko, *Chicago Sun-Times,* July 11, 1980. © News Group Chicago, Inc., 1980. Column by Mike Royko. Reprinted with the permission of the *Chicago Sun-Times.*

p. 88: "Who Cares about the Renaissance?" by Leslie S. P. Brown, *Newsweek,* April 11, 1983. Copyright 1983, by Newsweek, Inc. All rights reserved. Reprinted by permission.

p. 91: "Strike Out Little League" by Robin Roberts, *Newsweek,* 1975.

p. 94: "A Comeback for Commitment" by Linda Bird Francke. © 1978 by American Heritage Publishing Co., Inc. Reprinted by permission from HORIZON (September, 1978).

CONTENTS

PREFACE

This book is for college students who must learn to plan and write acceptable college examinations; it can help them to achieve reasonable mastery of spelling, usage, sentence structure, and conventional punctuation. It can also help them to do close, critical reading and analysis of modern expository prose.

And this book is for their instructors, who must teach large classes efficiently—rapidly reviewing fundamentals, systematically teaching essential skills, and fairly judging student achievement. It is the result of years of experience with the large classes that almost inevitably result from limited budgets and increasing enrollments.

For both students and teachers, *How to Read and Write in College* is a complete, economical, and convenient text. It is two books in one cover: an anthology of contemporary essays and articles, and a workbook of English fundamentals. This combination results in an obvious economy, but it also results in even greater convenience. Students need not carry two or more books to every class, and their teachers need not fear that many students will come to class carrying "the wrong book." Both students and teachers will appreciate the convenience of being able to move easily from anthology to workbook, from analysis of readings to exercises in the mechanics of English. The essential content of a unified course is all in one book.

The anthology is a collection of modern essays of more than usual literary value. Although all the readings are on subjects of current interest, they are arranged by rhetorical types so that they may be more easily incorporated into a class in English composition. Each essay is followed by exercises calling for understanding of vocabulary, form, and content, and each essay is followed by suggestions for writing and discussion.

These suggestions avoid the obviousness and emptiness of suggested titles like "My Summer Job" or "An Interesting Character." By including both easy and difficult assignments, the suggestions for writing and discussion challenge students to answer specific questions, to relate their reading to their own experience, and to write purposeful and thoughtful papers.

The workbook is a straightforward presentation of functional grammar, common sentence structure problems, troublesome points of usage, and conventional punctuation. It is conservative because it retains the content and terminology of conventional grammatical analysis, with which most students have some familiarity. It is modern because it is not dogmatic in matters of colloquial expressions or disputable language. It is efficient because it contains exercises that have been class tested and edited to avoid ambiguity or awkwardness that might obscure understanding of basic principles.

This book, together with the tests and teaching aids that accompany it, has been designed to give instructors assistance in teaching a necessary and difficult course. But it does nothing to limit their freedom to adapt the content of the course to the special requirements of a particular class. Although the book contains the materials for a complete first course in English, it does not necessarily impose its own organization upon that course. Every essay in the anthology and every section of the workbook text is independent of the rest of the book and may be introduced or omitted as the need or progress of a particular class dictates.

This new edition of *How to Read and Write in College, Second Series, Form 2,* is actually a new conception, carefully revised to incorporate suggestions from scores of college teachers

—both from colleagues and from generous correspondents in distant institutions. The anthology now precedes the workbook, not merely to incorporate the order of the book's title but also to encourage early consideration of rhetorical principles useful in both professional and student writing. A new section ("Which/Definition and Relationship") has been added to the anthology to provide materials for discussions of definition, classification, comparison, and contrast. The workbook now contains not only a carefully revised text but also many new exercises that have been printed in short units, prepared with greater variety of questions, and provided with answers in the back of the book. New exercises, called "Using Editing Skills," simulate—in simplified form—the kind of editing and revision students must learn to do when writing their own papers.

In preparing this new series of *How to Read and Write in College,* the author has received generous help from his colleagues in the English department of Santa Monica College, as well as from users of the book in many other communities and states. He is particularly indebted to Corinne Ising Dodge, who helped in the preparation of all phases of the manuscript; to the staffs of both the Santa Monica College Library and the UCLA Research Library; and to other directors of the UCLA/Santa Monica Writing Project for their assistance and encouragement.

Richard H. Dodge

PART ONE

How to Read in College

To succeed in any college work, you must learn to read efficiently. This means, first of all, that you must adapt your approach to the demands of the text and to your purpose in reading it. Some articles, like those found in newspapers prominently displayed at supermarket check-out stands, are little more than gossip, worth no more than casual attention, if that. Some fiction, similarly, is mass produced for easy entertainment and may be quickly read and quickly forgotten. But most of the material that you read in college courses is more challenging, more difficult, and more valuable.

The essays in this book vary in difficulty and purpose. But they are all, with few exceptions, the work of highly skilled professional writers expert in the exposition and development of facts and ideas. They are grouped in sections to facilitate comparison of techniques of description, definition, classification, narration, exposition, and argument. All of them, even the few that are lighthearted satire, whimsy, or burlesque, can repay careful attention.

In reading any college material in the humanities, social sciences, or fine arts, you are well advised to make a quick survey of the whole text in order to get an overall view of the author's subject, attitudes, and organization of the material. Good students beginning a new term frequently pick up an assigned textbook in economics, sociology, or psychology, for example, and read the preface or introduction, examine the table of contents, and then spend an afternoon or evening skimming through the whole book, paying particular attention to section headings, introductions, and conclusions, skipping lightly over material too complex or difficult for easy comprehension, but quickly getting a perspective on the subjects and problems presented. (This quick survey, obviously, is less practical if the text is one on calculus, physics, or chemistry, in which the development is frequently strictly sequential, with understanding of each chapter possible only after mastery of what has preceded it.)

In reading a brief essay, similarly, first read it quickly and alertly both to enjoy it and to identify its central idea and method of development or argument. Then reread it more slowly, making certain that you understand all of its vocabulary as well as key phrases and ideas. Finally, because you are working to improve your own writing, pay particular attention to introductory and concluding paragraphs, to development of description or argument, to the technique of definition or classification, and to the use of figurative language, anecdotes, dialogue, and transitional devices. Good writing begins with careful reading.

Finally, and probably most important, you must react to what you read—agree or disagree, like or dislike, reject or pursue further—for from this reaction will come the greater breadth of knowledge and feeling that is the most valuable result of a college education.

WHO

Character and Personality

A young boy's first lesson on the art of the firm handshake, an evening dress purposely ruined by a jealous sister, 2,000 advertising brochures dramatizing life in the Wild West, and a pair of beady eyes behind thick-lensed spectacles—these are significant details that influence and reveal character.

In the four essays printed here, four different authors describe the birth-to-death cycle of a father-son relationship, the emotional crosscurrents of a young woman's adolescence, an eccentric character who was both a lovable liar and a charming cheat, and an English teacher who was caricatured as a dragon lady with red hair.

Just as few experiences can be more important to a person than his or her relationships with other people, so few kinds of writing can be more challenging than biography and autobiography; the short essays printed here are excellent examples of both forms.

Dad

Andrew H. Malcolm

A working journalist, Andrew H. Malcolm is currently chief of The New York Times *Chicago bureau.*

Malcolm's moving memoir of his father focuses on two parts of the father-son relationship: the early years when the family lived together, and the later years after the author had established a life of his own. Through a series of anecdotes, arranged chronologically like a photograph album, Malcolm discusses his growing up and the role his dad played in the process; the second half concentrates on some bittersweet memories of the later years of the author's father. Note the effective use of quotations, the close attention to details, and the touching final scene of the sketch.

1. The first memory I have of him—of anything, really—is his strength. It was in the late afternoon in a house under construction near ours. The unfinished wood floor had large, terrifying holes whose yawning darkness I knew led to nowhere good. His powerful hands, then age 33, wrapped all the way around my tiny arms, then age 4, and easily swung me up to his shoulders to command all I surveyed.

2. The relationship between a son and his father changes over time. It may grow and flourish in mutual maturity. It may sour in resented dependence or independence. With many children living in single-parent homes today, it may not even exist.

3. But to a little boy right after World War II, a father seemed a god with strange strengths and uncanny powers enabling him to do and know things that no mortal could do or know. Amazing things, like putting a bicycle chain back on, just like that. Or building a hamster cage. Or guiding a jigsaw so it formed the letter F; I learned the alphabet that way in those pretelevision days, one letter or number every other evening plus a review of the collection. (The vowels we painted red because they were special somehow.)

4. He even seemed to know what I thought before I did. "You look like you could use a cheeseburger and chocolate shake," he would say on hot Sunday afternoons. When, at the age of 5, I broke a neighbor's garage window with a wild curve ball and waited in fear for 10 days to make the announcement, he seemed to know about it already and to have been waiting for something.

5. There were, of course, rules to learn. First came the handshake. None of those fishy little finger grips, but a good firm squeeze accompanied by an equally strong gaze into the other's eyes. "The first thing anyone knows about you is your handshake," he would say. And we'd practice it each night on his return from work, the serious toddler in the battered Cleveland Indian cap running up to the giant father to shake hands again and again until it was firm enough.

6. When my cat killed a bird, he defused the anger of a 9-year-old with a little chat about something called "instinked." The next year, when my dog got run over and the weight of sorrow was just too immense to stand, he was there, too, with his big arms and his own tears and some thoughts on the natural order of life and death, although what was natural about a speeding car that didn't stop always escaped me.

7. As time passed, there were other rules to learn. "Always do your best." "Do it now." "NEVER LIE!" And, most importantly, "You can do whatever you have to do." By my teens, he wasn't telling me what to do anymore, which was scary and heady at the same time. He provided perspective, not telling me what was around the great corner of life but letting me know there was a lot more than just today and the next, which I hadn't thought of.

8. When the most important girl in the world —I forget her name now—turned down a movie date, he just happened to walk by the kitchen phone. "This may be hard to believe right now," he said, "but someday you won't even remember her name."

9. One day, I realize now, there was a change. I wasn't trying to please him so much as I was trying to impress him. I never asked him to come to my football games. He had a high-pressure career, and it meant driving through most of Friday night. But for all the big games, when I looked over at the sideline, there was that familiar fedora. And, by God, did the opposing team captain ever get a firm handshake and a gaze he would remember.

10. Then, a school fact contradicted something he said. Impossible that he could be wrong, but there it was in the book. These accumulated over time, along with personal experiences, to buttress my own developing sense of values. And I could tell we had each taken our own, perfectly normal paths.

11. I began to see, too, his blind spots, his prejudices and his weaknesses. I never threw these up at him. He hadn't to me, and, anyway, he seemed to need protection. I stopped asking his advice; the experiences he drew from no longer seemed relevant to the decisions I had to make. On the phone, he would go on about politics at times, why he would vote the way he did or why some incumbent was a jerk. And I would roll my eyes to the ceiling and smile a little, though I hid it in my voice.

12. He volunteered advice for a while. But then, in more recent years, politics and issues gave way to talk of empty errands and, always, to ailments—his friends', my mother's and his own, which were serious and included heart disease. He had a bedside oxygen tank, and he would ostentatiously retire there during my visits, asking my help in easing his body onto the mattress. "You have very strong arms," he once noted.

13. From his bed, he showed me the many sores and scars on his misshapen body and all the bottles for medicine. He talked of the pain and craved much sympathy. He got some. But the scene was not attractive. He told me, as the doctor had, that his condition would only deteriorate. "Sometimes," he confided, "I would just like to lie down and go to sleep and not wake up."

14. After much thought and practice ("You can do whatever you have to do."), one night last winter, I sat down by his bed and remembered for an instant those terrifying dark holes in another house 35 years before. I told my father how much I loved him. I described all the things people were doing for him. But, I said, he kept eating poorly, hiding in his room and violating other doctor's orders. No amount of love could make someone else care about life, I said; it was a two-way street. He wasn't doing his best. The decision was his.

15. He said he knew how hard my words had been to say and how proud he was of me. "I had the best teacher," I said. "You can do whatever you have to do." He smiled a little. And we shook hands, firmly, for the last time.

16. Several days later, at about 4 A.M., my mother heard Dad shuffling about their dark room. "I have some things I have to do," he said. He paid a bundle of bills. He composed for my mother a long list of legal and financial what-to-do's "in case of emergency." And he wrote me a note.

17. Then he walked back to his bed and laid himself down. He went to sleep, naturally. And he did not wake up.

WORDS

What is the meaning of the italicized words in the following phrases?

1. "*uncanny* powers" (par. 3)
2. "which was scary and *heady*" (par. 7)
3. "that familiar *fedora*" (par. 9)
4. "to *buttress* my own developing sense of values" (par. 10)
5. "some *incumbent* was a jerk" (par. 11)
6. "he would *ostentatiously* retire" (par. 12)
7. "condition would only *deteriorate*" (par. 13)

FORM AND CONTENT

1. Is this memoir about a father, a son, or both men? Explain your answer.
2. Andrew Malcolm divides his essay into two distinct parts: paragraphs 1–8 and 9–17. What is his purpose in part 1? What function does sentence 1 in paragraph 9 serve? What is his purpose in part 2?
3. Explain the particular function of paragraph 2.
4. A firm handshake was the first "rule" taught by the father (par. 5). Cite and explain the effectiveness of two other handshake references in later paragraphs.
5. Although Malcolm's essay is sentimental, it is not without humor. Cite humorous details in paragraphs 6 and 8.

SUGGESTIONS FOR WRITING AND DISCUSSION

1. Write a sketch of a particular person, other than a family member, who has played an important role in your life. Use details to reveal his or her influence on your life and personality.
2. Describe in detail what constitutes an ideal parent. What specific characteristics would he or she have?
3. Describe a childhood experience in which you lied in order to save your skin, only to have your "crime" discovered by a parent or guardian.
4. Malcolm observes that the relationship between a son and his father changes over time. Discuss the changes that have occurred in your relationship with one of your parents or guardians. Begin with a description of the other person and then describe the nature of your changing relationship.
5. What kind of person amuses you? Antagonizes you? Disgusts you? Stirs your sympathy? Or rouses your admiration? Describe that person and discuss why he or she has this effect on you.

Competition

Nancy Friday

Nancy Friday is a journalist, an author, and a feminist. Her best-seller, My Mother/Myself, *is the source of the essay which follows.*

Beginning when she is a tall, awkward twelve year old, Friday introduces the reader to three generations of her family as she shares some intimate memories of her disturbed adolescence. She was two people. On the surface she was a popular, competitive young woman, the apple of her grandfather's eye. But secretly she was jealous and spiteful. While concentrating on her inner life, Friday describes her own motivations as well as those of the characters who participate in various family rivalries.

1. Although I didn't realize it at the time, my mother was getting prettier. My sister was a beauty. My adolescence was the time of our greatest estrangement.

2. I have a photo of the three of us when I was twelve: my mother, my sister, Susie, and I, on a big chintz sofa, each on a separate cushion, leaning away from one another with big spaces in between. I grew up fired with a sense of family spirit, which I loved and needed, with aunts and uncles and cousins under the omnipotent umbrella of my grandfather. "All for one and one for all," he would say at summer reunions, and no one took it more seriously than I. I would have gone to war for any one of them, and believed they would do the same for me. But within our own little nucleus, the three of us didn't touch much.

3. Now, when I ask her why, my mother sighs and says she supposes it was because that was how she was raised. I remember shrinking from her Elizabeth Arden night-cream kiss, mumbling from under the blanket that yes, I had brushed my teeth. I had not. I had wet the toothbrush in case she felt it, feeling that would get even with her. For what? The further we all get from childhood, the more physically affectionate we try to be with one another. But we are still shy after all these years.

4. I was a late bloomer, like my mother. But my mother bloomed so late, or had such a penetrating early frost, that she believed it even less than I would in my turn. When she was a freckled sixteen and sitting shyly on her unfortunate hands, her younger sister was already a famous beauty. That is still the relationship between them. Grandmothers both, in their eyes my aunt is still the sleek-haired belle of the ball, immaculately handsome on a horse. My mother's successes do not count. They will argue at 2:00 A.M. over whether one of my aunt's many beaux ever asked my mother out. My mother could never make up a flattering story about herself. I doubt that she so much as heard the nice things men told her once she had grown into the fine-looking woman who smiles at me in family photos. But she always gives in to my aunt, much I'm sure as she gave in to the old self-image after my father died. He—that one splendidly handsome man—may have picked her out from all the rest, but his death just a few years later must have felt like some punishment for having dared to believe for a moment that her father was wrong: who could possibly want her? She still blushes at a compliment.

5. I think she was at her prettiest in her early thirties. I was twelve and at my nadir. Her hair had gone a delicate auburn red and she wore it brushed back from her face in soft curls. Seated beside her and Susie, who inherited a raven version of her beautiful hair, I look like an adopted person. But I had already defended myself against my looks. They were unimportant. There was a distance between me and the mirror commensurate with the growing distance between me and my mother and sister. My success with my made-up persona was proof: I didn't need them. My titles at school, my awards and achievements, so bolstered my image of myself that until writing this book I genuinely believed that I grew up feeling sorry for my sister. What chance had she alongside The Great Achiever and Most Popular Girl in the World? I even worked up some guilt about outshining her. Pure survival instinct! My dazzling smile would divert the most critical observer from comparing me to the cute, petite girls with whom I grew up. I switched the contest: don't look at my lank hair, my 5′10″, don't notice that my right eye wanders bizarrely (though the eye doctor said it was useless to keep me in glasses); watch me tap dance, watch me win the game, let me make you happy! When I describe myself in those days my mother laughs. "Oh, Nancy, you were such a darling little girl." But I wasn't little any more.

6. I think my sister, Susie, was born beautiful, a fact that affected my mother and me deeply, though in different ways. I don't think it mattered so much until Susie's adolescence. She turned so lush one ached to look at her. Pictures of Susie then remind me of the young Elizabeth Taylor in *A Place in the Sun.* One has to almost look away from so much beauty. It scared my mother to death. Whatever had gone on between them before came to a head and has never stopped. Their constant friction determined me to get away from this house of women, to be free of women's petty competitions, to live on a bigger scale. I left home eventually but I've never gotten away from feeling how wonderful to be so beautiful your mother can't take her eyes off you, even if only to nag.

7. I remember an amazing lack of any feeling about my only sibling, with whom I shared a room for years, whose clothes were identical to mine until I was ten. Except for feelings of irritation when she tried to cuddle me when I was four, bursts of anger that erupted into fist fights which I started and won at ten, and after that, indifference, a calculated unawareness that has resulted in a terrible and sad absence of my sister in my life.

8. My husband says his sister was the only child his father ever paid any attention to; "You have done to Susie what I did to my sister," he says. "You made her invisible." Me, jealous of Susie, who never won a single trophy or had as many friends as I? I must have been insanely jealous.

9. I only allowed myself to face it twice. Both times happened in that twelfth year, when my usual defenses couldn't take the emotional crosscurrents of adolescence. When I did slash out it wasn't very glorious, no well-chosen words or contest on the tennis courts. I did it like a thief in the night. Nobody ever guessed it was I who poured the red nail polish down the front of Susie's new white eyelet evening dress the day of her first yacht club dance. When I stole her summer savings and threw her wallet down the sewer, mother blamed Susie for being so careless. I watched my sister accept the criticism with her mother's own resignation, and I felt some relief from the angry emotions that had hold of me.

10. When Susie went away to boarding school,

I made jokes about how glad I was to be rid of her. It was our first separation. Conflicting urges, angers, and envies were coming at me from every direction; I had nothing left over to handle my terrible feelings of loss at her going. It was the summer I was plagued by what I called "my thoughts."

11. I read every book in the house as a talisman against thinking. I was afraid that if my brain were left idle for even one minute, these "thoughts" would take over. Perhaps I feared they already had. Was my sister's going away the fulfillment of my own murderous wishes against her? I wrote in my first and only diary: "Susie, come home, please come home!!!!!!! I'm sorry, I'm sorry!!!!!!!"

12. When I outgrew the Nancy Drew books for perfect attendance at Sunday School, and the Girl Scout badges for such merits as selling the most rat poison door to door, I graduated to prizes at the community theater. I won a plastic wake-up radio for the I Speak for Democracy Contest. I was captain of the athletic association, president of the student government, and had the lead in the class play, all in the same year. In fact, I wrote the class play. It might have been embarrassing, but no one else wanted these prizes. Scoring home runs and getting straight A's weren't high on the list of priorities among my friends. (The South takes all prizes for raising noncompetitive women.) In the few cases where anyone did give me a run for the money, I had an unbeatable incentive: my grandfather's applause. It was he for whom I ran.

13. I can't remember ever hearing my grandfather say to my mother, "Well done, Jane." I can't remember my mother ever saying to my sister, "Well done, Susie." And I never gave my mother the chance to say it to me. She was the last to hear of my achievements, and when she did, it was not from me but from her friends. Did she really notice so little that I was leaving her out? Was she so hurt that she pretended not to care? My classmates who won second prize or even no prize at all asked their families to attend the award ceremonies. I, who won first prize, always, did so to the applause of no kin at all. Was I spiting her? I know I was spiting myself. Nothing would have made me happier than to have her there; nothing would induce me to invite her. It is a game I later played with men: "Leave!" I would cry, and when they did, "How could you hurt me so?" I'd implore.

14. If I deprived her of the chance to praise me, she never criticized me. Criticism was the vehicle by which she could articulate her relationship to my sister. No matter what it was, Susie could never get it right—in my mother's eyes. It continues that way to this day. Difficult as it is to think of my mother as competitive with anyone, how else could she have felt about her beautiful, ripe fourteen-year-old daughter? My mother was coming into her own mature, full bloom but perhaps that only made her more sensitive to the fact that Susie was simultaneously experiencing the same sexual flush. A year later, my mother remarried. Today, only the geography has changed: the argument begins as soon as they enter the same room. But they are often in the same room. They have never been closer.

15. How often the dinner table becomes the family battleground. When I met Bill he had no table you could sit around in his vast bachelor apartment. The dinner table was where his father waged war; it was the one time the family was together. In Charleston, dinner was served at 2:00. I have this picture of our midday meals: Susie on my right, mother on my left, and me feeling that our cook, Ruth, had set this beautiful table for me alone.

16. No one else seemed to care about the golden squash, the crisp chicken, the big silver pitcher of iced tea. While I proceeded to eat my way from one end of the table to the other,

Susie and mother would begin: "Susie, that lipstick is too dark. . . . Must you pluck your eyebrows? . . . Why did you buy high-heeled, open-toe shoes when I told you to get loafers? . . . Those pointy bras make you look like a, like a —" But my mother couldn't say the word. At this point one of them would leave the table in tears, while the other shuddered in despair at the sound of the slammed bedroom door. Meanwhile, I pondered my problem of whose house to play at that afternoon. I would finish both their desserts and be gone before Ruth had cleared the table. Am I exaggerating? Did it only happen once a week? Does it matter?

17. I was lucky to have escaped those devastating battles. "I never had to worry about Nancy," my mother has always said. "She could always take care of herself." It became true. Only my husband has been allowed to see the extent of my needs. But the competitive drive that made me so self-sufficient was fired by more than jealousy of my sister. If my mother wasn't going to acknowledge me, her father would. If she couldn't succeed in his eyes, I would. It's my best explanation for all those years of trophies and presidencies, for my ability to "reach" my grandfather as my mother never could. I not only won what she had wanted all her life—his praise—I learned with the canniness of the young that this great towering man loved to be loved, to be touched. He couldn't allow himself to reach out first to those he loved most, but he couldn't resist an overture of affection.

18. I greeted his visits with embraces, took the kisses I had won and sat at his feet like one of his Dalmatians, while my sister stood shyly in the background and my mother waited for his criticism. But I was no more aware of competing with my mother than of being jealous of my sister. Two generations of women in my family have struggled for my grandfather's praise. Perhaps I became his favorite because he sensed I needed it most. The price I paid was that I had to beat my mother and my sister. I am still guilty for that.

19. In the stereotyping of the sexes, men are granted all the competitive drives, women none. The idea of competitive women evokes disturbing images—the darker, dykey side of femininity, or cartoons of "ladies" in high heels, flailing at each other ineffectively with their handbags. An important step has been left out of our socialization: mother raises us to win people's love. She gives us no training in the emotions of rivalry that would lose it for us. With no practical experience in the rules that make competition safe, we fear its ferocity. Never having been taught to win, we do not know how to lose. Women are not raised to compete like gentlemen.

WORDS

What is the meaning of the italicized words in the following phrases?

1. "our greatest *estrangement*" (par. 1)
2. "on a big *chintz* sofa" (par. 2)
3. "the *omnipotent* umbrella" (par. 2)
4. "our own little *nucleus*" (par. 2)
5. "I was twelve and at my *nadir*" (par. 5)
6. "*commensurate* with the growing distance" (par. 5)
7. "my made-up *persona* (par. 5)

8. "eye wanders *bizarrely*" (par. 5)
9. "my only *sibling* (par. 7)
10. "a *talisman* against thinking" (par. 11)

FORM AND CONTENT

1. Who are the three people described in this essay? Is there a fourth significant person?
2. How does the photo (par. 2) sum up the information given in paragraph 1?
3. How does Friday use contrast in paragraphs 4 and 5?
4. Cite two examples of the author's jealousy toward her sister (par. 9). Was she proud of her actions?
5. For whose praise did two generations of the author's family struggle? What important step did Friday's mother leave out of her daughters' process of socialization (par. 19)?

SUGGESTIONS FOR WRITING AND DISCUSSION

1. This essay describes two rivalries: one between two sisters and one between a daughter and a mother. Have you experienced a rivalry with a brother, sister, or parent at any time in your life? If so, describe and explain it.
2. Nancy Friday says that she was least attractive when she was twelve. Was there a time in your life when you were a real "ugly duckling"? When and how did you outgrow this unhappy condition?
3. Have you ever known a person for whom you could never do anything right—a coach, a teacher, a relative? If so, describe him or her in detail and relate the outcome of the conflict.
4. Is there a member of your family—a single parent, a grandparent, an aunt or uncle—whom you have made particular efforts to please? Describe him or her and explain your relationship.
5. "Like a thief in the night" is how the author describes her actions toward her sister: ruining her sister's evening gown and stealing her sister's money, all because of jealousy. Have you ever done or wanted to do similarly spiteful things to a brother, sister, or friend? Confess all and explain.

Doc Marlowe

James Thurber

Long associated with The New Yorker *magazine, James Thurber (1894–1961) was one of America's best loved writers and considered by many our finest twentieth-century literary humorist.*

In his sketch of the character and personality of the lovable rascal, Doc Marlowe, Thurber pieces together a series of personal anecdotes, some revealing Doc's good side and some his bad. These are presented in chronological order and cover Thurber's recollections from age eleven to sixteen. Through quoted material, the author allows the reader to hear Doc, his manner of speaking, and the words he utters when he gets excited. Although Thurber is aware of and infuriated by some of Doc's actions, he proudly describes the special impact that Doc had on his life.

1. I was too young to be other than awed and puzzled by Doc Marlowe when I knew him. I was only sixteen when he died. He was sixty-seven. There was that vast difference in our ages and there was a vaster difference in our backgrounds. Doc Marlowe was a medicine-show man. He had been a lot of other things, too: a circus man, the proprietor of a concession at Coney Island, a saloon-keeper; but in his fifties he had traveled around with a tent-show troupe made up of a Mexican named Chick-alilli, who threw knives, and a man called Professor Jones, who played the banjo. Doc Marlowe would come out after the entertainment and harangue the crowd and sell bottles of medicine for all kinds of ailments. I found out all this about him gradually, toward the last, and after he died. When I first knew him, he represented the Wild West to me, and there was nobody I admired so much.

2. I met Doc Marlowe at old Mrs. Willoughby's rooming house. She had been a nurse in our family, and I used to go and visit her over week-ends sometimes, for I was very fond of her. I was about eleven years old then. Doc Marlowe wore scarred leather leggings, a bright-colored bead vest that he said he got from the Indians, and a ten-gallon hat with kitchen matches stuck in the band, all the way around. He was about six feet four inches tall, with big shoulders, and a long, drooping mustache. He let his hair grow long, like General Custer's. He had a wonderful collection of Indian relics and six-shooters, and he used to tell me stories of his adventures in the Far West. His favorite expressions were "Hay, boy!" and "Hay, boy-gie!," which he used the way some people now use "Hot dog!" or "Doggone!" He told me once that he had killed an Indian chief named Yellow Hand in a tomahawk duel on horseback. I thought he was the greatest man I had ever seen. It wasn't until he died and his son came on from New Jersey for the funeral that I found out he had never been in the Far West in his life. He had been born in Brooklyn.

3. Doc Marlowe had given up the road when

I knew him, but he still dealt in what he called "medicines." His stock in trade was a liniment that he had called Snake Oil when he traveled around. He changed the name to Blackhawk Liniment when he settled in Columbus. Doc didn't always sell enough of it to pay for his bed and board, and old Mrs. Willoughby would sometimes have to "trust" him for weeks at a time. She didn't mind, because his liniment had taken a bad kink out of her right limb that had bothered her for thirty years. I used to see people whom Doc had massaged with Blackhawk Liniment move arms and legs that they hadn't been able to move before he "treated" them. His patients were day laborers, wives of streetcar conductors, and people like that. Sometimes they would shout and weep after Doc had massaged them, and several got up and walked around who hadn't been able to walk before. One man hadn't turned his head to either side for seven years before Doc soused him with Blackhawk. In half an hour he could move his head as easily as I could move mine. "Glory be to God!" he shouted. "It's the secret qualities in the ointment, my friend," Doc Marlowe told him, suavely. He always called the liniment ointment.

4. News of his miracles got around by word of mouth among the poorer classes of town—he was not able to reach the better people (the "tony folks," he called them)—but there was never a big enough sale to give Doc a steady income. For one thing, people thought there was more magic in Doc's touch than in his liniment, and, for another, the ingredients of Blackhawk cost so much that his profits were not very great. I know, because I used to go to the wholesale chemical company once in a while for him and buy his supplies. Everything that went into the liniment was standard and expensive (and well-known, not secret). A man at the company told me he didn't see how Doc could make much money on it at thirty-five cents a bottle. But even when he was very low in funds Doc never cut out any of the ingredients or substituted cheaper ones. Mrs. Willoughby had suggested it to him once, she told me, when she was helping him "put up a batch," and he had got mad. "He puts a heap of store by that liniment being right up to the mark," she said.

5. Doc added to his small earnings, I discovered, by money he made gambling. He used to win quite a few dollars on Saturday nights at Freck's saloon, playing poker with the market-men and the railroaders who dropped in there. It wasn't for several years that I found out Doc cheated. I had never heard about marked cards until he told me about them and showed me his. It was one rainy afternoon, after he had played seven-up with Mrs. Willoughby and old Mr. Peiffer, another roomer of hers. They had played for small stakes (Doc wouldn't play cards unless there was some money up, and Mrs. Willoughby wouldn't play if very much was up). Only twenty or thirty cents had changed hands in the end. Doc had won it all. I remember my astonishment and indignation when it dawned on me that Doc had used the marked cards in playing the old lady and the old man. "You didn't cheat *them,* did you?" I asked him. "Jimmy, my boy," he told me, "the man that calls the turn wins the money." His eyes twinkled and he seemed to enjoy my anger. I was outraged, but I was helpless. I knew I could never tell Mrs. Willoughby about how Doc had cheated her at seven-up. I liked her, but I liked him, too. Once he had given me a whole dollar to buy fireworks with on the Fourth of July.

6. I remember once, when I was staying at Mrs. Willoughby's, Doc Marlowe was roused out of bed in the middle of the night by a poor woman who was frantic because her little girl was sick. This woman had had the sciatica driven out of her by his liniment, she reminded

Doc. He placed her then. She had never been able to pay him a cent for his liniment or his "treatments," and he had given her a great many. He got up and dressed, and went over to her house. The child had colic, I suppose. Doc couldn't have had any idea what was the matter, but he sopped on liniment; he sopped on a whole bottle. When he came back home, two hours later, he said he had "relieved the distress." The little girl had gone to sleep and was all right the next day, whether on account of Doc Marlowe or in spite of him I don't know. "I want to thank you, Doctor," said the mother, tremulously, when she called on him that afternoon. He gave her another bottle of liniment, and he didn't charge her for it or for his "professional call." He used to massage, and give liniment to, a lot of sufferers who were too poor to pay. Mrs. Willoughby told him once that he was too generous and too easily taken in. Doc laughed—and winked at me, with the twinkle in his eye that he had had when he told me how he had cheated the old lady at cards.

7. Once I went for a walk with him out Town Street on a Saturday afternoon. It was a warm day, and after a while I said I wanted a soda. Well, he said, he didn't care if he took something himself. We went into a drugstore, and I ordered a chocolate soda and he had a lemon phosphate. When we had finished, he said, "Jimmy, my son, I'll match you to see who pays for the drinks." He handed me a quarter and he told me to toss the quarter and he would call the turn. He called heads and won. I paid for the drinks. It left me with a dime.

8. I was fifteen when Doc got out his pamphlets, as he called them. He had eased the misery of the wife of a small-time printer and the grateful man had given him a special price on two thousand advertising pamphlets. There was very little in them about Blackhawk Liniment. They were mostly about Doc himself and his "Life in the Far West." He had gone out to Franklin Park one day with a photographer—another of his numerous friends—and there the photographer took dozens of pictures of Doc, a lariat in one hand, a six-shooter in the other. I had gone along. When the pamphlets came out, there were the pictures of Doc, peering around trees, crouching behind bushes, whirling the lariat, aiming the gun. "Dr. H. M. Marlowe Hunting Indians" was one of the captions. "Dr. H. M. Marlowe after Hoss-Thieves" was another one. He was very proud of the pamphlets and always had a sheaf with him. He would pass them out to people on the street.

9. Two years before he died Doc got hold of an ancient, wheezy Cadillac somewhere. He aimed to start traveling around again, he said, but he never did, because the old automobile was so worn out it wouldn't hold up for more than a mile or so. It was about this time that a man named Hardman and his wife came to stay at Mrs. Willoughby's. They were farm people from around Lancaster who had sold their place. They got to like Doc because he was so jolly, they said, and they enjoyed his stories. He treated Mrs. Hardman for an old complaint in the small of her back and wouldn't take any money for it. They thought he was a fine gentleman. Then there came a day when they announced that they were going to St. Louis, where they had a son. They talked some of settling in St. Louis. Doc Marlowe told them they ought to buy a nice auto cheap and drive out, instead of going by train—it wouldn't cost much and they could see the country, give themselves a treat. Now, he knew where they could pick up just such a car.

10. Of course, he finally sold them the decrepit Cadillac—it had been stored away somewhere in the back of a garage whose owner kept it there for nothing because Doc had relieved his mother of a distress in the groins, as Doc explained it. I don't know just how the garage man doctored up the car, but he did. It actually chugged along pretty steadily when Doc took the Hardmans out for a trial spin. He told them he hated to part with it, but he finally let them have it for a hundred dollars. I knew, of course, and so did Doc, that it couldn't last many miles.

11. Doc got a letter from the Hardmans in St. Louis ten days later. They had had to abandon the old junk pile in West Jefferson, some fifteen miles out of Columbus. Doc read the letter aloud to me, peering over his glasses, his eyes twinkling, every now and then punctuating the lines with "Hay, boy!" and "Hay, boy-gie!" "I just want you to know, Dr. Marlowe," he read, "what I think of low-life swindlers like you [Hay, boy!] and that it will be a long day before I put my trust in a two-faced lyer and imposture again [Hay, boy-gie!]. The garrage man in W. Jefferson told us your old rattle-trap had been doctored up just to fool us. It was a low down dirty trick [Hay, boy!]." Far from being disturbed by the letter, Doc Marlowe was plainly amused. He took off his glasses, after he finished it and laughed, his hand to his brow and his eyes closed. I was pretty mad, because I had liked the Hardmans, and because they had liked him. Doc Marlowe put the letter carefully back into its envelope and tucked it away in his inside coat pocket, as if it were something precious. Then he picked up a pack of cards and began to lay out a solitaire hand. "Want to set in a little seven-up game, Jimmy?" he asked me. I was furious. "Not with a cheater like you!" I shouted, and stamped out of the room, slamming the door. I could hear him chuckling to himself behind me.

12. The last time I saw Doc Marlowe was just a few days before he died. I didn't know anything about death, but I knew that he was dying when I saw him. His voice was very faint and his face was drawn; they told me he had a lot of pain. When I got ready to leave the room, he asked me to bring him a tin box that was on his bureau. I got it and handed it to him. He poked around in it for a while with unsteady fingers and finally found what he wanted. He handed it to me. It was a quarter, or rather it looked like a quarter, but it had heads on both sides. "Never let the other fella call the turn, Jimmy, my boy," said Doc, with a shadow of his old twinkle and the echo of his old chuckle. I still have the two-headed quarter. For a long time I didn't like to think about it, or about Doc Marlowe, but I do now.

WORDS

What is the meaning of the italicized words in the following phrases?

1. "*harangue* the crowd" (par. 1)
2. "Doc *soused* him with Blackhawk" (par. 3)
3. "Doc told him, *suavely*" (par. 3)
4. "the *sciatica* driven out of her" (par. 6)
5. "The child had *colic*" (par. 6)
6. "said the mother, *tremulously*" (par. 6)
7. "a *lariat* in one hand" (par. 8)
8. "the *decrepit* Cadillac" (par. 10)

FORM AND CONTENT

1. What two aspects of Doc Marlowe's character does James Thurber emphasize in the sketch? The words "awed" and "puzzled" in paragraph 1 should help you.

WHO—Character and Personality

2. Why does Thurber place quotation marks around the words "medicines" and "treated" (par. 3) and "treatments" and "professional call" (par. 6)?
3. Explain the author's references to "medicine-show man" (par. 1) and "General Custer's hair" (par. 2).
4. How does the event described in paragraph 7 relate to the final scene of the essay?
5. Contrast the author's tone in paragraph 11 with that found in paragraph 12.

SUGGESTIONS FOR WRITING AND DISCUSSIONS

1. Describe the physical characteristics and the personality of someone like Doc Marlowe, one who possesses both positive and negative qualities.
2. Describe the personality and physical qualities of a person whom you earnestly despise.
3. Describe a doctor or a dentist, one whose job it is to make you well. Using appeals to the senses (smell, sight, hearing, and touch), describe his or her office and your feelings while you are there.
4. Sometimes cars, usually old ones, take on human characteristics. Describe in detail such a vehicle. Be sure to give it a name.
5. Sometimes it is satisfying to be someone else's follower, allowing him or her to lead the way. Describe a "leader" whom you have admired and your role as "follower."

The Teacher as Dragon

Anna Tuttle Villegas

Anna Tuttle Villegas is a member of the English faculty at the University of the Pacific, Stockton, California.

The essay which follows is actually about two women, one real and the other a vicious caricature. The former is a dedicated, highly principled composition instructor and the latter a bizarre "fire-breathing dragon" of a high school English teacher, the subject of a student essay. The character and personality of both women are revealed through the use of powerful negative adjectives, anecdotes, and comparison and contrast. The author delves below the surface of stereotype and offers reasons why some teachers find it easier to "torment than to teach." She recognizes, understands, and occasionally identifies with the sour, bitter "red-haired vixen"; however, her conclusion contains a positive reaffirmation of professional faith.

1. A few semesters ago, in fulfillment of a descriptive paper assignment, I received a student essay describing a high school English teacher. To this day I vividly recall the image it created. It was of a stout, ham-like body perched atop two trunkish legs that ended in toes having not toenails but yellow, calcified claws (which were always, the student noted, causing damage to hosiery). On top of this lumbering figure was planted a savage, baleful countenance fringed with sparse, kinky, red hair. Behind the inevitable thick-lensed spectacles glared beady porcine eyes whose sole purpose, it seems, was to seek out ne'er-do-wells and inflict on them stinging lashes of shame and guilt.

2. The indelible impression I have of the essay (and the woman) is the intricately painted relationship between appearance and character. True, I had emphasized to my students that they describe their subjects along thematic lines, but there was something supernaturally real and uncannily familiar to me about this fire-breathing dragon of an English teacher. I caught, in the reflections of her horn-rims, an image of myself.

3. In appearance I am nothing like her. Where she is short and stout, I am tall and leaning to the skinny side. Where she wears gaudy and sackish dresses, I wear informal pants and shirts, not unlike those of my students. The closest my hair comes to red are the few rusty strands left over from the chlorine bleach of last summer's daily swimming. I am blind as a bat, and my prescription is strong—but I don't wear horn-rimmed glasses. And my eyes are blue, not beady black.

4. Why, then, in the midst of midnight insomnia or the predawn stirrings of the soul, do I see myself in this red-haired vixen?

5. The teaching of writing, of good writing, is the teaching of thinking—not thinking presented in a general, abstracted, grandiose way, but thinking applied to the individual mind. When, as a writing teacher, I ask for an argumentative essay that springs from a student's interest in a subject, I am not asking for a legislative document or a psychological treatise. I am asking for reasonable thought on a limited topic conveyed from a unique perspective, the student's own.

6. To ask for reasonable thought—to ask for any individual thought—is a very risky business. It means that what will finally be evaluated by the teacher is a projection of the student's self, and, unless the student is that rare one who enters a writing class articulate, skilled and independently thoughtful, that part of the self tends to be particularly vulnerable.

7. No matter how often a writing teacher chants that "receiving a D grade doesn't mean you are a D person," students interpret a grade as a grade on their characters, and they react much like a calf whose flank is singed with a hot iron: bawling and kicking and protesting throatily against convention and authority, in their pained rage mistaking blue eyes for black ones.

8. No one likes to be told, or even have hinted at, that his mind is cluttered, untidy, disordered, lacking purpose. Yet when I comment that an essay fails to meet the objectives the writer has set for it, that it dawdles from point to point without developing any one idea, I have the unpleasant task of pointing a finger at the clutter.

9. I believe myself to be an expert at supportive tact, but it is in this aspect of my job and my relationship to my students that I find my kinship with the red-haired dragon. We are both concerned with the nurturing of creative thought, and in our attempts to bribe and cajole thought from our students we sometimes have to point out where it is wilting from the neglect of haste or lack of commitment. Then we become sisters: dragon ladies who bleed red ink instead of blood.

10. Our genealogy follows a long engagement in the profession. Although I don't yet resemble the red-haired teacher in person, in spirit I am beginning to. In her youth she, like me, must have entertained the belief that in teaching her students to write she was endowing them with an enduring tool for discovering themselves and their relationship to their world. She must have felt the thrill of discovery herself when she received papers that rewarded her with the richness of shared experience.

11. Unfortunately, long before I stood nervously before my first expository class, she must have encountered the disappointment of failed expectations. Subconsciously perhaps, she rallied by convincing herself that with gentle and persistent prodding of her students' minds she could extract from them substance for good essays and sustenance for her belief in their capacity to think. This, I speculate, may have delayed her eventual disenchantment with the human imagination for a few years. But as time and students passed by her, she was forced to accept the decay of her initial illusion about the rational animal's ability to communicate. It was at this time that her eyes got bad, her prescription thicker and her hair unruly. She was transforming herself into a person who was impervious to disappointment. She began to shield herself in her scales.

12. One doesn't have to count the dragon ladies one has known to realize that the constant failure of expectations creates bitterness, sours the appeal of meeting new minds, and physically transforms a person. The dragon teacher is an understandable product of many years of a gradual lowering of standards. Ultimately she found it easier to torment than to teach. With tormenting she could see at least an emotional response, while with teaching she despaired of ever finding an intellectual one.

13. I remember reading amid cheers that essay to my class. After reviewing the descriptive techniques the writer had used, we turned to a discussion of the relationship between thesis and descriptive detail. In a class of twenty students from widely varying geographic backgrounds, I found that fifteen of them had been taught high school English, if not by the dragon lady herself, by her identical sister. Her attitude and her appearance, even down to the fine detail of the calcified toenails, were those of an entire nation of English schoolmarms. And I am of the same breed.

14. I admit that I read the essay to my class with the intention of milking from it every ounce of humor that it had. In retrospect I see that what I was really doing, in a sneaky and lowdown way, was saying to my students: Look, here is what you might have had for a writing teacher. But you didn't. You have me—and aren't I different? Aren't I breaking the mold? Won't you write your hearts out for me?

15. I don't like the image of myself that I caught reflected in that essay. I don't like the image of my profession that appeared there, either. Writing well is the most powerful intellectual tool that a person—student or teacher or layman—can develop. I go to school every day, talk about conventions and rhetorical modes and ideas, drag home stacks of student essays, comment on conventions and modes and ideas and return to school the next day to begin again because I believe in the written word's power. And I refuse to succumb to the stereotype the outside world has of me.

16. I have great sympathy for the red-haired woman whom I have used so badly. I understand how she has evolved into her present state. But I am sorry she gave up. Our job is too important, our students' minds too precious, for me to give up too. My hair will not turn red.

WORDS

What is the meaning of the italicized words in the following phrases?

1. "a savage, *baleful* countenance" (par. 1)
2. "a savage, baleful *countenance*" (par. 1)
3. "beady *porcine* eyes" (par. 1)
4. "The *indelible* impression" (par. 2)
5. "*uncannily* familiar" (par. 2)
6. "this red-haired *vixen*" (par. 4)
7. "in a general, abstracted, *grandiose* way" (par. 5)
8. "it *dawdles* from point to point" (par. 8)
9. "attempts to bribe and *cajole*" (par. 9)
10. "who was *impervious*" (par. 11)

FORM AND CONTENT

1. In what paragraph does Villegas state her thesis?
2. List a few negative adjectives the author uses to characterize the dragon teacher (par. 1).
3. What is the function of paragraph 4? How is this paragraph related to the thesis of the article?
4. What does the author establish in paragraphs 5–8?
5. What caused the dragon teacher to become bitter and sour (par. 12)?

SUGGESTIONS FOR WRITING AND DISCUSSION

1. Describe a teacher of science or mathematics who, like the dragon teacher, appears to have grown bitter and sour, who has found it "easier to torment than to teach." Do you have any ideas as to why he or she became disillusioned?
2. Have you ever had a teacher who became your guru? If so, describe his or her personality, emphasizing the special qualities that he or she possessed.
3. Have you ever had a teacher whom you found impossible to please, with whom you were in passionate disagreement? If so, describe him or her.
4. The author describes herself as one who is an "expert in supportive tact." Define this quality and describe a teacher, past or present, who was or is equally expert.
5. Describe the character and personality of a deeply committed person, one who is willing to stand up for what he or she believes, no matter how difficult and frustrating the task or one-sided the situation.

WHERE

Place and Appearance

A land that is flat and bleak and cheerless, baked by merciless sun and lashed by frozen rain; a grove of crooked aspens on the North Rim of the Grand Canyon; a busy street, traveled by many people and watched by many eyes; and a nice, dull, old Chicago neighborhood threatened by change—these are special places with special appearances.

Different in size, geography, and character, they challenge description. To communicate a personal perception of each place, a writer must select, arrange, and interpret details that reveal a larger pattern. One writer may describe how an isolated and cheerless land can lead a disaffected generation to boredom and purposeless action; another writer may describe an old street to demonstrate that its varied life and movement produce better results than the sterile courtyards of new planned cities. Alone in a wood, another writer may find feeling, awareness, and even companionship in trees; while still another may describe a neighborhood to mourn its passing.

In doing these things, writers must transcend mere physical description. They are describing human environments, scenes of action, stages of plays. Just as a room, or a home, or an institution reflects and molds the characters of those who live in it, so does a near desert, an isolated aspen grove, or a small part of a large city. Even a single street may help "to keep the peace because there are plenty of eyes on it."

Loving County, Texas

Larry L. King

Larry L. King, a native Texan, is a highly respected journalist, novelist, and essayist.

Using vigorous verbs, vivid adjectives, colorful similes ("the summer sun is as merciless as a loan shark"), King describes a barren, windswept place and the quality of life found there. Note the effectiveness of the topic sentences that introduce five of his paragraphs and the use of specific details that support them. King introduces lines from a country song, humorous irony ("exotic Kansas City"), frustrated teenagers, and complacent old men; all of these illustrate the curse of Loving County—boredom.

1. The land is stark and flat and treeless, altogether as bleak and spare as mood scenes in Russian literature, a great dry-docked ocean with small swells of hummocky tan sand dunes or humpbacked rocky knolls that change colors with the hour and the shadows: reddish brown, slate gray, bruise colored. But it is the sky—God-high and pale, like a blue chenille bedspread bleached by seasons in the sun—that dominates. There is simply *too much* sky. Men grow small in its presence and—perhaps feeling diminished—they sometimes are compelled to proclaim themselves in wild or berserk ways. Alone in those remote voids, one may suddenly half believe he is the last man on earth and go in frantic search of the tribe. Desert fever, the natives call it.

2. And while the endless dry doomed land and eternal sky may bring on the fever, so, too, can the weather. The wind, persistent and unengageable for half the year, swooshes unencumbered from the northernmost Great Plains, howling, whining, singing off-key and covering everything with a maddening grainy down. Court records attest that during the windy seasons the natives are quicker to lift their voices, or their fists, or even their guns, in rage.

3. The summer sun is as merciless as a loan shark: a blinding, angry orange explosion baking the land's sparse grasses and quickly aging the skin. In winter there are nights to ache the bone; cold, stinging lashings of frozen rain. Yet even the weather is not the worst natural enemy. Outside the industrial sprawl of the prairie's minicities—on the occasional ranches or oil leases or in the flawed little country towns—the great curse is boredom. Teenagers in the faded jeans and glistening ducktail hairstyles of another day wander in restless packs to the roller rink or circle root beer stands sounding their mating calls by a mighty revving of engines. Old men shuffle dominoes in the shade of service stations or feedstores. There is the television, of course, and the joys of small-town gossip—and in season a weekly high school football game may secretly be considered more important than even Vacation Bible School. Newt Keen laments the passing of country socials where people reveled all night at one ranch house or another: "Now you got to go over to Pecos to them fightin' and dancin' clubs. But, you know, it ain't near as much fun to fight with strangers."

4. The young and the imaginative in Loving

County are largely disaffected, strangers in Jerusalem. And those who can, move on when they can. Today's desert youths belong to a transitional generation. Born to an exhausted frontier where there are no more Dodge Citys to tame, no more wild rivers to ford, no more cattle trails to ride or oil booms to follow, theirs is a heritage beyond preserving. The last horseman has passed by, leaving only myths and fences. Industrialization has come and gone: having drilled and robbed the earth, the swaggering two-fisted oil boomer, heir apparent to the earlier cowboy or Indian fighter, has clattered off to the next feverish adventure, leaving behind sterile sophisticated pumps and gauges and storage tanks that automatically record their own dull technological accomplishments. Only the land remains, the high sky, the eerie isolation. The wind hums mocking tunes of loss and the jukeboxes echo it: *"Just call Lonesome-seven-seven-two-oh-three . . ." "I'd trade all of my tomorrows for just one yesterday. . . ."*

5. The songs are of rejection, disappointment, aborted opportunities . . . of finishing second. And the music is everywhere, incessantly jangling, the call of the lonely. Even many graybeards who have trimmed back their dreams—if they ever had any—cannot sit still unless the jukebox or radio is moaning to them of old loves lost, of the tricks of the wicked cities, of life's rough and rocky traveling. Few know that the music says more about them than they say of themselves.

6. The young sense the loss of a grander and more adventurous past. It is these—the young and those who secretly know they never will be truly young again—who prove most susceptible to fits of desert fever. And so they sometimes go lickety-splitting down the rural highways at speeds dizzy enough to confuse the ambidextrous, running like so many Rabbit Angstroms, leaving behind a trail of sad country songs, beer vapors and the echo of some feverish, senseless shout. Some may find themselves at dawn howling in the precincts of a long-forgotten girl friend, or tempting the dangers of "fightin' and dancin' clubs" with names like Blue Moon Bar or Texas Taddy Jo's. Some keep running: to the army or to a Fort Worth factory or maybe to exotic Kansas City. Others, their fevers cooled and with no place to go, drive back slowly—a bit sheepishly—to rejoin the private chaos and public tediums of their lives.

WORDS

What is the meaning of the italicized words in the following phrases?

1. "*hummocky* tan sand dunes" (par. 1)
2. "in wild or *berserk* ways" (par. 1)
3. "baking the land's *sparse* grasses (par. 3)
4. "stinging *lashings* of frozen rain" (par. 3)
5. "The young . . . are largely *disaffected"* (par. 4)
6. "a *heritage* beyond preserving" (par. 4)
7. "the high sky, the *eerie* isolation" (par. 4)
8. "songs are of . . . *aborted* opportunities" (par. 5)
9. "running to . . . *exotic* Kansas City" (par. 6)
10. "public *tediums* of their lives" (par. 6)

FORM AND CONTENT

1. Both the land and the climate (except for the winds) that the author describes are much like those of Las Vegas, Nevada. But how, do you believe, do the populations of Las Vegas and Loving County differ from each other.
2. The author says that the young people in Loving County "sense the loss of a grander and more adventurous past." Why should they feel such a loss more keenly than the young people of London, Paris, or Rome?
3. Some forms of irony are very like sarcasm. Why is the phrase "exotic Kansas City" clearly ironical?
4. There is one metaphor (a rather strange one) as well as one simile in the first paragraph. Identify them and comment on their effect.
5. The topic sentence of paragraph 3 is not the first sentence. What sentence is the topic sentence?

SUGGESTIONS FOR WRITING AND DISCUSSION

1. Using King as a guide, describe the lives of people in a particular neighborhood—a small town or an industrial city or an urban ghetto.
2. If you have ever experienced the lost loneliness of desert fever or cabin fever, describe the place you were in and the feelings it produced in you.
3. Write a character sketch of a person trapped by an environment or special circumstances.
4. If ever you have known and loved a particular bit of forest, meadow, or desert, describe it. Why was it important to you?
5. Can a person be just as lonely in New York City as in Loving County, Texas? If so, why? If not, why not?

The Crooked Wood

Edward Abbey

A naturalist and conservationist, Edward Abbey worked for a time as a National Park Service ranger. He has written extensively on deserts of the American Southwest.

Abbey boasts that he is a hard-nosed empiricist, one who believes only in what he can see, hear, smell, grab, or bite into, but he also claims that trees have feelings, emotions, and personalities. As he remembers walking through a grove of aspen trees on the North Rim of the Grand Canyon, he tells of the lives of trees and how they are as aware of our presence as we are of theirs. Abbey's description of place and appearance is philosophical. Note the commitment he makes in the final paragraph.

1. For four seasons I worked as a fire lookout on the North Rim of the Grand Canyon. To get to my job I walked for a mile and a half each morning on a trail through a dense grove of quaking aspens. I called this grove "the crooked wood" because the trees there, nearly all of them, have been curiously deformed. The trunks are bent in shapes that seem more whimsical than natural: dog legs, S-curves, elbows, knees. The deformity is always found in the lower part of the trunk, four or five feet above the ground. Above that level the trunks assume the vertical attitude normal to aspens, supporting the usual symmetric umbrella of graceful, delicately suspended, dancing leaves which gives this tree its specific name, *tremuloides.*

2. Why the deformation? The explanation is simple. On the North Rim, at an elevation of 8,000 to 9,000 feet above sea level, winter snows are heavy. In well-shaded places, such as the ridge where my crooked grove is found, massive drifts of snow survive through May and into June, overlapping part of the growing season. Under the creeping weight and pressure of these snowdrifts the young aspens—seedling and sapling—grow as best they can, in whatever direction they must, through spring after spring, seeking the sunlight that is their elixir, until they reach a height where their growth is not affected by the snow.

3. The life of trees. We know so little about this strange planet we live on, this haunted world where all answers lead only to more mystery. The character of trees, for example, their feelings, emotions, personalities—Shelley was not the first to speak of "the sensitive plant." The mandrake, they believed, screams when uprooted. Contemporary researchers suggest that plants respond to music (preferring Mozart to the Rolling Stones, I'm not surprised to hear) and to human emotions. I'm inclined to believe it. And I'm the type inclined to doubt. But three seasons of solitary walking under those aspen trees, through the green translucence of summer and the golden radiance of autumn, alone in the stillness of the forest, can do queer things to a man's common sense.

4. We think we perceive character or "personality" in the shape, face, eyes of our fellow humans; why not find something similar in the appearance of plants—especially trees? How avoid it? Obvious analogies come at once to mind: the solemnity of the dark, heavy, brooding spruce; the honest, hopeful nobility of the yellow pine; the anxiety of white fir; the remote grandeur of the bristlecone pine; the brightness, the gaiety, the charm, the feminine sensitivity, the aspiring joyousness of *Populus tremuloides*. (Our name; what the aspen calls itself we may never know.)

5. I can hear the laughter down in the pit and up in the peanut gallery as I write these vulnerable words. (I'm a hard-nosed empiricist myself, one who believes only in what he can hear, see, smell, grab, bite into, so I understand.) But—I repeat—if you could spend as I did the sweeter part of three good years in that forest, scanning a sea of treetops for a twist of smoke, walking beneath that canopy of leaves in the chill clear mornings and again in the evenings—evenings sometimes full of golden peace and sometimes charged with storm and lightning—you too might begin to wonder, not only about yourself but also about those *beings,* alive, sentient, transpiring, which surround you. Especially the aspens, the quaking aspens, always so vibrant with light and motion, forever restless, always whispering, in tune like ballerinas to the music of the air. Walking there day after day, among those slim trim trees, so innocent (it seems) in their white and green or white and gold, you become aware after a while not only of the trees but of the trees' awareness of you. What they felt I had no notion of; I never got to know them well as individuals. But their conscious presence was unmistakable. I was not alone.

6. My father has been a logger, sawyer, and woodsman for most of his life. I myself have put in a fair share of time with ax, crosscut saw, chain saw, sledge, and wedge at the reduction of trees into fuel, post, and lumber. I understand and sympathize with the reasonable needs of a reasonable number of people on a finite continent. All men and women require shelter. All life depends upon other life. But what is happening today, in North America, is not rational use but irrational massacre. Man the Pest, multiplied to the swarming stage, is attacking the remaining forests like a plague of locusts on a field of grain. Knowing now what we have learned, unless the need were urgent, I could no more sink the blade of an ax into the tissues of a living tree than I could drive it into the flesh of a fellow human.

WORDS

What is the meaning of the italicized words in the following phrases?

1. "more *whimsical* than natural" (par. 1)
2. "sunlight . . . is their *elixir*" (par. 2)
3. "the *mandrake* . . . screams" (par. 3)
4. "the green *translucence* of summer" (par. 3)
5. "*analogies* come . . . to mind" (par. 4)
6. "*aspiring* joyousness" (par. 4)
7. "these *vulnerable* words" (par. 5)
8. "I'm a hard-nosed *empiricist*" (par. 5)
9. "beings, alive, *sentient,* transpiring" (par. 5)
10. "on a *finite* continent" (par. 6)

FORM AND CONTENT

1. First in paragraph 3, and then again, parenthetically, in paragraph 5, the author insists that he is ordinarily a skeptic, a doubter. What is the value of these self-appraisals in the development of this essay?
2. Does the author insist (par. 6) that all woodcutting is bad and that he himself would never chop down a tree?
3. In paragraph 5, the author says that the crooked aspens were not only sentient but also conscious. Does he offer any evidence for this belief?
4. How do the first two paragraphs of this essay, which contain an objective description and explanation by a trained naturalist, contribute to the argument of the rest of the essay?
5. How persuasive do you find the evidence in paragraph 3 (the allusion to one of Shelley's poems, the reference to an old bit of folklore about the mandrake root, and the citing of an undocumented study of the response of plants to music)? Does your conclusion perhaps help you to explain the last sentence of the paragraph?

SUGGESTIONS FOR WRITING AND DISCUSSION

1. The author characterizes different kinds of trees as solemn, noble, anxious, or joyous. Describe and characterize different kinds of houses in the same way.
2. The author spent "the sweeter part of three good years" among the aspens on the North Rim of the Grand Canyon. Describe the place where you spent the sweeter part of any year.
3. In justifying the cutting of trees to satisfy "the reasonable needs of a reasonable number of people," the author says, "All life depends upon other life." How is this truth demonstrated, for instance, by the way we eat and dress?
4. Do you or anyone you know spend time talking to pets or plants? Why, do you think, people do this?
5. If you hold, or have ever held, a belief that most people would consider an illusion, a myth, or a superstition, describe it and explain how you came to believe it.

In the Neighborhood

Joseph Epstein

Joseph Epstein is a native of Chicago, where he still makes his home. He teaches at Northwestern and is editor of The American Scholar.

In a sometimes irritable tone, Epstein describes the characteristics of his neighborhood, a place currently undergoing a change he finds distasteful. His use of colorful examples captures the area and its people. In language that is both witty and sarcastic, he contrasts the rhythms of the neighborhood on weekdays and on weekends and goes on to introduce the eccentric characters and the shopkeepers who share his Chicago turf.

1. If anyone senses that this essay is written out of personal grievance, his instincts are near perfect. My own neighborhood is, alas, currently undergoing boutiquification. Such a nice dull neighborhood it is, too. Or rather *was,* till one day large signs were posted on neighborhood shop windows announcing, Paul Revere-like, "The Main Is Coming," "The Main Is Coming." The Main turns out to be a Boutique America shopping center on Main Street. I shall provide a tour of it presently, but first I shall attempt to get at what I so like about my neighborhood and what about it seems to me so worth saving.

2. What, really, is wanted from a neighborhood? Convenience, certainly; an absence of major aggravation, to be sure. But perhaps most of all, ideally, what is wanted is a comfortable background, a breathing space of intermission between the intensities of private life and the calculations of public life. In the neighborhood, relationships need not become entangled, behavior need not be triggered by motive. In the neighborhood—between the drama of the household and the battlefield of the career—the casual reigns, the quotidian dominates. In the neighborhood, life mercifully flows on.

3. Like the tides of the moon, the neighborhood in which I live has its own regular rhythms. In the early morning hours, there are the nattering of squirrels, the twittering of birds, the creaking of the newspaper delivery man's steel-wheeled cart. Things pick up around eight o'clock, as people set off for work. Showered and shined, ready for drama or dullness as the case may be, they step off to offices and shops. Yellow buses pull up to take children to day-care centers or nursery school, and in the summer to day camp. The majority of the kids go off to grade school three blocks away, or to the junior high school six blocks away, or to the high school a few miles distant. The neighborhood settles down. A young mother walks by with her infant in a pram. A truck from United Parcel stops for a delivery. A cat pads across a lawn. An elderly woman, a cane in one hand, a shopping bag in the other, trudges by. Near eleven, the postman is on the block. After three, school out, children take over the block: a boy bangs a tennis ball against a garage wall, two younger children chase a dog, bikes are everywhere. Around five-thirty, adults begin to return from downtown, some having stopped along the way for groceries or for dry cleaning.

Dampened and rumpled after the day downtown and the subway ride home, they have roughly fourteen hours to give over to dinner, television, reading, lovemaking, and sleep, before starting out again. With the dark, a new quiet sets in. Teenagers gather at the park or down at the lake; they leave behind them a clinging odor of pot or a few empty beer cans. The streets empty out, and only an occasional dog-walker appears after ten. Safe though the neighborhood generally is, this is still the 1970s, and even here paranoia is the better part of valor. The next day the same rhythm will begin again.

4. Weekends the rhythm changes. Saturday morning the street jumps with people on errands: much toting of laundry, dry cleaning, groceries. A more fervid energy is given over to the serious business of play. Couples glide by on bicycles. Tennis rackets are unscrewed from presses, unsheathed from covers. Camping equipment is loaded into trunks or onto car carriers. (In winter, skis replace camping equipment.) A slower, more dispersed traffic is on the street Sundays: people lug home their three or four pounds of *New York Times* or *Chicago Tribune.* In warm weather three couples living in an apartment building north of mine used to bring their breakfasts out to their building's small front lawn—in training for the more spacious life of the suburbs to which they have doubtless by now repaired.

5. A more than adequate supply of characters is about. A Negro cowboy roams these streets: a man who looks to be late into his sixties, he strolls about in sheepskin coat, a ten-gallon hat broken in at the brim, curly white sideburns, a bandana round his neck. An elderly woman, pale and frail, walks about wrapped up in an overly large blue raincoat, black men's socks covering her thin legs, a babushka over her head tucked in snugly under the chin. Sitting on the small bench outside the neighborhood news kiosk is a man of glistening ebony color, with a slender head upon which are deployed features of an extraordinary delicacy and elegance. So handsome, so photogenic, so much the grist for a certain kind of art photography does he seem that more than once I have watched a stranger with a camera ask permission to photograph him. He invariably complies, smiling exuberantly, revealing several missing teeth. A woman a few buildings down my block feeds squirrels by hand at her high first-floor window. Five or six squirrels scale the wall to reach her ledge, and the tableau there presented makes it all too easy to imagine them taking over her apartment. A man in a beret, scraggly gray beard, and matching long hair lives around the corner; he wears all black in the winter, all white in the summer, and does I know not what for a living. Central Casting is to be congratulated for supplying these characters.

6. "Nice day, Mr. Steadman."

7. "Not if you've bet on the Cardinals it isn't, Mr. Epstein."

8. He is a neighborhood shopkeeper, runs a dry cleaning establishment, a solitary man with a solitary vice: gambling on ball games. Unmarried, of middle age, neither an addict nor a fanatic, he is a man who, quite simply, enjoys his gambling. Across the street from Steadman's is the shop of Mr. William Richardson, shoe repair. (Will there be men in future generations who will do such jobs, or will shoes be made to be thrown out when the heels wear down or a hole is worn in the sole?) Mr. Richardson is a Negro, a man of perfect diction and high dignity. Adorning the wall of his shop is a commendatory plaque citing his efforts in behalf of the NAACP. Up the street is Wulf's, a Certified Grocery Store, now in its second generation of ownership. Mr. Wulf, Jr., in his middle forties, is quiet, competent, and roughly six feet six. He once played basketball for Michigan State: one imagines him not much of a scorer but very strong off the boards. Next door to Wulf's, at the corner, is Leo's Pharmacy. Leo's specialties are cameras, which sell pretty well, and flattery of his female customers, which doesn't always sell. "A beautiful day, now that you're here," he will say to one of them. Or "Where is that beautiful smile this morning?" A block away, on Main Street, used to be Joe's Laundromat. A furiously hard worker and an unshakably cheerful man, Joe carries a tattooed number on his forearm, memento of years in a Nazi concentration camp. When Boutique America came into the neighborhood, rents went up all around, and Joe chose to move. Into his place has since been inserted Sawdust, Inc., a shop that sells wooden toys and offers classes in woodcarving.

9. I do not want any wooden toys, I do not want any lessons in woodcarving, though I did like to have my laundry done at a reasonable price.

WORDS

What is the meaning of the italicized words in the following phrases?

1. "a *Boutique* America shopping center" (par. 1)
2. "the *quotidian* dominates" (par. 2)
3. "the *nattering* of squirrels" (par. 3)
4. "her infant in a *pram*" (par. 3)
5. "*paranoia* is the better part of valor" (par. 3)
6. "more *fervid* energy" (par. 4)
7. "a *babushka* over her head" (par. 5)
8. "outside the neighborhood news *kiosk*" (par. 5)
9. "smiling *exuberantly*" (par. 5)
10. "man of perfect *diction*" (par. 8)

FORM AND CONTENT

1. The author's personal grievance is that his neighborhood is undergoing "boutiquification." What is that (the author neither defines nor describes it)?
2. Explain what the author means when he defines a *neighborhood* as "a breathing space of intermission between the intensities of private life and the calculations of public life."
3. Clearly, the last sentence of paragraph 5 is not literally true. What does it mean, and what is its effect?
4. What single specific result of "boutiquification" does the author give in paragraph 8? What other neighborhood changes is it likely to foreshadow?
5. The author's neighbors are described in paragraphs 3 and 4. How do they seem to differ from the "characters" (par. 5) and the shopkeepers (par. 8)?

SUGGESTIONS FOR WRITING AND DISCUSSION

1. Both cities and rural areas seem to change character during different times of day and night. Choose a place you know well and describe the changes it undergoes.

2. What changes in your own neighborhood have you been sorry to see? Which have you welcomed? On balance, do you think that your neighborhood is being improved?
3. "A neighborhood that is not constantly changing is probably dead or dying." Do you agree or disagree? Explain.
4. In some parts of the country, large enclosed shopping centers seem to have become the gathering places and playgrounds for teenagers. What is the attraction for very young people of such places?
5. If there are people in your neighborhood who seem to be unusual characters, describe them. Are they necessarily poorer, weaker, and less educated than you? Why does the description of such people, like that in paragraph 5, frequently seem patronizing and condescending?

The Use of Sidewalks

Jane Jacobs

Jane Jacobs, who has been a newspaper reporter and an associate editor of The Architectural Forum, *is the author of* The Death and Life of Great American Cities, *the well-known book from which the following excerpt is taken.*

In it she describes the street where she lives. Unlike other such descriptions, which may be written to show that an area is beautiful, lovely, or quaint, this description is written to prove a thesis: that a busy street with multiple uses is safe because it is constantly being watched by many eyes. Hence her descriptions of tradesmen, people leaving or returning from work, housewives on shopping expeditions, working men and playing children, and even a late-night bagpiper are all purposeful. Her description of what she calls a frenetic street ballet makes it very clear that her street is not a hospitable place for secret, stealthy crime.

1. Under the seeming disorder of the old city, wherever the old city is working successfully, is a marvelous order for maintaining the safety of the streets and the freedom of the city. It is a complex order. Its essence is intricacy of sidewalk use, bringing with it a constant succession of eyes. This order is all composed of movement and change, and although it is life, not art, we may fancifully call it the art form of the city and liken it to the dance—not to a simple-minded precision dance with everyone kicking up at the same time, twirling in unison and bowing off *en masse,* but to an intricate ballet in which the individual dancers and ensembles all have distinctive parts which miraculously reinforce each other and compose an orderly whole. The ballet of the good city sidewalk never repeats itself from place to place, and in any one place is always replete with new improvisations.

2. The stretch of Hudson Street where I live is each day the scene of an intricate sidewalk ballet. I make my own first entrance into it a little after eight when I put out the garbage can, surely a prosaic occupation, but I enjoy my part, my little clang, as the droves of junior high school students walk by the center of the stage dropping candy wrappers. (How do they eat so much candy so early in the morning?)

3. While I sweep up the wrappers I watch the other rituals of morning: Mr. Halpert unlocking the laundry's handcart from its mooring to a cellar door, Joe Cornacchia's son-in-law stacking out the empty crates from the delicatessen, the barber bringing out his sidewalk folding chair, Mr. Goldstein arranging the coils of wire which proclaim the hardware store is open, the wife of the tenement's superintendent depositing her chunky three-year-old with a toy mandolin on the stoop, the vantage point from which he is learning the English his mother cannot speak. Now the primary children, heading for St. Luke's, dribble through to the south; the children for St. Veronica's cross, heading to the west, and the children for P.S. 41, heading toward the east. Two new entrances are being made from the wings: well-dressed and even elegant women and men with briefcases emerge from doorways and side streets. Most of these are heading for the bus and subways, but some hover on the curbs, stopping taxis which have miraculously appeared at the right moment, for the taxis are part of a wider morning ritual: having dropped passengers from midtown in the downtown financial district, they are now bringing downtowners up to midtown. Simultaneously, numbers of women in housedresses have emerged and as they crisscross with one another they pause for quick conversations that sound with either laughter or joint indignation, never, it seems, anything between. It is time for me to hurry to work too, and I exchange my ritual farewell with Mr. Lofaro, the short, thick-bodied, white-aproned fruit man who stands outside his doorway a little up the street, his arms folded, his feet planted, looking solid as earth itself. We nod; we each glance quickly up and down the street, then look back to each other and smile. We have done this many a morning for more than ten years, and we both know what it means: All is well.

4. The heart-of-the-day ballet I seldom see, because part of the nature of it is that working people who live there, like me, are mostly gone, filling the roles of strangers on other sidewalks. But from days off, I know enough of it to know that it becomes more and more intricate. Longshoremen who are not working that day gather at the White Horse or the Ideal or the International for beer and conversation. The executives and business lunchers from the industries just to the west throng the Dorgene restaurant and the Lion's Head coffee house; meat-market workers and communications scientists fill the bakery lunchroom. Character dancers come on, a strange old man with strings of old shoes over his shoulders, motor-scooter riders with big beards and girl friends who bounce on the back of the scooters and wear their hair long in front of their faces as well as behind, drunks who follow the advice of the Hat Council and are always turned out in hats, but not hats the Council would approve. Mr. Lacey, the locksmith, shuts up his shop for a while and goes to exchange the time of day with Mr. Slube at the cigar store. Mr. Koochagian, the tailor, waters the luxuriant jungle of plants in his window, gives them a critical look from the outside, accepts a compliment on them from two passers-by, fingers the leaves on the plane tree in front of our house with a thoughtful gardener's appraisal, and crosses the street for a bite at the Ideal where he can keep an eye on customers and wigwag across the message that he is coming. The baby carriages come out, and clusters of everyone from toddlers with dolls to teenagers with homework gather at the stoops.

5. When I get home after work, the ballet is reaching its crescendo. This is the time of roller skates and stilts and tricycles, and games in the lee of the stoop with bottletops and plastic cowboys; this is the time of bundles and packages, zigzagging from the drug store to the fruit stand and back over to the butcher's; this is the time when teenagers, all dressed up, are pausing to ask if their slips show or their collars look right; this is the time when beautiful girls get out of MG's; this is the time when the fire engines go through; this is the time when anybody you know around Hudson Street will go by.

6. As darkness thickens and Mr. Halpert moors the laundry cart to the cellar door again, the ballet goes on under lights, eddying back and forth but intensifying at the bright spotlight pools of Joe's sidewalk pizza dispensary, the bars, the delicatessen, the restaurant and the drug store. The night workers stop now at the delicatessen, to pick up salami and a container of milk. Things have settled down for the evening but the street and its ballet have not come to a stop.

7. I know the deep night ballet and its seasons best from waking long after midnight to tend a baby and, sitting in the dark, seeing the shadows and hearing the sounds of the sidewalk. Mostly it is a sound like infinitely pattering snatches of party conversation and, about three in the morning, singing, very good singing. Sometimes there is sharpness and anger or sad, sad weeping, or a flurry of search for a string of beads broken. One night a young man came roaring along, bellowing terrible language at two girls whom he had apparently picked up and who were disappointing him. Doors opened, a wary semicircle formed around him, not too close, until the police came. Out came the heads, too, along Hudson Street, offering opinion, "Drunk . . . Crazy . . . A wild kid from the suburbs."*

8. Deep in the night, I am almost unaware how many people are on the street unless something calls them together, like the bagpipe. Who the piper was and why he favored our street I have no idea. The bagpipe just skirled out in the February night, and as if it were a signal the random, dwindled movements of the sidewalk took on direction. Swiftly, quietly, almost magically a little crowd was there, a crowd that evolved into a circle with a Highland fling inside it. The crowd could be seen on the shadowy sidewalk, the dancers could be seen, but the bagpiper himself was almost invisible because his bravura was all in his music. He was a very little man in a plain brown overcoat. When he finished and vanished, the dancers and watchers applauded, and applause came from the galleries too, half a dozen of the hundred windows on Hudson Street. Then the windows closed, and the little crowd dissolved into the random movements of the night street.

*He turned out to be a wild kid from the suburbs. Sometimes, on Hudson Street, we are tempted to believe the suburbs must be a difficult place to bring up children.

9. The strangers on Hudson Street, the allies whose eyes help us natives keep the peace of the street, are so many that they always seem to be different people from one day to the next. That does not matter. Whether they are so many always-different people as they seem to be, I do not know. Likely they are. When Jimmy Rogan fell through a plate-glass window (he was separating some scuffling friends) and almost lost his arm, a stranger in an old T shirt emerged from the Ideal bar, swiftly applied an expert tourniquet and, according to the hospital's emergency staff, saved Jimmy's life. Nobody remembered seeing the man before and no one has seen him since. The hospital was called in this way: a woman sitting on the steps next to the accident ran over to the bus stop, wordlessly snatched the dime from the hand of a stranger who was waiting with his fifteen-cent fare ready, and raced into the Ideal's phone booth. The stranger raced after her to offer the nickel too. Nobody remembered seeing him before, and no one has seen him since. When you see the same stranger three or four times on Hudson Street, you begin to nod. This is almost getting to be an acquaintance, a public acquaintance, of course.

10. I have made the daily ballet of Hudson Street sound more frenetic than it is, because writing it telescopes it. In real life, it is not that way. In real life, to be sure, something is always going on, the ballet is never at a halt, but the general effect is peaceful and the general tenor even leisurely. People who know well such animated city streets will know how it is. I am afraid people who do not will always have it a little wrong in their heads—like the old prints of rhinoceroses made from travelers' descriptions of rhinoceroses.

11. On Hudson Street, the same as in the North End of Boston or in any other animated neighborhoods of great cities, we are not innately more competent at keeping the sidewalks safe than are the people who try to live off the hostile truce of Turf in a blind-eyed city. We are the lucky possessors of a city order that makes it relatively simple to keep the peace because there are plenty of eyes on the street. But there is nothing simple about that order itself, or the bewildering number of components that go into it. Most of those components are specialized in one way or another. They unite in their joint effect upon the sidewalk, which is not specialized in the least. That is its strength.

WORDS

What is the meaning of the italicized words in the following phrases?

1. "*replete* with new improvisations" (par. 1)
2. "the *vantage* point" (par. 3)
3. "exchange my *ritual* farewell" (par. 3)
4. "ballet is reaching its *crescendo* (par. 5)
5. "a *wary* semicircle formed" (par. 7)
6. "his *bravura* was all in his music" (par. 8)
7. "sound more *frenetic* than it is" (par. 10)
8. "general *tenor* even leisurely" (par. 10)
9. "any other *animated* neighborhoods" (par. 11)
10. "not *innately* more competent" (par. 11)

FORM AND CONTENT

1. In describing the details of what she has called "an intricate ballet," the author (in par. 3) uses many specific "action" verbs and verbals. In the first sentence she uses *sweep, unlocking, stacking, bringing, arranging, depositing,* and *learning.* List five more such verbs or verbals in the rest of paragraph 3.
2. The thesis that the author is illustrating is stated at the beginning and again at the end of the essay. Select two sentences, one from the first paragraph and one from the last, that state her thesis.
3. Why does the author compare city sidewalk use to an intricate ballet rather than to the precision of a chorus line?
4. What natural changes in the scene the author is describing are indicated by dividing the description into four paragraphs (pars. 3–6)?
5. What is the rhetorical effect of the short sentences that end paragraphs 3 and 11?

SUGGESTIONS FOR WRITING AND DISCUSSION

1. What kind of neighborhood would you most prefer to live in—a farming community, a small town, an affluent suburb, or a city apartment or town house? Explain.
2. The oldest cliché about New York City is that it is a great place to visit but no place to live. If you have (or reject) this opinion of New York (or any other city or country), explain your attitude.

WHERE—Place and Appearance

3. How have population growth and pressure affected a town, a lake, a beach, or a park that you have known for a long time? Describe what has happened.
4. Many writers have believed that living in wilderness or wide open spaces influences men and women to become better, braver, and more noble. Do you agree? Why, or why not?
5. Describe a place that has always had some kind of effect on your mood and feelings.

Definition and Relationship

Which of the common diseases leads to death on the highway, in the home, and at the beach? Which of two great generals embodied an ideal image of an aristocratic society? Which myth will best justify the big mess in your house or apartment? And which method will be used by your furnace, your purse, or your cigarette lighter to resist and defeat you?

In the essays printed here, one author defines and describes a disease, and another compares two great men. Much more lightheartedly, two other authors classify both the ways we rationalize our untidiness and the ways we are bedeviled and frustrated by our possessions.

Thus these four essays offer a good example of definition, an excellent demonstration of comparison and contrast, and two skillful classifications of problems in everyday living. All are worthy of study, for defining, comparing, and classifying are operations required in almost every kind of expository writing done in college.

Living with Jellinek's Disease

Kathleen Whalen FitzGerald

Kathleen Whalen FitzGerald, writer and novelist, is a contributor to Newsweek.

In this essay she defines Jellinek's disease in two ways: first, she describes it and distinguishes it from other diseases; and second, she gives its more common and easily recognized name. The essay is more than a mere exercise in definition; it is also an argument against the use of the familiar name for the disease—a name burdened by many misconceptions, misunderstandings, and prejudices.

1. My name is Kathleen. I have Jellinek's disease. As a woman discovers a malignancy buried in her breast when she bathes, I, too, discovered my disease in private. Ironically, I had been to the doctor only two weeks before and he had missed it. So subtle, so deadly is Jellinek's disease.

2. How could this horrible thing have happened to me, struck by Jellinek's disease just as my father before me? He died of Jellinek's, and I thought I knew all about it and was smart enough to avoid this insidious illness. Not so, for Jellinek's is no respecter of persons. It strikes young and old, rich and poor, black, brown and white—any that fall within its ravaging path.

3. How could this have happened to me? I live in a good neighborhood and have beautiful children, a successful husband and go to mass every Sunday. I've been to college and read and pray and lead a good life, yet I contracted Jellinek's disease.

4. As I began to realize the scope of my illness, I was plunged into grief, for never again would I be like ordinary people. I railed against my God for having done this to me, and I shook my clenched fists at my genes, my heredity, my father, for had I not been programmed long before my birth to be a Jellinek's victim? As Tay-Sachs disease strikes Jews and sickle-cell anemia strikes blacks, so Jellinek's disease visits the Irish with unfair regularity. Yet we Irish are far from alone in this illness.

5. I knew the statistics. Jellinek's ranks with heart disease and cancer as the country's three major health problems. There are an estimated 12 million of us who suffer from Jellinek's disease; nearly 25 percent of us are teenagers. The average Jellinek's victim is in his or her 40s with a family and a job. Many of us do not know we have Jellinek's disease, and many of us are ashamed that we do. We try to hide it from ourselves and from the rest of you.

6. Jellinek's disease is responsible for:

- 50 percent of all auto fatalities.
- 80 percent of all home violence.
- 30 percent of all suicides.
- 60 percent of all child abuse.
- 65 percent of all drownings.

7. It is estimated that when a woman contracts the disease, her husband leaves her in 9 out of 10 cases; when a man contracts it, his wife leaves in 1 out of 10 cases.

8. Jellinek's disease costs the nation $54.1 billion annually; half of this is paid for by industry in lost time, health and welfare benefits, property damage, medical expenses and overhead costs of insurance and lost wages.

9. My disease was named after Dr. E. M. Jellinek (1890–1963), who conducted his research at Yale University and served as a consultant to the World Health Organization. Dr. Jellinek was the first to define medically and to chart the progression of the fatal disease into its various stages: early, prodromal, crucial, chronic.

10. Jellinek's disease is another name for alcoholism, the most neglected health problem in the United States today. Neglect springs from denial, the hallmark of alcoholism. In other words: if I say that I am not an alcoholic, then I am not an alcoholic and I do not need help. Consequently, it is a fact that only 5 to 10 percent of alcoholics recover. (Not that we can ever drink again, but we can learn to live happily without it.)

11. Medical science is making headway into the denial morass. Not long ago, alcoholism was rejected as a disease because it did not show up on an X-ray or a CAT scan. Hard information is now available to show that alcoholics are genetically predisposed to this disease and that their blood chemistry and brain electricity demonstrate a pathological response to the ingestion of alcohol.

12. Nationally, we deny the existence of Jellinek's disease and minimize the impact it has on the health of our citizens. In 1977 the federal government spent twice as much on dental research as it did on alcoholism research. How many murders and fatal accidents are accounted for by impacted wisdom teeth or an unsightly overbite?

13. One of the major causes for the denial, shame and neglect is the name by which we call it: *alcoholism.* It is replete with negative social and moral implications: skid row; bag ladies; a crazed, drunken father murdering his seven children; a priest stumbling on the altar; red roses for a very blue lady; William Holden cracking his head and dying alone.

14. As we have become more mature and wiser in our understanding of physical, genetic and accidental handicaps, our language has become more sophisticated, more reflective of this maturity. No longer do we say Mongoloid, but Down's syndrome; a cripple is a paraplegic; a child slow to learn is no longer retarded, but exceptional; the insane have become manic-depressive or schizophrenic.

15. To the degree that myth, misconception and misunderstanding surround an illness, recovery is inhibited. The myth of alcoholism is that its victims are weak-willed, sinful and selfish. As if we sought and reveled in our illness. As if we felt no pain. As if we ought to control ourselves. It is easier to control diarrhea than to assert the will over alcoholism.

16. For over 25 years, the American Medical Association has recognized alcoholism as a disease with identifiable, progressive symptoms that, if untreated, lead to mental damage, physical incapacity and early death. Our lives are cut short by 10 to 12 years. Yet alcoholism is an *ism,* like names of doctrines or theories or styles: fascism; imperialism; cubism; Thomism; realism; heroism. What other disease is an *ism?* Cancerism? Diabetesism? Herpesism? Alcoholism is not a theory or doctrine or style. It is a disease that kills its victims and its victims' victims.

17. As long as we cling to the name alcoholism we relegate the disease to the dark chambers of sin and shame and preclude its righteous acceptance as an illness. The name, likewise, resonates as an ism, an abstract, theoretical entity that deflects from the reality of a disease that can be treated and healed.

18. Sticks and stones will break my bones and names, indeed, do hurt me.

19. My name is Kathleen. I have Jellinek's disease.

WORDS

What is the meaning of the italicized words in the following phrases?

1. "So *subtle*" (par. 1)
2. "this *insidious* illness" (par. 2)
3. "its *ravaging* path" (par. 2)
4. "I *railed* against my God" (par. 4)
5. "its various stages: early, *prodromal*" (par. 9)
6. "the *hallmark* of alcoholism" (par. 10)
7. "the denial *morass*" (par. 11)
8. "are genetically *predisposed* to this disease" (par. 11)
9. "the *ingestion* of alcohol" (par. 11)
10. "the name, likewise, *resonates*" (par. 17)

FORM AND CONTENT

1. In this essay, Kathleen FitzGerald explains what Jellinek's disease really is; however, she is dissatisfied with the name society has given the disease. Why?
2. What two personal reasons make the author a reliable and knowledgeable authority (pars. 1 and 2)?
3. What is the function of the opening nine paragraphs? Why is the word "Jellinek" repeated so often and what is gained by this repetition?
4. What information found in paragraph 11 should refute one of the "myths" of alcoholism (par. 15)?
5. What is the function of paragraph 17? Would this information have more impact if it had been stated earlier in the essay?

SUGGESTIONS FOR WRITING AND DISCUSSION

1. Write an essay defining a well-known *ism*—patriotism, socialism, realism, vegetarianism. First describe what the term represents; then reveal the actual term itself at the conclusion of the essay.
2. Define a word or a term or a piece of slang that is currently used almost exclusively by young people.
3. When is a man or a woman old? Define *old age.*
4. What steps if any should a high school administrator or a school board take to protect students from drug pushers?
5. Someone who has a problem with drugs or alcohol is said to have an "addictive personality." How does such a person differ from someone with normal appetites?

Grant and Lee

Bruce Catton

Bruce Catton (1899–1978) was a respected and admired historian of the American Civil War, a winner of both the Pulitzer Prize for nonfiction and the National Book Award.

In this selection, he first contrasts the two greatest generals of the war, explaining their differences in background and philosophy, and then he compares their even more important similarities. This extended exercise in comparison and contrast helps the reader to understand both men better, just as a brief metaphor or simile can give a line of prose or poetry a heightened meaning.

1. When Ulysses S. Grant and Robert E. Lee met in the parlor of a modest house at Appomattox Court House, Virginia, on April 9, 1865, to work out the terms for the surrender of Lee's Army of Northern Virginia, a great chapter in American life came to a close, and a great new chapter began.

2. These men were bringing the Civil War to its virtual finish. To be sure, other armies had yet to surrender, and for a few days the fugitive Confederate government would struggle desperately and vainly, trying to find some way to go on living now that its chief support was gone. But in effect it was all over when Grant and Lee signed the papers. And the little room where they wrote out the terms was the scene of one of the poignant, dramatic contrasts in American history.

3. They were two strong men, these oddly different generals, and they represented the strengths of two conflicting currents that, through them, had come into final collision.

4. Back of Robert E. Lee was the notion that the old aristocratic concept might somehow survive and be dominant in American life.

5. Lee was tidewater Virginia, and in his background were family, culture, and tradition . . . the age of chivalry transplanted to a New World which was making its own legends and its own myths. He embodied a way of life that had come down through the age of knighthood and the English country squire. America was a land that was beginning all over again, dedicated to nothing much more complicated than the rather hazy belief that all men had equal rights and should have an equal chance in the world. In such a land Lee stood for the feeling that it was somehow of advantage to human society to have a pronounced inequality in the social structure. There should be a leisure class, backed by ownership of land; in turn, society itself should be keyed to the land as the chief source of wealth and influence. It would bring forth (according to this ideal) a class of men with a strong sense of obligation to the community; men who lived not to gain advantage for themselves, but to meet the solemn obligations which had been laid on them by the very fact that they were privileged. From them the country would get its leadership; to them it could look for the higher values—of thought, of conduct, of personal deportment—to give it strength and virtue.

6. Lee embodied the noblest elements of this

aristocratic ideal. Through him, the landed nobility justified itself. For four years, the Southern states had fought a desperate war to uphold the ideals for which Lee stood. In the end, it almost seemed as if the Confederacy fought for Lee; as if he himself was the Confederacy . . . the best thing that the way of life for which the Confederacy stood could ever have to offer. He had passed into legend before Appomattox. Thousands of tired, underfed, poorly clothed Confederate soldiers, long since past the simple enthusiasm of the early days of the struggle, somehow considered Lee the symbol of everything for which they had been willing to die. But they could not quite put this feeling into words. If the Lost Cause, sanctified by so much heroism and so many deaths, had a living justification, its justification was General Lee.

7. Grant, the son of a tanner on the Western frontier, was everything Lee was not. He had come up the hard way and embodied nothing in particular except the eternal toughness and sinewy fiber of the men who grew up beyond the mountains. He was one of a body of men who owed reverence and obeisance to no one, who were self-reliant to a fault, who cared hardly anything for the past but who had a sharp eye for the future.

8. These frontier men were the precise opposites of the tidewater aristocrats. Back of them, in the great surge that had taken people over the Alleghenies and into the opening Western country, there was a deep, implicit dissatisfaction with a past that had settled into grooves. They stood for democracy, not from any reasoned conclusion about the proper ordering of human society, but simply because they had grown up in the middle of democracy and knew how it worked. Their society might have privileges, but they would be privileges each man had won for himself. Forms and patterns meant nothing. No man was born to anything, except perhaps to a chance to show how far he could rise. Life was competition.

9. Yet along with this feeling had come a deep sense of belonging to a national community. The Westerner who developed a farm, opened a shop, or set up in business as a trader, could hope to prosper only as his own community prospered—and his community ran from the Atlantic to the Pacific and from Canada down to Mexico. If the land was settled, with towns and highways and accessible markets, he could better himself. He saw his fate in terms of the nation's own destiny. As its horizons expanded, so did his. He had, in other words, an acute dollars-and-cents stake in the continued growth and development of his country.

10. And that, perhaps, is where the contrast between Grant and Lee becomes most striking. The Virginia aristocrat, inevitably, saw himself in relation to his own region. He lived in a static society which could endure almost anything except change. Instinctively, his first loyalty would go to the locality in which that society existed. He would fight to the limit of endurance to defend it, because in defending it he was defending everything that gave his own life its deepest meaning.

11. The Westerner, on the other hand, would fight with an equal tenacity for the broader concept of society. He fought so because everything he lived by was tied to growth, expansion, and a constantly widening horizon. What he lived by would survive or fall with the nation itself. He could not possibly stand by unmoved in the face of an attempt to destroy the Union. He would combat it with everything he had, because he could only see it as an effort to cut the ground out from under his feet.

12. So Grant and Lee were in complete contrast, representing two diametrically opposed elements in American life. Grant was the modern man emerging; beyond him, ready to come on the stage, was the great age of steel and machinery, of crowded cities and a restless burgeoning vitality. Lee might have ridden down from the old age of chivalry, lance in hand, silken banner fluttering over his head. Each man was the perfect champion of his cause, drawing both his strengths and his weaknesses from the people he led.

13. Yet it was not all contrast, after all. Different as they were—in background, in personality, in underlying aspiration—these two great soldiers had much in common. Under everything else, they were marvelous fighters. Furthermore, their fighting qualities were really very much alike.

14. Each man had, to begin with, the great virtue of utter tenacity and fidelity. Grant fought his way down the Mississippi Valley in spite of acute personal discouragement and profound military handicaps. Lee hung on in the trenches at Petersburg after hope itself had died. In each man there was an indomitable quality . . . the born fighter's refusal to give up as long as he can still remain on his feet and lift his two fists.

15. Daring and resourcefulness they had, too; the ability to think faster and move faster than the enemy. These were the qualities which gave Lee the dazzling campaigns of Second Manassas and Chancellorsville and won Vicksburg for Grant.

16. Lastly, and perhaps greatest of all, there was the ability, at the end, to turn quickly from war to peace once the fighting was over. Out of the way these two men behaved at Appomattox came the possibility of a peace of reconciliation. It was a possibility not wholly realized, in the years to come, but which did, in the end, help the two sections to become one nation again . . . after a war whose bitterness might have seemed to make such a reunion wholly impossible. No part of either man's life became him more than the part he played in their brief meeting in the McLean house at Appomattox. Their behavior there put all succeeding generations of Americans in their debt. Two great Americans, Grant and Lee—very different, yet under everything very much alike. Their encounter at Appomattox was one of the great moments of American history.

WORDS

What is the meaning of the italicized words in the following phrases?

1. "one of the *poignant,* dramatic contrasts" (par. 2)
2. "to have a *pronounced* inequality" (par. 5)
3. "*sanctified* by so much heroism" (par. 6)
4. "*sinewy* fiber of the men" (par. 7)
5. "the great virtue of utter *tenacity*" (par. 14)

FORM AND CONTENT

1. What advantage did people like Lee see in having a landed aristocracy in American society (par. 5)?
2. How did privileges in the Confederacy differ from privileges on the Western frontier (pars. 5–8)?
3. In comparing Lee and Grant, does Catton show a preference for either? Why, or why not?

4. How does the last paragraph of this selection use echoes of the first paragraph to achieve an effective conclusion?
5. What is the difference between paragraphs 3 to 12 and paragraphs 13 to 16?

SUGGESTIONS FOR WRITING AND DISCUSSION

1. Contrast the appearance and classroom style of any two markedly different high school or college teachers.
2. Compare two automobiles, one domestic and one foreign. Choose the one that you prefer.
3. Contrast the different attitudes of your parents' generation and your own toward relations between men and women.
4. Contrast the attitudes toward courtesy held by two different cultures or two different age groups.
5. Contrast two places you like to visit, places that are totally dissimilar.

On Being a Mess

Elizabeth Ames

Elizabeth Ames, who lives in New York, contributed this essay to Newsweek.

The following selection is an unpretentious and amusing treatment of the shortcomings and problems of Messy People [the initial capitalizations are the author's]. But it is also a good example of the usefulness of classification—separating things by kind. Here the author classifies the myths that Messy People use to justify their sloppiness. The classification may not be completely comprehensive, but it helps to contrast a number of ingenious rationalizations.

1. I am one of those people who simply cannot clean up. To me, the prospect of an orderly living space is as remote—and problematic—as trying to climb Mount Kilimanjaro.

2. There's a definite syndrome of sloppiness. Many people, I've noticed, go about being sloppy in much the same way. I'm not sure what to call us. Mess-aholics? Mess-addicts? Whatever we are, the one thing we are *not* is slobs. Slobs wallow in their mess. Messy People (for want of a better label) groan over it. We're continually apologizing to the tune of, "My apartment is such a pigsty. My house is such a mess." We are always embarrassed.

3. When my place is at its worst, I frequently invite another Messy Person over. We'll engage in an odd one-upmanship that is both competition and consolation. "I'm sorry, the place is terrible." "You should see *mine.* It's ten times worse." "Oh, no, it isn't." "Yes, it is." Etc.

4. Messy People want to clean up, but we can't. Not that we don't try. We do, and probably more strenuously than most Neat People. I have scoured and dusted my tiny apartment on more sunny Saturdays than I can count. I have slogged through three-day marathons (attacking the kitchen, the living room, the bedroom and bathroom in turn). Yet somehow the apartment will not come to order. Soon after I've thrown in the sponge, I'm again tripping on the same sneakers and piles of underwear.

5. We can never quite conquer the Mess. Rout it from the living room, and it withdraws to the bedroom. From there it may retreat under the bed or into dresser drawers. A protean monster, it forever changes form to evade us.

6. To complicate matters, it is also omnivorous. It eats my keys (usually before I go out). It eats my shoes. And worst of all, it eats my bills. That can have sticky consequences because who, after all, misses bills? Occasionally, it takes the threat of legal action for me to discover that the Mess devoured my bills before I had a chance to pay them.

7. Often the Mess seems to rule our lives. I have declined dozens of casual engagements because "I have to get rid of that Mess." Then there are the potential visitors I've had to meet in restaurants "because there is a giant Mess in my apartment."

8. Other times, the only way to subdue the Mess is to invite people to dinner. But even when I've labored over my apartment all afternoon—even when I think I have it licked—the Mess rears its ugly head.

9. "What about the newspapers on the floor?" a well-meaning friend will chide. "What about those files and legal pads on the dining-room table?"

10. "But I haven't *finished* those newspapers and I *work* on the dining-room table." My friends shake their heads sadly. I am surely a lost cause.

11. And that's on a good day. On bad days, the Mess takes over completely. There is no space at all on that dining-room table, or anywhere else for that matter. Everything I own is lost under the rubble. On tiptoe, I pick my way around the books and assorted papers, trying not to step on anything important.

12. On bad days I frequently cannot decide what to wear, partly because half my wardrobe—the clothes I wore last week—is heaped on the bedroom desk.

13. As for the kitchen, it can be downright scary. I dread opening the dark refrigerator, certain that some forgotten tomatoes have metamorphosed into new forms of life. Who knows what lurks in the sink? The dishes there form towers that lean precariously. They usually manage to fall over between 2 and 3 A.M.

14. I'm convinced that on one bad day I will enter my apartment and suddenly panic—thinking I've been robbed when I haven't. After all, how could a normal person wreak such havoc? I must be living with some invisible maniac, or a crazed gorilla.

15. Perhaps that is why so many Messy People feel "exposed" when a stranger glimpses their Mess. Beneath our attempts at denial, we have seen the enemy and he is certainly no crazed gorilla . . .

16. Reality, however, is not always easy to face. Thus we have devised several ingenious myths to justify our Mess—and ourselves. They are:

- ***The Clean Mess.*** This myth is our primary protection against the gruesome label, "slob." Slobs, of course, live in filth. Messy People live amid a profusion of sterile objects. "What's wrong," we ask, "with some basically clean clothes lying around? At least they're not fungus."
- ***The Intellectual Mess.*** According to this one, we are too busy pondering the state of the universe to bother with such earthly realities as unmade beds. We are creative nonconformists whose order is disorder. People with Intellectual Messes look down their noses at unimaginative organized souls. There's no challenge, they insist, in finding a dictionary *right away.* How routine. How dull.
- ***It's My Mother's Fault.*** Behind nearly every Messy Person is a Meticulous Mother. We love to recount our childhood torment at her hands and bemoan its effects: "She ordered me to do the bathroom so many times! I now have convulsions at the sight of window cleaner . . . So much talk about eating off her floors warped my subconscious. I'm acting out delusions of being an animal." And so on.
- ***It's My Apartment's Fault.*** People who rely on this complain, "There's no place left to put anything. My closets are full. What would I do with those things I'm saving for the Salvation Army? What would I do with my stuffed giraffe, Snookie? And those old broiler pans belonged to my grandfather!"

17. Such are the myths of Mess. Myths, because there are plenty of neat folks with brains, badgering mothers and small apartments. Being a mess is no blessing. The only way out is to probe your true motives, discard the excuses and accept responsibility. For me, that was a gut-wrenching process. It was so powerful, in fact, that I didn't wash dishes for two weeks.

WORDS

What is the meaning of the italicized words in the following phrases?

1. "a definite *syndrome*" (par. 2)
2. "an odd *one-upmanship*" (par. 3)
3. "I have *scoured*" (par. 4)
4. "A *protean* monster" (par. 5)
5. "it is also *omnivorous*" (par. 6)
6. "a . . . friend will *chide*" (par. 9)
7. "tomatoes have *metamorphosed*" (par. 13)
8. "*wreak* such havoc" (par. 14)
9. "several *ingenious* myths" (par. 16)
10. "a *Meticulous* Mother" (par. 16)
11. "acting out *delusions*" (par. 16)

FORM AND CONTENT

1. The author organizes her essay into three parts: paragraphs 2–10, 11–15, and 16–17. What is the general topic discussed in each of the three parts?
2. Comment on Ames' humorous use of capitalization throughout her essay.
3. Explain the effectiveness of the "protean monster" reference in paragraphs 5 and 6.
4. In four separate sentences, summarize each of the author's myths (par. 16).
5. Note the play on words in paragraph 15: "We have seen the enemy . . ." Who, then, is the enemy?

SUGGESTIONS FOR WRITING AND DISCUSSION

1. Most family garages contain large collections of various things. Write an essay classifying the possessions in your garage, closet, or storage room.
2. Many people like the author boast of their faults. If you have a fault of which you can boast or that you can make entertaining, describe it.
3. Neil Simon once wrote a play called *The Odd Couple* about two men, one of whom was very neat and one very messy. Which of these characters would you find it harder to live with?
4. Some people "keep up with the Joneses" by imitating their expenditures, possessions, or life-styles. Classify the people you know who try to "keep up with the Joneses."
5. As a younger person you were probably asked by your parents to clean up your room. Why do most, if not all, young people have messy rooms that they are reluctant to clean?

The Plot Against People

Russell Baker

Russell Baker, the author of Growing Up, *a moving autobiography, is one of America's best-known writers of humor and a columnist for* The New York Times.

This brief essay is essentially a burlesque of scientific classification, dividing inanimate objects into three classes—"those that don't work, those that break down, and those that get lost." And this classification helps to wring humor out of frequent irritations everyone has experienced. Yet it is this kind of classification that is indispensable in sciences like botany, in professions like law and medicine, and in much of the business of the world.

1. Washington, June 17—Inanimate objects are classified scientifically into three major categories—those that don't work, those that break down and those that get lost.

2. The goal of all inanimate objects is to resist man and ultimately to defeat him, and the three major classifications are based on the method each object uses to achieve its purpose. As a general rule, any object capable of breaking down at the moment when it is most needed will do so. The automobile is typical of the category.

3. With the cunning typical of its breed, the automobile never breaks down while entering a filling station with a large staff of idle mechanics. It waits until it reaches a downtown intersection in the middle of the rush hour, or until it is fully loaded with family and luggage on the Ohio Turnpike.

4. Thus it creates maximum misery, inconvenience, frustration and irritability among its human cargo, thereby reducing its owner's life span.

5. Washing machines, garbage disposals, lawn mowers, light bulbs, automatic laundry dryers, water pipes, furnaces, electrical fuses, television tubes, hose nozzles, tape recorders, slide projectors—all are in league with the automobile to take their turn at breaking down whenever life threatens to flow smoothly for their human enemies.

6. Many inanimate objects, of course, find it extremely difficult to break down. Pliers, for example, and gloves and keys are almost totally incapable of breaking down. Therefore, they have had to evolve a different technique for resisting man.

7. They get lost. Science has still not solved the mystery of how they do it, and no man has ever caught one of them in the act of getting lost. The most plausible theory is that they have developed a secret method of locomotion which they are able to conceal the instant a human eye falls upon them.

8. It is not uncommon for a pair of pliers to climb all the way from the cellar to the attic in its single-minded determination to raise its owner's blood pressure. Keys have been known to burrow three feet under mattresses. Women's purses, despite their great weight, frequently travel through six or seven rooms to find hiding space under a couch.

9. Scientists have been struck by the fact that things that break down virtually never get lost, while things that get lost hardly ever break down.

10. A furnace, for example, will invariably break down at the depth of the first winter cold wave, but it will never get lost. A woman's purse, which after all does have some inherent capacity for breaking down, hardly ever does; it almost invariably chooses to get lost.

11. Some persons believe this constitutes evidence that inanimate objects are not entirely hostile to man, and that a negotiated peace is possible. After all, they point out, a furnace could infuriate a man even more thoroughly by getting lost than by breaking down, just as a glove could upset him far more by breaking down than by getting lost.

12. Not everyone agrees, however, that this indicates a conciliatory attitude among inanimate objects. Many say it merely proves that furnaces, gloves and pliers are incredibly stupid.

13. The third class of objects—those that don't work—is the most curious of all. These include such objects as barometers, car clocks, cigarette lighters, flashlights and toy-train locomotives. It is inaccurate, of course, to say that they never work. They work once, usually for the first few hours after being brought home, and then quit. Thereafter, they never work again.

14. In fact, it is widely assumed that they are built for the purpose of not working. Some people have reached advanced ages without ever seeing some of these objects—barometers, for example—in working order.

15. Science is utterly baffled by the entire category. There are many theories about it. The most interesting holds that the things that don't work have attained the highest state possible for an inanimate object, the state to which things break down and things that get lost can still only aspire.

16. They have truly defeated man by conditioning him never to expect anything of them, and in return they have given man the only peace he receives from inanimate society. He does not expect his barometer to work, his electric locomotive to run, his cigarette lighter to light or his flashlight to illuminate, and when they don't it does not raise his blood pressure.

17. He cannot attain that peace with furnaces and keys and cars and women's purses as long as he demands that they work for their keep.

——— WORDS

What is the meaning of the italicized words in the following phrases?

1. "*Inanimate* objects" (par. 1)
2. "*cunning* typical of its breed" (par. 3)
3. "*idle* mechanics" (par. 3)
4. "The most *plausible* theory" (par. 7)
5. "some *inherent* capacity" (par. 10)
6. "*infuriate* a man" (par. 11)
7. "a *conciliatory* attitude" (par. 12)
8. "*incredibly* stupid" (par. 12)
9. "utterly *baffled*" (par. 15)
10. "*attained* the highest state" (par. 15)

FORM AND CONTENT

1. This essay depends for its humor partly on the use of personification. What is *personification* and how is it used here?
2. Baker's essay classifies inanimate objects into three categories. How is the transition between the second and third made (pars. 6 and 7)?
3. Baker's humor depends in part on "mock seriousness." That is, he pretends to be more serious than he really is. Evaluate his use of the words "scientifically," "science," and "scientists" in paragraphs 1, 7, 9, and 15.
4. In what paragraph is the thesis of the essay stated?
5. How is overstatement used for comic effect in this essay? The single sentence in paragraph 4 is a good example of this technique.

SUGGESTIONS FOR WRITING AND DISCUSSION

1. If you have had a long feud with a particular inanimate object, describe your difficulties, frustrations, and attempts to conquer.
2. Classify your friends by degree of importance to you, by your importance to them, or by any similarities that a number of them share.
3. Classify your hobbies in a way that will suggest something about you and your personality.
4. Write an essay in which you classify people by types: types of teachers, students, administrators, or business people.
5. When you buy a used car, how can you best evaluate its condition and serviceability?

Action and Outcome

An odd group of Maine men go on a coon hunt, the heavyweight champion of the world defends his title, a future president of the United States fights for his honor, and a twenty-eight-year-old woman is murdered in full view of thirty-eight witnesses. These are accounts of conflict and resolution, interesting of and for themselves.

But they are also interesting because of their larger significance. For one of the coon hunters, this was his first experience, as it was for a puppy who also made the trip. For a young black child in rural Arkansas, Joe Louis' championship had a very special significance. For American history, the early morning duel proved that Andrew Jackson could not be frightened by a boast or stopped by a bullet. And for thirty-eight people in Queens, New York, the need not to get involved was fatal for a young woman.

Thus all the action of the four narratives printed here is meaningful. The authors are concerned not only with what happened, but also with what it meant. And the technique of each narrator is perfectly adapted to his or her purpose.

Coon Hunt

E. B. White

E. B. White is one of America's most respected essayists, humorists, and social critics. Two of his children's books— Charlotte's Web *and* Stuart Little*—have become classics.*

Telling a story is as natural and familiar an act as describing a person or a place. In the following essay, White demonstrates his skill in narrative writing by setting forth a series of events and sprinkling them with wry humor, tongue-in-cheek irony, "down country" dialect, understatement, and figurative language. It is obvious from the start that White is an observer, not a genuine hunter. But he accompanies the "odd lot" of hunters and dogs and writes gracefully about the first night he went coon hunting.

1. There were two dogs with us the night we went coon hunting. One was an old hound, veteran of a thousand campaigns, who knew what we were up to and who wasted no time in idle diversions. The other was a puppy, brought along to observe and learn; to him the star-sprinkled sky and the deep dark woods and the myriad scents and the lateness of the hour and the frosty ground were intoxicating. The excitement of our departure was too much for his bowels. Tied in the truck, he was purged all the way over to Winkumpaw Brook and was hollow as a rotten log before the night was well under way. This may have had something to do with what happened.

2. It was great hunting that night, perfect for man and beast, a fateful night for coon. The stars leaned close, and some lost their hold and fell. I was amazed at how quickly and easily the men moved through the woods in strange country, guided by hunches and a bit of lantern gleam. The woods hit back at you if you let your guard down.

3. We were an odd lot. A couple of the men were in coveralls—those bunny suits garage mechanics wear. One old fellow had been all stove to pieces in a car accident; another was down with a hard cold and a racking cough; another had broken two ribs the day before and had been strapped up that afternoon by a doctor. He had killed the pain with a few shots of whisky and the spirits had evidently reminded him of coon hunting. This fellow had a terrible thirst for water all during the night and he had a way of straying off from the main party and hugging the water courses where he could kneel and drink when the need was great. We could sometimes follow the progress of his thirst in the winking of his buglight, in some faraway valley. After a bit he would rejoin us. "I'm drier'n a covered bridge," he would say disconsolately.

4. I felt a strong affinity for the puppy because he and I were the new ones to this strange game, and somehow it seemed to me we were sharing the same excitement and mystery of a night in the woods. I had begun to feel the excitement back in the kitchen of the farmhouse, where the hunters had gathered, dropping in and standing about against the walls of the room. The talk began right away, all the cooning lore, the tales of being lost from three in the

morning until six, and the tricks a coon would play on a dog. There was a woman in the room, wife of the owner of the old dog, and she was the only one for whom the night held no special allure. She sat knitting a huge mitten. Mostly, the hunters paid no attention to her. Only one remark went her way. One of the men, observing the mitten, asked:

5. "Gettin' that man o'yours ready for winter?"

6. She nodded.

7. "I should kill him before winter if he was mine—he's no good for anything else," the fellow continued, pleasantly.

8. The woman raised a grudging smile to this sure-fire witticism. She plied the needles without interruption. This obviously was not the first time she had been left at home while men and dogs went about their business, and it wasn't going to be the last time either. For her it was just one night in a long succession of nights. This was the fall and in the fall the men hunted coon. They left after sundown and returned before sunup. That was all there was to that.

9. The best coon country is always far away. Men are roamers, and getting a long way from home is part of the sport. Our motorcade consisted of two vehicles, a truck for the dogs and owners, and a sedan for the hangers-on, lantern-bearers, and advisory committee. The old dog jumped into place the minute he was let out of the barn; the puppy was hoisted in and tied. The two of them sat on a pile of straw just behind the cab. The man with the broken ribs got into the sedan. Nobody seemed to think it was in the least odd that he was going coon hunting, to walk twelve or fifteen miles in rough country. He said the adhesive tape held everything O.K. and anyway, he said, the only time his chest hurt was when he breathed.

10. We advanced without stealth, the truck leading. The headlights of our car shone directly in the faces of the dogs. The old dog leaned back craftily against the sideboards, to steady himself against the motion. He half closed his eyes and was as quiet on the journey as a middle-aged drummer on a way train. The pup crouched uneasily and was frequently thrown. He would rare up and sniff, then crouch again, then a curve would throw him and he would lose his balance and go down. He found a hole in the sideboards and occasionally would press his nose through to sniff the air. Then the excitement would attack his bowels and he would let go all over everything—with some difficulty because of the violent motion of the truck. The old dog observed this untidiness with profound contempt.

11. We got away from the highway after a while and followed a rough back road up into some country I had never been into. At last we got out and let the old hound go. He went to work instantly, dropping downhill out of sight. We could hear his little bell tinkling as he ranged about in the dim valley between us and a night-struck lake. When he picked up a scent, suddenly his full round tones went through you, and the night was a gong that had been struck. The old dog knew his business. The men, waiting around, would discuss in great detail his hunting and would describe what he was doing off there, and what the coon was doing; but I doubted that they knew, and they just kept making things up the way children do. As soon as the hound barked tree, which is a slightly different sound than the sound of the running, we followed his voice and shot the coon.

12. Once the dog led us to an old apple tree in an almost impenetrable thicket, and when the flashlights were shined up into the topmost branches no coon was there. The owner was puzzled and embarrassed. Nothing like this had ever happened before, he said. There was a long period of consultation and speculation, all sorts of theories were advanced. The most popular was that the coon had climbed the apple tree, then crossed, squirrel-like, into the branches of a nearby hackmatack, then descended, fooling the hound. Either this was the case or the dog had made an error. Upward of an hour was spent trying every angle of this delicious contretemps.

13. The puppy was held in leash most of the time, but when the first coon was treed he was allowed to watch the kill. Lights from half a dozen flashlights swept the tree top and converged to make a halo, with the coon's bright little sharp face in the center of the luminous ring. Our host lethargically drew his pistol, prolonging the climax with a legitimate sense of the theater. No one spoke while he drew a bead. The shot seemed to puncture first the night, then the coon. The coon lost his grip and landed with a thud, still alive and fighting. The old hound rushed in savagely, to grab him by the throat and finish him off. It was a big bull coon; he died bravely and swiftly, and the hound worked with silent fury. Then the puppy, in leash, was allowed to advance and sniff. He was trembling in every muscle, and was all eyes and ears and nose—like a child being allowed to see something meant only for grownups. (I felt a little that way myself.) As he stretched his nose forward timidly to inhale the heady smell of warm coon, the old hound, jealous, snarled and leaped. The owner jerked back. The puppy yelped in terror. Everyone laughed. It was a youngster, getting burned by life—that sort of sight. Made you laugh.

14. After midnight we moved into easier country about ten miles away. Here the going was better—old fields and orchards, where the little wild apples lay in thick clusters under the trees. Old stone walls ran into the woods, and now and then there would be an empty barn as a ghostly landmark. The night grew frosty and the ground underfoot was slippery with rime. The bare birches wore the stars on their fingers, and the world rolled seductively, a dark symphony of brooding groves and plains. Things had gone well, and everyone was content just to be out in the small hours, following the musical directions of a wise and busy dog.

15. The puppy's owner had slipped the leash and allowed his charge to range about a bit. Nobody was paying much attention to him. The pup stayed with the party mostly, and although he was aware of the long-range operations of the older dog, he seemed to know that this was out of his class; he seemed timid of the woods and tended to stay close, contenting himself with sniffing about and occasionally jumping up to kiss someone's face. We were stepping along through the woods, the old hound near at hand, when the thing happened. Suddenly the puppy (who had not made a sound up to this point) let out a loud whoop and went charging off on a tangent. Everybody stopped dead in surprise.

16. "What goes on here anyway?" said somebody quietly.

17. The old hound was as mystified as the rest of us. This was a show-off stunt apparently, this puppy trying to bark coon. Nobody could make it out. Obviously there was no coon scent or the old dog would have picked it up instantly and been at his work.

18. "What in *the* devil?" asked somebody.

19. The puppy was howling unmercifully as though possessed. He charged here and there and came back along his own track passing us at a crazy mad pace, and diving into the woods on the other side of the trail. The yelps sounded hysterical now. Again the puppy charged back. This time as he passed we could see that he had a queer look in his eye and that his movements were erratic. He would dive one way at a terrible clip, then stop and back off as though ducking an enemy, half cringing; but he kept putting up this terrible holler and commotion.

Once he came straight at me. I stepped aside and he went by screaming.

20. "Runnin' fit," said his owner. "That's the trouble. I can tell now by the way he acts. He's took with cramps in his bowwils and he don't know anythin' to do 'cept run and holler. C'mon, Dusty, c'mon, boy!"

21. He kept calling him softly. But Dusty was in another world and the shapes were after him. It was an eerie business, this crazy dog tearing around in the dark woods, half coming at you, half running from you. Even the old dog seemed disturbed and worried, as though to say: "You see—you *will* bring a child along, after his bedtime."

22. The men were patient, sympathetic now.

23. "That's all it is, he's took with a fit."

24. Dusty charged into the midst of us, scattering us. He stopped, bristling, his eyes too bright, a trace of froth at his mouth. He seemed half angry, half scared and wanting comfort. "Nothing much you can do, he'll run it off," they said.

25. And Dusty ran it off, in the deep dark woods, big with imaginary coons and enormous jealous old hounds, alive with the beautiful smells of the wild. His evening had been too much for him; for the time being he was as crazy as a loon. Someone suggested we go home.

26. We started moving up toward the cars, which were two or three fields away over where you could see the elms black against the sky. The thought of home wasn't popular. A counter suggestion was made to prolong the hunting, and we separated off into two parties, one to return to the cars, the other to cut across country with the old dog and intercept the main body where a certain woods road met the highway. I walked several more miles, and for the first time began to feel cold. It was another hour before I saw Dusty again. He was all right. All he needed was to be held in somebody's arms. He was very, very sleepy. He and I were both sleepy. I think we will both remember the first night we ever went coon hunting.

WORDS

What is the meaning of the italicized words in the following phrases?

1. "he would say *disconsolately*" (par. 3)
2. "a strong *affinity*" (par. 4)
3. "no special *allure*" (par. 4)
4. "She *plied* the needles" (par. 8)
5. "advanced without *stealth*" (par. 10)
6. "an almost *impenetrable* thicket" (par. 12)
7. "this delicious *contretemps*" (par. 12)
8. "*lethargically* drew his pistol" (par. 13)
9. "slippery with *rime*" (par. 14)
10. "off on a *tangent*" (par. 15)

FORM AND CONTENT

1. E. B. White sprinkles his narrative with figurative language, especially similes. Explain his "drummer" simile in paragraph 10. Identify the similes in paragraphs 13, 19, and 25.

WHAT—Action and Outcome

2. What is White's general feeling about his fellow hunters?
3. What is the one distinguishing characteristic of each of the "odd lot" who go on the hunt (par. 3)?
4. What is peculiar about the way some of White's characters talk (pars. 3, 7, and 20)? What does this add to the narrative?
5. Summarize briefly the controlling idea, or theme, of White's story. Paragraphs 4 and 26 should help you.

SUGGESTIONS FOR WRITING AND DISCUSSION

1. Write a narrative of a surprisingly humorous event that you experienced, an event that was not what you expected it to be.
2. Observe the public behavior of a small group of people engaged in a cooperative effort: singing, playing music, leading cheers at a college game, demonstrating for a particular cause. Narrate the event and describe the participants.
3. Write a first-person narrative from an animal's point of view. For instance, let a family pet describe you or other members of your family.
4. People often act unpredictably at times of extreme stress. If you have ever experienced a stressful event, tell what happened and how you reacted under pressure.
5. E. B. White vividly remembers his very first coon hunt. What happened on your first day on a new job, your first rehearsal for a play, your first day of practice with a team? Try to capture your sense of nervousness or fear of failure.

Champion of the World

Maya Angelou

Maya Angelou has been a successful dancer, actress, producer, and writer; the recipient of several honors and prizes, she is the author of I Know Why the Caged Bird Sings, *from which the following selection was taken.*

In this essay Angelou tells of an important event in the 1930s: Joe Louis is defending his heavyweight boxing championship against the Italian challenger, Primo Carnera. She quickly builds up suspense in the opening paragraphs by juggling the radio report of the fight, the reactions of the listeners who have gathered in a small store in the rural South, and her own philosophical musings on the event's importance to the listeners and to black Americans throughout the country. Dialogue is used effectively, as is the dramatic account of the fight itself.

1. The last inch of space was filled, yet people continued to wedge themselves along the walls of the Store. Uncle Willie had turned the radio up to its last notch so that youngsters on the porch wouldn't miss a word. Women sat on kitchen chairs, dining-room chairs, stools and upturned wooden boxes. Small children and babies perched on every lap available and men leaned on the shelves or on each other.

2. The apprehensive mood was shot through with shafts of gaiety, as a black sky is streaked with lightning.

3. "I ain't worried 'bout this fight. Joe's gonna whip that cracker like it's open season."

4. "He gone whip him till that white boy call him Momma."

5. At last the talking was finished and the string-along songs about razor blades were over and the fight began.

6. "A quick jab to the head." In the Store the crowd grunted. "A left to the head and a right and another left." One of the listeners cackled like a hen and was quieted.

7. "They're in a clinch, Louis is trying to fight his way out."

8. Some bitter comedian on the porch said, "That white man don't mind hugging that niggah now, I betcha."

9. "The referee is moving in to break them up, but Louis finally pushed the contender away and it's an uppercut to the chin. The contender is hanging on, now he's backing away. Louis catches him with a short left to the jaw."

10. A tide of murmuring assent poured out the doors and into the yard.

11. "Another left and another left. Louis is saving that mighty right . . ." The mutter in the Store had grown into a baby roar and it was pierced by the clang of a bell and the announcer's "That's the bell for round three, ladies and gentlemen."

12. As I pushed my way into the Store I wondered if the announcer gave any thought to the fact that he was addressing as "ladies and gentlemen" all the Negroes around the world who sat sweating and praying, glued to their "master's voice."

13. There were only a few calls for R. C. Colas, Dr. Peppers, and Hires root beer. The real festivities would begin after the fight. Then even the old Christian ladies who taught their children and tried themselves to practice turning the other cheek would buy soft drinks, and if the Brown Bomber's victory was a particularly bloody one they would order peanut patties and Baby Ruths also.

14. Bailey and I laid the coins on top of the cash register. Uncle Willie didn't allow us to ring up sales during a fight. It was too noisy and might shake up the atmosphere. When the gong rang for the next round we pushed through the near-sacred quiet to the herd of children outside.

15. "He's got Louis against the ropes and now it's a left to the body and a right to the ribs. Another right to the body, it looks like it was low. . . . Yes, ladies and gentlemen, the referee is signaling but the contender keeps raining the blows on Louis. It's another to the body, and it looks like Louis is going down."

16. My race groaned. It was our people falling. It was another lynching, yet another Black man hanging on a tree. One more woman ambushed and raped. A Black boy whipped and maimed. It was hounds on the trail of a man running through slimy swamps. It was a white woman slapping her maid for being forgetful.

17. The men in the Store stood away from the walls and at attention. Women greedily clutched the babes on their laps while on the porch the shufflings and smiles, flirtings and pinching of a few minutes before were gone. This might be the end of the world. If Joe lost we were back in slavery and beyond help. It would all be true, the accusations that we were lower types of human beings. Only a little higher than apes. True that we were stupid and ugly and lazy and dirty and, unlucky and worst of all, that God Himself hated us and ordained us to be hewers of wood and drawers of water, forever and ever, world without end.

18. We didn't breathe. We didn't hope. We waited.

19. "He's off the ropes, ladies and gentlemen. He's moving towards the center of the ring." There was no time to be relieved. The worst might still happen.

20. "And now it looks like Joe is mad. He's caught Carnera with a left hook to the head and a right to the head. It's a left jab to the body and another left to the head. There's a left cross and a right to the head. The contender's right eye is bleeding and he can't seem to keep his block up. Louis is penetrating every block. The referee is moving in, but Louis sends a left to the body and it's an uppercut to the chin and the contender is dropping. He's on the canvas, ladies and gentlemen."

21. Babies slid to the floor as women stood up and men leaned toward the radio.

22. "Here's the referee. He's counting. One, two, three, four, five, six, seven . . . Is the contender trying to get up again?"

23. All the men in the store shouted, "NO."

24. "—eight, nine, ten." There were a few sounds from the audience, but they seemed to be holding themselves in against tremendous pressure.

25. "The fight is all over, ladies and gentlemen. Let's get the microphone over to the referee . . . Here he is. He's got the Brown Bomber's hand, he's holding it up . . . Here he is . . ."

26. Then the voice, husky and familiar, came to wash over us—"The winnah, and still heavyweight champeen of the world . . . Joe Louis."

27. Champion of the world. A Black boy. Some Black mother's son. He was the strongest man in the world. People drank Coca-Colas like ambrosia and ate candy bars like Christmas. Some of the men went behind the Store and poured white lightning in their soft-drink bottles, and a few of the bigger boys followed them. Those who were not chased away came back blowing their breath in front of themselves like proud smokers.

28. It would take an hour or more before the people would leave the Store and head for home. Those who lived too far had made arrangements to stay in town. It wouldn't do for a Black man and his family to be caught on a lonely country road on a night when Joe Louis had proved that we were the strongest people in the world.

WORDS

What is the meaning of the italicized words in the following phrases?

1. "The *apprehensive* mood" (par. 2)
2. "pushed the *contender*" (par. 9)
3. "tide of murmuring *assent*" (par. 10)
4. "the *accusations* that we were lower" (par. 17)
5. "*hewers* of wood" (par. 17)
6. "Coca-Colas like *ambrosia*" (par. 27)

FORM AND CONTENT

1. Suggest a meaning for the following references: "cracker" (par. 3); "string-along songs about razor blades" (par. 5); "master's voice" (par. 12); "Brown Bomber" (par. 13); "Carnera" (par. 20).
2. There are three distinct "voices" found in Maya Angelou's essay: the author's, the crowd's, and the radio's. Comment on the kind of language used by each.
3. For what special reason does the author include paragraphs 16, 17, and 18? What do they add to the drama?
4. Cite examples of figurative language found in paragraphs 2, 10, and 11.
5. Cite an example of bitter irony found in paragraph 28.

SUGGESTIONS FOR WRITING AND DISCUSSION

1. Each generation has its heroes, its idols: singers, actors, and athletes, among others. Write an essay in which you try to capture the special reverence you felt for some hero or heroine when you were in your early teens.
2. Recount a moment or situation in which you realized that you had lost a cherished childhood belief.
3. You are present at a place where a dramatic event is about to take place: a Martian visitor is about to land, you will soon walk on the moon, you are going to be discovered by a movie producer or a television network. Describe your impressions as you record the details.
4. Assume that you have applied for a job, one you really want. You realize, however, that the competition is rough and you must make a first-rate impression. Tell what happens when you arrive at the interview, see the others who have also applied, and meet your interviewer. Build up the tension. You, of course, will receive the position.
5. Describe a particular sporting event—a football game, tennis match, championship fight. Use vivid language to capture the drama of the event. Comment on the conduct of the crowd.

Duel at Red River

Marquis James

Marquis James (1891–1955), a journalist and biographer, twice was awarded the Pulitzer Prize for excellence in historical writing.

Occasionally using dated terms that send the reader scurrying to the dictionary, James captures a particular time in American history by using some of the expressions from that period—the turn of the nineteenth century. He arranges his story in two parts: a glimpse into the character and personality of Andrew Jackson, and the actual duel itself. James is successful in intriguing the reader as he builds up the element of suspense. Note how his readers actually ride with the general as he and his entourage approach Red River. Part 2 features the actual duel (the story's climactic scene) and the immediate aftermath.

1

1. On Thursday, May 29, 1806, Andrew Jackson rose at five o'clock, and after breakfast told Rachel that he would be gone for a couple of days and meanwhile he might have some trouble with Mr. Dickinson. Rachel probably knew what the trouble would be and she did not ask. Rachel had her private channels of information. At six-thirty Jackson joined Overton at Nashville. Overton had the pistols. With three others they departed for the Kentucky line.

2. Mr. Dickinson and eight companions were already on the road. "Good-by, darling," he told his young wife. "I shall be sure to be at home to-morrow evening." This confidence was not altogether assumed. He was a snap shot. At the word of command and firing apparently without aim, he could put four balls in a mark twenty-four feet away, each ball touching another. The persistent tradition on the countryside, that to worry Jackson he left several such examples of his marksmanship along the road, is unconfirmed by any member of the Dickinson or Jackson parties. But the story that he had offered on the streets of Nashville to wager he would kill Jackson at the first fire was vouchsafed by John Overton, the brother of Jackson's second, a few days after the duel.

3. Jackson said he was glad that "the other side" had started so early. It was a guarantee against further delay. Jackson had chafed over the seven days that had elapsed since the acceptance of the challenge. At their first interview, Overton and Dr. Hanson Catlett, Mr. Dickinson's second, had agreed that the meeting should be on Friday, May thirtieth, near Harrison's Mills on Red River just beyond the Kentucky boundary. Jackson protested at once. He did not wish to ride forty miles to preserve the fiction of a delicate regard for Tennessee's unenforceable statute against dueling. He did not wish to wait a week for something that could be done in a few hours. Dickinson's excuse was that he desired to borrow a pair of pistols. Overton offered the choice of Jackson's pistols, pledging Jackson to the use of the other.

These were the weapons that had been employed by Coffee and McNairy.

4. As they rode Jackson talked a great deal, scrupulously avoiding the subject that burdened every mind. Really, however, there was nothing more to be profitably said on that head. General Overton was a Revolutionary soldier of long acquaintance with the Code. With his principal he had canvassed every possible aspect of the issue forthcoming. "Distance . . . twenty-four feet; the parties to stand facing each other, with their pistols down perpendicularly. When they are READY, the single word FIRE! to be given; at which they are to fire as soon as they please. Should either fire before the word is given we [the seconds] pledge ourselves to shoot him down instantly." Jackson was neither a quick shot, nor an especially good one for the western country. He had decided not to compete with Dickinson for the first fire. He expected to be hit, perhaps badly. But he counted on the resources of his will to sustain him until he could aim deliberately and shoot to kill, if it were the last act of his life.

5. On the first leg of the ride they traversed the old Kentucky Road, the route by which, fifteen years before, Andrew Jackson had carried Rachel Robards from her husband's home, the present journey being a part of the long sequel to the other. Jackson rambled on in a shrill voice. Thomas Jefferson was "the best Republican in theory and the worst in practice" he had ever seen. And he lacked courage. How long were we to support the affronts of England —impressment of seamen, cuffing about of our ocean commerce? Perhaps as long as Mr. Jefferson stayed in office. Well, that would be two years, and certainly his successor should be a stouter man. "We must fight England again. In the last war I was not old enough to be any account." He prayed that the next might come "before I get too old to fight."

6. General Overton asked how old Jackson reckoned he would have to be for that. In England's case about a hundred, Jackson said.

7. He spoke of Burr. A year ago, this day, Jackson had borne him from the banquet in Nashville to the Hermitage. He recalled their first meeting in 1797 when both were in Congress. Jackson also met General Hamilton that winter. "Personally, no gentleman could help liking Hamilton. But his political views were all English." At heart a monarchist. "Why, did he not urge Washington to take a crown!"

8. Burr also had his failings. He had made a mistake, observed Jackson with admirable detachment, a political mistake, when he fought Hamilton. And about his Western projects the General was none too sanguine. Burr relied overmuch on what others told him. Besides, there was Jefferson to be reckoned with. "Burr is as far from a fool as I ever saw, and yet he is as easily fooled as any man I ever knew."

9. The day was warm, and a little after ten o'clock the party stopped for refreshment. Jackson took a mint julep, ate lightly and rested until mid-afternoon. The party reached Miller's Tavern in Kentucky about eight o'-clock. After a supper of fried chicken, waffles, sweet potatoes and coffee, Jackson repaired to the porch to chat with the inn's company. No one guessed his errand. At ten o'clock he knocked the ashes from his pipe and went to bed. Asleep in ten minutes, he had to be roused at five in the morning.

2

10. The parties met on the bank of the Red River at a break in a poplar woods. Doctor Catlett won the toss for choice of position, but as the sun had not come through the trees this signified nothing. The giving of the word fell to Overton. Jackson's pistols were to be used after all, Dickinson taking his pick. The nine-inch barrels were charged with ounce balls of seventy caliber. The ground was paced off, the principals took their places. Jackson wore a dark-blue frock coat and trousers of the same material; Mr. Dickinson a shorter coat of blue, and gray trousers.

11. "Gentlemen, are you ready?" called General Overton.

12. "Ready," said Dickinson quickly.

13. "Yes, sir," said Jackson.

14. *"Fere!"* cried Overton in the Old-Country accent.

15. Dickinson fired almost instantly. A fleck of dust rose from Jackson's coat and his left hand clutched his chest. For an instant he thought himself dying, but, fighting for self-command, slowly he raised his pistol.

16. Dickinson recoiled a step horror-stricken. "My God! Have I missed him?"

17. Overton presented his pistol. "Back to the mark, sir!"

18. Dickinson folded his arms. Jackson's spare form straightened. He aimed. There was a hollow "clock" as the hammer stopped at half-cock. He drew it back, sighted again and fired. Dickinson swayed to the ground.

19. As they reached the horses Overton noticed that his friend's left boot was filled with blood. "Oh, I believe that he pinked me," said Jackson quickly, "but I don't want those people to know," indicating the group that bent over Dickinson. Jackson's surgeon found that Dickinson's aim had been perfectly true, but he had judged the position of Jackson's heart by the set of his coat, and Jackson wore his coats loosely on account of the excessive slenderness of his figure. But I should have hit him," he exclaimed, "if he had shot me through the brain."

20. With a furrow through his bowels Charles Dickinson tossed in agony until evening when friends eased him with a story that Jackson had a bullet in his breast and was dying. At ten o'clock he asked who had put out the light.

WORDS

What is the meaning of the italicized words in the following phrases?

1. "was *vouchsafed* by Overton" (par. 2)
2. "Jackson had *chafed* over the seven days" (par. 3)
3. "Tennessee's unenforceable *statute"* (par. 3)
4. "*scrupulously* avoiding the subject" (par. 4)
5. "the *affronts* of England" (par. 5)
6. "At heart a *monarchist"* (par. 7)
7. "the General was none too *sanguine"* (par. 8)
8. "Jackson *repaired* to the porch" (par. 9)
9. "a dark-blue *frock* coat" (par. 10)
10. "a *furrow* through his bowels" (par. 20)

FORM AND CONTENT

1. What story telling technique does Marquis James employ in paragraphs 5–8? What information do these paragraphs reveal concerning Andrew Jackson's personality and character?
2. Why wasn't the duel fought in Jackson's home state of Tennessee (par. 3)?

3. Why was Dickinson confident of victory over Jackson (par. 2)? What was Jackson's dueling strategy (par. 4)?
4. What does Jackson's conduct the night before the duel suggest about his personality (par. 9)?
5. This narration is written in two parts. What is the function of part 1? Why is it important for the reader to have this information? What is revealed in part 2?

SUGGESTIONS FOR WRITING AND DISCUSSION

1. Retell the Jackson-Dickinson duel from Dickinson's point of view.
2. Recount an episode from your own life in which you were a definite "underdog" and yet emerged the victor.
3. Recall an episode in which you or a friend had to defend your honor or reputation. What events created the problem? What was the eventual outcome?
4. Describe an episode in which your first impressions of a person or a place turned out to be just the opposite of the truth.
5. In life, many misunderstandings are caused by gossip. Describe a personal experience in which you (or a friend) were the victim of malicious and hurtful rumor. How did you face the issue? What was the eventual outcome?

38 Who Saw Murder Didn't Call the Police

Martin Gansberg

Martin Gansberg has been a reporter and an editor for The New York Times. *For fifteen years he was a college teacher and is now a successful free-lance writer.*

Using a deceptively simple news reporting style, the author tells two stories. He first objectively relates the events of a murder, never resorting to a melodramatic or sentimental tone. Next he gives some of the witnesses a chance to defend their inaction and quotes them directly. Here he shifts from objective reporting and includes carefully selected quotes in order to share his outrage with the reader. He also selects short quotes from police investigators that sum up the essay's sense of disgust and despair.

1. For more than half an hour 38 respectable, law-abiding citizens in Queens watched a killer stalk and stab a woman in three separate attacks in Kew Gardens.

2. Twice their chatter and the sudden glow of their bedroom lights interrupted him and frightened him off. Each time he returned, sought her out, and stabbed her again. Not one person telephoned the police during the assault; one witness called after the woman was dead.

3. That was two weeks ago today.

4. Still shocked is Assistant Chief Inspector Frederick M. Lussen, in charge of the borough's detectives and a veteran of 25 years of homicide investigations. He can give a matter-of-fact recitation on many murders. But the Kew Gardens slaying baffles him—not because it is a murder, but because the "good people" failed to call the police.

5. "As we have reconstructed the crime," he said, "the assailant had three chances to kill this woman during a 35-minute period. He returned twice to complete the job. If we had been called when he first attacked, the woman might not be dead now."

6. This is what the police say happened beginning at 3:20 A.M. in the staid, middle-class, tree-lined Austin Street area:

7. Twenty-eight-year-old Catherine Genovese, who was called Kitty by almost everyone in the neighborhood, was returning home from her job as manager of a bar in Hollis. She parked her red Fiat in a lot adjacent to the Kew Gardens Long Island Rail Road Station, facing Mowbray Place. Like many residents of the neighborhood, she had parked there day after day since her arrival from Connecticut a year ago, although the railroad frowns on the practice.

8. She turned off the lights of her car, locked the door, and started to walk the 100 feet to the entrance of her apartment at 82–70 Austin Street, which is in a Tudor building, with stores in the first floor and apartments on the second.

9. The entrance to the apartment is in the rear of the building because the front is rented to retail stores. At night the quiet neighborhood is shrouded in the slumbering darkness that marks most residential areas.

10. Miss Genovese noticed a man at the far end of the lot, near a seven-story apartment house at 82–40 Austin Street. She halted. Then, nervously, she headed up Austin Street toward Lefferts Boulevard, where there is a call box to the 102nd Police Precinct in nearby Richmond Hill.

11. She got as far as a street light in front of a bookstore before the man grabbed her. She screamed. Lights went on in the 10-story apartment house at 82–67 Austin Street, which faces the bookstore. Windows slid open and voices punctuated the early-morning stillness.

12. Miss Genovese screamed: "Oh, my God, he stabbed me! Please help me! Please help me!"

13. From one of the upper windows in the apartment house, a man called down: "Let that girl alone!"

14. The assailant looked up at him, shrugged and walked down Austin Street toward a white sedan parked a short distance away. Miss Genovese struggled to her feet.

15. Lights went out. The killer returned to Miss Genovese, now trying to make her way around the side of the building by the parking lot to get to her apartment. The assailant stabbed her again.

16. "I'm dying!" she shrieked. "I'm dying!"

17. Windows were opened again, and lights went on in many apartments. The assailant got into his car and drove away. Miss Genovese staggered to her feet. A city bus, Q–10, the Lefferts Boulevard line to Kennedy International Airport, passed. It was 3:35 A.M.

18. The assailant returned. By then, Miss Genovese had crawled to the back of the building, where the freshly painted brown doors to the apartment house held out hope for safety. The killer tried the first door; she wasn't there. At the second door, 82–62 Austin Street, he saw her slumped on the floor at the foot of the stairs. He stabbed her a third time—fatally.

19. It was 3:50 by the time the police received their first call, from a man who was a neighbor of Miss Genovese. In two minutes they were at the scene. The neighbor, a 70-year-old woman, and another woman were the only persons on the street. Nobody else came forward.

20. The man explained that he had called the police after much deliberation. He had phoned a friend in Nassau County for advice and then he had crossed the roof of the building to the apartment of the elderly woman to get her to make the call.

21. "I didn't want to get involved," he sheepishly told the police.

22. Six days later, the police arrested Winston Moseley, a 29-year-old business-machine operator, and charged him with homicide. Moseley had no previous record. He is married, has two children and owns a home at 133–19 Sutter Avenue, South Ozone Park, Queens. On Wednesday, a court committed him to Kings County Hospital for psychiatric observation.

23. When questioned by the police, Moseley also said that he had slain Mrs. Annie May Johnson, 24, of 146–12 133rd Avenue, Jamaica, on Feb. 29 and Barbara Kralik, 15, of 174–17 140th Avenue, Springfield Gardens, last July. In the Kralik case, the police are holding Alvin L. Mitchell, who is said to have confessed to that slaying.

24. The police stressed how simple it would have been to have gotten in touch with them. "A phone call," said one of the detectives, "would have done it." The police may be reached by dialing "O" for operator or SPring 7-3100.

25. Today witnesses from the neighborhood, which is made up of one-family homes in the $35,000 to $60,000 range with the exception of the two apartment houses near the railroad station, find it difficult to explain why they didn't call the police.

26. A housewife, knowingly if quite casually, said, "We thought it was a lover's quarrel." A husband and wife both said, "Frankly, we were afraid." They seemed aware of the fact that events might have been different. A distraught woman, wiping her hands on her apron, said, "I didn't want my husband to get involved."

27. One couple, now willing to talk about that night, said they heard the first screams. The husband looked thoughtfully at the bookstore where the killer first grabbed Miss Genovese.

28. "We went to the window to see what was happening," he said, "but the light from our bedroom made it difficult to see the street." The wife, still apprehensive, added: "I put out the light and we were able to see better."

29. Asked why they hadn't called the police, she shrugged and replied: "I don't know."

30. A man peeked out from the slight opening in the doorway to his apartment and rattled off an account of the killer's second attack. Why hadn't he called the police at the time? "I was tired," he said without emotion. "I went back to bed."

31. It was 4:25 A.M. when the ambulance arrived to take the body of Miss Genovese. It drove off. "Then," a solemn police detective said, "the people came out."

WORDS

What is the meaning of the italicized words in the following phrases?

1. "the *borough's* detectives" (par. 4)
2. "a matter-of-fact *recitation*" (par. 4)
3. "a *Tudor* building" (par. 8)
4. "after much *deliberation* (par. 20)
5. "a *solemn* police detective" (par. 31)

FORM AND CONTENT

1. What general purpose do the opening six paragraphs serve? Why does the author set "good people" in quotation marks (par. 4)? Why are the three descriptive words "staid, middle-class, tree-lined" especially effective (par. 6)?
2. The actual narrative begins on paragraph 7. Cite the paragraph where it ends.
3. What consistent pattern runs through the use of directly quoted material found in paragraphs 21, 26, 28, 29, and 30?
4. Gansberg's style is well suited to a narrative of this type. Which of the following terms best sums up his style: (a) simple and matter-of-fact; (b) sentimental; (c) sensational; (d) outraged and condemning. Defend your selection.
5. The events described in this narrative took place more than twenty years ago, and the essay has been frequently reprinted. How do you account for its popularity in light of the gruesome nature of the subject matter? How important is the author's narrative technique?

SUGGESTIONS FOR WRITING AND DISCUSSION

1. Have you ever passed the scene of an accident or a fight without stopping to help? Tell what happened and defend your inaction.
2. Why do you believe that many police officers after a few years on the force become very cynical about their fellow citizens? Explain.

3. This article describes and implicitly condemns citizens who did not interfere to stop a murder. Have you ever had an acquaintance or a neighbor who interfered too much with other people's lives? Describe and evaluate what he or she did.
4. Assume that you had been a witness to the attack on Katherine Genovese. What do you sincerely believe you would have done and why?
5. Why are seemingly senseless assaults against women more common than such assaults against men? Are they sexually motivated, are they caused by the belief that women are weaker than men, or are they rooted in the attitudes and organization of our society?

HOW

Method and Detail

How do Massachusetts drivers qualify for the title of America's rudest? How do potential terrorist targets and their chauffeurs learn to foil attempts to kill or capture them on the open road? How does a patient husband react when his wife of many years launches a new career? How does a woman who loves eating and loathes exercise resist the pressure exerted by her stretching, jogging, dieting friends?

These are questions answered in the four articles that follow. The answers are illustrated by comparison, statistical evidence, process analysis, and anecdote. Each essay can be understood by any reader, even if the reader is not touring New England in a rented car, a student at a counter-terrorist driving school, a confused husband shopping at a supermarket or waiting for a plumber, or a lover of rich food in a world possessed by the fitness craze. These essays are examples of clear exposition written by professional writers.

This kind of exposition—straightforward presentation and explanation of facts and ideas—is one of the most difficult and most important kinds of writing students can study. For in their college work and professional life—although they may never attempt to write a novel, a short story, or a drama—they will be forced to write thousands of pages of exposition, trying always to present facts and ideas clearly and accurately.

Massachusetts Drivers: Heels on Wheels

Caskie Stinnett

Caskie Stinnett has written several books and has been editor-in-chief of Holiday *and* Travel and Leisure; *in recent years he has been a regular contributor to the* Atlantic Monthly.

In this essay he describes how badly most of the people in Massachusetts drive. The problem is a serious one, as Stinnett shows by quoting alarming statistics. And he uses brief anecdotes not only to show how Massachusetts drivers disregard the law but also to make his essay humorous and entertaining.

1. Massachusetts drivers are my enemy, and I would say they are the enemy of almost everybody operating an automobile on the nation's highways. One sees them hurtling along roads in Connecticut, Ohio, Pennsylvania, and states far from home; they are easy to spot, crossing median strips, passing on the right or the left, sounding their horns ceaselessly, plunging into traffic from side streets without pausing, making abruptly left turns from right-hand lanes, fracturing every law designed by man for safety, and carrying in their hearts a strange and soaring sense of pride for being what they are—the outlaws of the highways.

2. Stated very simply and without exaggeration, the Massachusetts driver will do anything, or at least will *try* anything. He or she possesses no sufferance, no loyalty, no sense of group identity. If the late Justice Cardoza's admonition, "Mutual forebearance is the first law of the highway," is understood by Massachusetts drivers at all, it is thought of as a quaint and obsolete point of view. Weakness, hesitation, or even worse, politeness on the part of another driver is received with scorn and unconcealed contempt. The Massachusetts driver dislikes, indeed loathes, all other drivers. He especially loathes other Massachusetts drivers.

3. On a quiet residential street in Boston recently, I saw a driver pull up beside a red sign saying EMERGENCY NO PARKING TODAY. Getting out of his car, he glanced cautiously up and down the street, opened his trunk, placed the sign, concrete base and all, on the floor of the trunk, slammed the top down, and departed. I wasn't there when he returned, but I am sure he replaced the sign and drove away. To him it was a simple solution to a parking problem.

4. I became a resident of Boston only recently, coming from New York City, where aggressive driving is not unknown. On my first trip through Boston streets, I realized the pitiful base of experience I possessed; fifteen years of driving in midtown Manhattan had done nothing to prepare me for the reckless dive and swoop of Boston traffic, the arrogant weaving in and out in the traffic pattern, the horn-blowing, the sudden stops, the crunching of fenders and the splintering of tail-lights, the ceaseless struggle to arrive at the next intersection a few seconds before any other car. I have been told that the primary ambition of the Boston driver, once he has pulled away from the curb, is to prevent any other car from doing so; transportation and destination become secondary motives. Overtaking, passing, and, if possible, eliminating from the face of the earth all other cars is the real reason for turning on the ignition in the first place.

5. Why the deadly competition of the highway so stirs the blood of the Massachusetts driver is puzzling to me, since I've found the average citizen of the state to be a highly responsible and friendly individual, and one encounters in Boston a level of culture and charm that exists perhaps no place else in this country. Yet behind the wheel of the car that cuts in front of me quickly and causes me to slam my brakes. I recognize the man who dined at the table next to me in my club last night, or the lady with whom I had a fine conversation at a cocktail party over the weekend. Only a crumpled fender or a tortured grille, bespeaking some minor traffic disaster, reveals a trace of the gladiator spirit that seems to lie just beneath the surface of the man or woman who owns and operates an automobile in Massachusetts. I find it hard to believe that my mailman, one of the gentlest of men, who goes out of his way to do me kindnesses, starts blowing his horn before he turns on his ignition, but I know that it's true. One Sunday I saw him, in street clothes, cut across a grass-covered median strip on one of Boston's main arteries simply because he was momentarily stalled in traffic. That's the one thing a Boston driver can't tolerate: motionlessness. It isn't important where he's going so long as he's moving and moving ahead of anybody else.

6. In Boston, one doesn't park a car, one abandons it. If there is a place at a curb, fine; if not, the driver fits the car into whatever space is available and worries about the consequences upon return. I have a leased parking area on a back street for which a monthly payment is made. It was during my first week in Boston that I learned the pathetic inadequacy of the large sign designating the area as privately leased. Now I lock a chain across it when I leave, and experience has taught me that the chain must be very taut. If there is sufficient slack, one person will hold the chain up while the other drives under it. I've confronted some of these trespassing car owners when they returned for their cars, and their explanation invariably was, "There was no place else to park." To them, that seemed reason enough.

7. The driver, as well as the car, can be recalled by his maker, but this fact seems to weigh lightly in the thoughts of the Massachusetts driver. Although he has most certainly mechanized his aggressions, and is capable of striking terror in the hearts of other drivers who may be tasting for the first time the full extravagance of Massachusetts highway behavior, the Massachusetts driver is no killer. Rather, he is a fender-crusher, a close-call artist, who averts disaster by inches or seconds. The National Safety Council frankly acknowledges that it cannot compare state accident rates, because of the lack of uniformity in reporting. "In some states an accident is reportable if there is as little as fifty dollars in damage to the vehicle," asserts Janet M. Wantroba, of the council's motor vehicle statistics unit, "while in other states the dollar amount could be as high as $450. Therefore, an accident that occurs in one state may not be reportable in another. This poses many problems where reporting accidents and comparing states is concerned."

8. Lemuel H. Devers, president of the Massachusetts Auto Racing and Accident Prevention Bureau, possesses his own statistics, and he acknowledges that Massachusetts drivers bump into each other about 10 percent more frequently than drivers anywhere else in the United States. This figure is more or less supported by insurance companies who say they have the figures to prove that Massachusetts is the collision capital of America. " 'Rude' is the most frequently used term applied to Massachusetts drivers," says Richard E. McLaughlin, who was secretary of public safety under former Governor Francis W. Sargent. "They are the most undisciplined drivers in the United States because there has never been an effective highway patrol. There is an unconscious contempt for the whole concept of motor vehicle law enforcement. We are three generations into the motor vehicle era in Massachusetts and the carelessness has been passed from parents to children."

9. Just why the drivers of one state should be more aggressive and undisciplined than those of any other is not easy to pinpoint, and McLaughlin's theory is open to challenge. But the Massachusetts driver most certainly regards traffic laws of all fifty states as suggestive only, not to be taken too seriously, and this point of view must surely be rooted in police permissiveness. In almost all of the reckless behavior of Massachusetts drivers one finds an absence of anxiety over the prospect of being brought to court or having driving privileges suspended.

10. Meter maids in the city of Boston daily festoon cars with tickets for illegal parking, but these are usually found in gutters at the end of the day, casually thrown there by owners who are irritated to discover under their windshield wipers this symbol of police intrusion into their rights. Occasionally one encounters a car on the front wheel of which has been fastened a large device rendering the vehicle immobile, and on the windshield a prominent sign asserting that the car has been temporarily seized by the Police Department. This happens only to cars owned by notorious scofflaws, and is rare; in the time that I have lived in Boston I have seen only two instances when these devices were used.

11. The virus of irresponsible driving is contagious; once it enters the bloodstream of a city or state, it spreads rapidly. A driver who sees another run through a red light will most likely be tempted to do so too. One day I was somewhat startled to see a truck of the New England Telephone Company run a red light and then speed down a one-way street against oncoming traffic. For some reason—we were all young and innocent once—I expected a commercial vehicle to obey the law, but then I realized that a truck driver would most likely do what he saw other drivers doing.

12. A few months after I had settled in Boston, the lady sitting next to me at a dinner party inquired graciously how I liked the city. I replied that I liked it immensely but with one exception; I was terrified by the recklessness of Boston drivers. "Oh," she said lightly but with a touch of pride, "I'm one of them." Shortly after that, I gather, some of the humor if not the pride vanished from the situation when Massachusetts automobile insurance rates soared to a point where they were among the highest in the nation. The Boston *Globe* published the results of a study of insurance rates in the seven highest-priced regions: Boston and its environs ranked number one. The owner of a Pontiac whose book value was $1630 found that his insurance premium for the year came to—oddly enough—$1630. What a typical Massachusetts motorist paid for a package of collision insurance was twice what it cost in Chicago and two and a half times what it cost in Philadelphia. For fire, theft, and vandalism coverage, the typical Bostonian paid three and a half times what the Chicagoan did and six times the Philadelphian's bill. In general, collision and comprehensive (fire and theft) rates in Massachusetts are nearly twice the national average. The theft of cars in Boston is so commonplace that owners gaze out of their windows every morning to see if their cars are still there. Whether the casual manner with which cars are stolen is intertwined with the casual disregard for traffic laws is a matter of conjecture; some public safety officials think so.

13. One day this past spring, I was crossing an overpass on Storrow Drive, an expressway along the Charles River, with a Boston friend when we witnessed what appeared almost certain to develop into an ugly accident. A speeding car swerved around another, ricocheted against a concrete wall, turned completely around in the road, righted itself miraculously, and sped on. It wrung a gasp of admiration from my friend. "Wow!" he said. "I would never have the nerve to try that." Being a Boston driver himself, he didn't recognize it as accidental, and I decided against telling him. He would never have believed it.

WORDS

What is the meaning of the italicized words in the following phrases?

1. "Justice Cardoza's *admonition*" (par. 2)
2. "Mutual *forbearance* is the first law" (par. 2)
3. "a trace of the *gladiator* spirit" (par. 5)
4. "cars owned by notorious *scofflaws*" (par. 10)
5. "a matter of *conjecture*" (par. 12)

FORM AND CONTENT

1. How do the first sentences of paragraphs 1 and 2 work to capture a reader's attention?
2. What is the anecdote in paragraph 3 intended to illustrate?
3. What do the examples of paragraph 5 demonstrate about the nature of Massachusetts drivers?
4. What explanation is suggested for the bad driving in Massachusetts (pars. 8 and 9)?
5. How does much of the evidence offered in paragraph 12 differ from that in the rest of the essay?

SUGGESTIONS FOR WRITING AND DISCUSSION

1. How can police and courts cooperate to discourage the kind of driving described in this essay?
2. How could an accident that you experienced or observed have been prevented? Describe both the accident and your remedy.
3. Describe the objectionable and obnoxious behavior of some drivers in your own community.
4. Is it fair that automobile insurance rates in many states are lower for young women than for young men? Explain.
5. What is the best way to plan, schedule, and conduct a long automobile trip?

Driving for Dear Life

Robert C. Wurmstedt

Robert C. Wurmstedt has been a reporter and free-lance writer; he is now the Cairo bureau chief for Time.

In this essay he tells how the BSR Counter-Terrorist Driving School trains its students to avoid or destroy attacks from ambush. He first gets and holds the reader's attention by describing violent evasive driving, complete with "horrible screeching and the hot stink of brake pads and burning tires." Then he reveals that this frantic action has been only a part of a student's final examination. Thereafter he systematically describes the work of the school and how it trains counter-terrorist drivers.

1. The night is balmy. The highway is lit by a full moon. Suddenly, as the car crests a hill, there it is, just 50 yards ahead, a terrorist roadblock: two small foreign cars, parked across the pavement. With only a second to react, the driver lunges at the emergency brake to lock the rear wheels, then jams down hard on the brake pedal too. He jerks the steering wheel to the right. The rear of the car twists savagely in a 180° "bootleg" turn.

2. There is a horrible screeching and the hot stink of brake pads and burning tires. Heart pounding, the driver guns his motor, racing away from the barricade. But another car pulls out of a dark side road to cut him off. Though half blinded by the lights, he jams on the brakes again, and just as his car is shuddering to a stop, he slams it into reverse and guns the engine. Seconds later he takes his foot off the gas and turns the steering wheel hard. Tires screaming, the car spins around again, but faces the roadblock. There is no choice now but to pray, step on the gas and try to ram through.

3. He hits. But no deafening crash occurs. On impact, the two cars swing away easily, for they are on casters and covered with polyurethane foam pads. The terrorist threat was not real, but still there is genuine sweat on the driver's palms. This is part of the final exam given at the BSR Counter-Terrorist Driving School. It is the culmination of a four-day course held at Summit Point, W. Va., about 80 miles west of Washington. Instructor Bill Scott, 42, a Yale Ph.D. in geology and an ex-champion Formula Super Vee race-car driver, started the course in 1976 after the Air Force asked him to provide driver training for some of its officers. Since then, Scott and three other instructors, backed by a team of mechanics, have trained hundreds of chauffeurs and corporation executives in how to foil attempts to kill or capture them on the road. The basic course, including films and lectures plus actual driving, costs $1,495.

4. Scott does not advertise. Many of his clients demand that their names be kept secret. Information about the course is passed along through an old-boy network of corporate security chiefs and ex-CIA and Secret Service types. "Worldwide, attacks on cars happen every day," says Scott. "They don't even make news any more. About 90% take place in European suburbs. About 90% are successful."

5. There are six or eight drivers in most of Scott's classes. The first day is devoted to shooting up an old Buick with a 9-mm machine gun, an automatic pistol and a 12-gauge shotgun so the students will be familiar with the firepower available to the "opposition." Most slugs easily penetrate the side of the car. Then four of the class put on crash helmets and seat belts for an initiation run around the track in one of Scott's four new, high-performance Chevrolet Malibu police cars.

6. It's the white-knuckle express. Scott does straightaways at 110 m.p.h. and rarely corners at less than 65 m.p.h. The car seems to be flying out of control. Passengers are jerked around hard as Scott throws the Chevy into bootleg and J turns. Tires scream. Heads (and stomachs) spin. Everyone is scared. "This is hardball out here," shouts Scott in the understatement of the week, "but you'll be doing it in a few days." No way, each student groans to himself. But only 10% fail the course.

7. The next three days are a kind of Outward Bound for driving. At the speeds required (70 to 80 m.p.h.), students at first have no sense of how to control the car—or whether they have it in control at all. Many Americans are defensive drivers, quite content to putt around in an underpowered, six-year-old sedan, carefully navigating the maniacal freeway traffic that surrounds many cities. And every sensible and safe reflex built up for that kind of driving must be violated in Scott's course.

8. Skid control comes first, performed by going through a slalom course on an inch of loose gravel. The trick is to accelerate and brake and countersteer the car as the rear end skids violently. You must use the skid. It's like driving on ice. The best way to stop a car is to brake steadily and very hard, not pump the brakes. Next comes emergency braking and swerving to avoid objects at high speeds. Each student is ordered to drive absolutely flat out toward a sharp curve until the last possible second. Just when he is convinced that the car will shoot off the road, just when every instinct and a lifetime of conditioning demand that he brake and slow down, Scott shouts: "Gun it! Faster! Faster!"

9. "We want to jam you right into the middle of it," says Scott. "Whether you are normally cautious on the road or a hot-shot, it upsets nearly everyone. Especially the macho types. It's a heavy landing for them to find out they really can't drive and are nowhere near the limits of the car." For reassurance, the student looks at the brake pedal installed on the passenger side of Scott's Malibu for the instructor to use if a student panics and freezes.

10. The class learns to make fast, tight turns so the terrorists cannot get "inside" and force their quarry off the road. "Driving a car is a very sensuous thing," says Bruce Reichel, 33, one of Scott's instructors. "You have a lot of feedback from a car. Be aware of it."

11. The feedback from the car-ramming exercise is anything but sensuous. "Use the car as a weapon, if necessary," insists Scott. To learn what that means students take turns driving a beat-up 1974 Cadillac into an old bronze Buick special. Proper technique: slow down, then slam on the brakes to make the terrorists think you are stopping. Then gun the car, aiming for the front or rear axle. At 30 m.p.h. this barely rattles the Cadillac. But it spins the Buick into a full 360° turn and produces a very satisfying roar, crumpling metal and shattering glass. The Cadillac is hardly dented, but anyone inside the Buick will be badly shaken up.

12. Ramming is almost the last alternative to consider. In an ambush the two basic maneuvers are the bootleg and J turns, which students practice for hours. The worst thing is to do nothing. During "confrontation and chase," a sort of midterm exam on wheels, each student jockeys one Malibu around the track, trying to anticipate, and avoid, ambushes by "terrorist" instructors in three other cars.

13. In one pattern the student drives at 30 m.p.h., with two cars following. Over a hill and 50 yards ahead a barricade looms. At the same time one of the cars behind passes, distracting the student driver. He grows breathless, loses control, can't think. Can't do anything, in fact. Finally he just stops the car. "All you learned just dropped out of your head," Scott chides. The next try is much better. He spins the car into a good J turn, evading a sudden roadblock, and escapes. When Scott concedes that the move was a "reasonable reaction," the student feels as proud as a small boy the first time he manages to stay up on a two-wheeler. Fear turns into exhilaration. He can hardly wait for the next ambush.

14. Scott advises students "to be suspicious of anything unusual." In the Third World, for example, where official police roadblocks are common, it is not difficult for terrorists to get weapons and government uniforms. But it is hard for them to get police cars. "That could be the tip-off," Scott warns. "Look at the vehicle in the roadblock. In the Middle East or Italy, if a van, baby carriage or wheelchair appears in front of you, you can be statistically assured you are being attacked."

15. To be useful, the reflexes of antiterrorism must be instantaneous. And though they have saved several of Scott's graduates from trouble, on occasion they can be dangerous. A corporate chauffeur confronted by a man pushing a rack of clothes across a downtown street in Pittsburgh was suspicious enough to gun the car onto the sidewalk, smashing several parking meters in an escape attempt. It was not an attack. Luckily no pedestrians were injured. Though trying to drive around a roadblock is the worst thing to do—it exposes you to broadside fire—the chauffeur's startled boss gave him a $5,000 bonus and paid for the parking meters.

WORDS

1. "the car *crests* a hill" (par. 1)
2. "It is the *culmination*" (par. 3)
3. "*maniacal* freeway traffic" (par. 7)
4. "a *slalom* course" (par. 8)
5. "reflexes of antiterrorism must be *instantaneous*" (par. 15)

FORM AND CONTENT

1. Suggest a meaning for the following references: "an old-boy network" (par. 4); "white-knuckle express" (par. 6); "hardball" (par. 6); "macho types" (par. 9); "Third World" (par. 14).
2. In presenting the step-by-step process that drivers go through at Bill Scott's school, the author first has to gain his readers' attention. What interest-arousing method does he use in the opening three paragraphs?
3. How do Scott's direct quotations used in paragraphs 8, 9, 13, and 14 add to the effectiveness of the process analysis?
4. Give several examples of words and phrases that suggest vivid sense impressions, such as "hot stink of brake pads" in paragraph 2.
5. What technique does the author use in closing his essay and what does it add to the effectiveness of the piece?

SUGGESTIONS FOR WRITING AND DISCUSSION

1. Write a paper in which you give a step-by-step explanation of an everyday process such as painting a house, cooking a meal, or getting a driver's license.
2. What driving skills are necessary for one who drives on narrow mountain roads or on a dangerous street or highway?
3. How do television programs and motion pictures demonstrate the importance of automobiles in American lives?
4. How have you learned one of the following survival skills: swimming, rock climbing, defensive driving, or first aid?
5. If you have ever lived or visited in a country that uses another language, discuss how you learned to get around and make your wishes known.

On-the-Job Training

Harvey J. Fields

Harvey J. Fields is a rabbi of the Wilshire Boulevard Temple in Los Angeles; he is also a writer, and he is now working on his first novel.

In the following essay, the author is not describing an orderly process like a course of instruction or the conduct of a scientific experiment. Instead, he is telling how he and his wife are working to adjust themselves and their marriage to new circumstances. This process is untidy, unpredictable, and bewildering; and the author uses both brief narratives and short explanations to communicate his confusion and insecurity.

1. It is 6:30 A.M. and my wife just left for work. Three months ago, she launched a new career as a stockbroker. Together we concluded that it was a good idea. It would boost our income; perhaps more importantly, it would provide a creative outlet for her talents. "We have a solid marriage. You are young and capable. Look around," I advised, "there are all kinds of opportunities."

2. We reasoned that her time had arrived. Two of our children are at college; a third is a self-sufficient high-school student. For the last 22 years, my wife has cared for our needs, run thousands of errands, driven millions of carpool miles, kept our family finances, been there when the plumber arrived to fix our leaking faucets and at my side, looking radiant, for a constant stream of professional-social obligations.

3. Now all of that has changed. And it is not as easy as I thought it would be. Accommodations have to be made. Worries, doubts, little aching jealousies and resentments, and big ones as well, have emerged. Then, while driving to my office and brooding over this transformation erupting in my life, I happened to hear a commentator announce that new research has determined that husbands with working wives have a shorter life expectancy than those with traditional homemaker wives. Icing on the cake, as they say.

4. During the first few weeks, certain tasks just fell into place. She could no longer deliver and pick up at the cleaners, or make it to our bank. They were out of her way, but happily right on my route to the office. So were the pharmacy and supermarket.

5. The supermarket. I love the supermarket, but on Sundays. Never during the week, all dressed up in a business suit. Sunday is when a man is supposed to visit the supermarket and fill his cart with all sorts of whims and his favorite beer.

6. Did I feel queasy pushing a cart around on Tuesday afternoon, holding a long list written on a pink sheet of paper, and with all those women and children staring at me? I did. And I wanted to evaporate when Gwen Sommers cornered me holding a large box of Tide in one hand and a big bottle of Era Plus in the other. With sympathy pouring from her compassionate brown eyes, she asked, "Is everything all right with Sybil?" By that she meant: "You are supposed to be at your office doing a man's job, and Sybil should be here shopping." Of course I wanted to explain, defend, send her home to read "The Feminine Mystique," but I didn't. Instead, I headed for the checkout line gripping my six-pack of beer, hoping to indicate that all the boxes, cans, fruits and vegetables in my cart were simply the unbridled enthusiasm of a mad male on a shopping spree.

7. When I reached home, her car was not in the driveway. Another trauma. She was always there to greet me at the door with a warm hug and kiss. Now she was late getting home. The house was dark and empty. No sweet aromas of dinner prepared. Just silence, and all those groceries to bring into the house and put away, and bothersome doubts about how our emerging new arrangement will affect us.

8. It already has, but you grin and bear the first frustrations. A week after she was hired, we sat down to talk about vacation time. I am tired. It's been a tension-filled year. I need a few weeks to unwind. We have always vacationed together. We would never have considered going off alone. Not us. We are "together" kind of people.

9. But she is committed to a training program, 16 weeks of rigorous study. She is flowering with new enthusiasm, and her career demands most of her energy, time and attention. So what about me? A vacation alone? By myself? It hurts, fills me with resentment. What are we married for, anyway?

10. "What about coming up for long weekends?" I suggest. "I will have to check with my boss." It's an innocent remark, but I want to explode. "Her boss?" I am supposed to be No. 1 in her life. Now, suddenly, she has to get permission from someone else to spend time with me. The gall starts to ooze. I whine inside: "Are we giving up too much? Are we to become roommates sharing the conveniences of a home, the warm memories of rearing our kids, and nothing else?"

11. One evening, she tells me: "I had lunch today with Tom, George and Steve. We went to this fancy sushi bar. Tom suggested I try it. George says we are going to make a dynamite team. Steve says this. Tom . . . Steve . . . George . . ."

12. I am not listening to what she is saying. All I hear are male names. All I see are new men in her life: associates, partners, colleagues, customers. All male. All aggressive. All with claims on her.

13. "Do you know what Jim asked me the other day?" she inquires. I want to stuff my ears, pretend nothing has changed. "What?" I answer, already angry at what I might hear. "I was shocked," she says. "He asked me what I was going to do when the first client came on strong with a proposition and made it clear that, if I wasn't willing, he would take his business elsewhere."

14. My stomach tightens into an ache. I feel as if I have been hit in the groin. Creeping doubts rumble inside me. I am silent, reflective about it all. The propositions won't be that straightforward. They will come subtly, twisted into all sorts of temptations. The devil always wears angel's garb and his voice is sweet and innocent, even naïve.

15. Later, I laugh at my fears and anxieties. All those years, all my trips, conventions, speaking appearances, alone in hotel rooms in new cities, did she have the same flurry of doubts? Did she wonder about whom I was meeting, and where? How did she make it through all those years, and I can't seem to bear all the questions and confusions for even a month?

16. And there are other questions. Whose number should be given at the high school in case of emergency? Who is responsible for banking, cleaning, shopping, cooking? How much help can I expect from her when it comes to attending functions related to my career? And is she expecting me to go out and make nice to her clients, rub elbows at office parties with her associates? How shall all of these be sorted out? Who calls the shots?

17. My stress level is rising. I liked the way we were. We had negotiated a comfortable arrangement. It was smooth, seldom a surprise. Now it's all in flux, and I am scared.

18. I see myself being stripped of my masculine, dominant, father, success image. There it is. I have said it. We were programmed by parents into believing that the male was the breadwinner. His job was top priority. He was to earn, protect and preside over his family. He was the senior partner; she was the junior partner. But the curtain has fallen on those old assumptions, and it's painful and bewildering.

19. So I am afraid for us. Human relationships are delicate affairs. Their circuitry is complex and bewildering. They jam, overload and burn out in the most inexplicable ways. The future is no sure bet. That may be tough, but it is the truth.

20. Who knows, if we are lucky, and do our job at communicating, sharing, listening and loving, the fact that my wife just went to work may not shorten my life at all. It may add qualities and dimensions that surprise and enrich us. Let's hope so, because I have just rushed home at lunch time to meet the plumber, and something has got to make that worthwhile.

WORDS

What is the meaning of the italicized words in the following phrases?

1. "all sorts of *whims*" (par. 5)
2. "I feel *queasy*" (par. 6)
3. "the *unbridled* enthusiasm" (par. 6)
4. "Another *trauma*" (par. 7)
5. "*gall* starts to ooze" (par. 10)
6. "it's all in *flux*" (par. 17)

FORM AND CONTENT

1. Contrast the tone of paragraph 1 to that of paragraph 20. What one detail does Fields include in both paragraphs 2 and 20?
2. Note the author's method of organizing material: paragraphs 1 and 2 reveal him as a reasonable modern husband. What details does he include in paragraphs 3–8?
3. What important change in tone takes place in paragraph 9? Choose one verb that highlights this change.
4. Classify the details found in paragraphs 14–20. What takes place in paragraphs 11, 12, and 13 to trigger this reaction?
5. What particularly significant statement does the author make in paragraph 18?

SUGGESTIONS FOR WRITING AND DISCUSSION

1. Supermarket managers know that men do more impulse buying than women, buying from special displays that catch their eyes. Why is this true? Do they have more money, less experience, or less responsibility?

HOW—Method and Detail

2. What is there about the position of men in our society that would make the author ashamed of vegetables in his shopping cart but not of a six-pack of beer?
3. Why did the author and his wife agree that she should have a career? Should all women when their children have grown resume old careers or begin new ones? Explain and defend your answer.
4. How should a married couple, both of whom are working outside the home, best divide household chores and responsibilities?
5. Discuss your experiences in a job that demanded "on-the-job training." Explain what you did and how well you did it?

It's Getting Hard to Ride the Gravy Boat

Enid Nemy

Enid Nemy is a humorous observer of modern manners and mores; this essay, in which she reports on the current enthusiasm for physical fitness programs, was first published in The New York Times Magazine.

Unlike many articles now being published, this one does not give instructions on how to lose weight or how to exercise or how to supplement a diet with vitamins or minerals. It is rather a witty description of how the healthful activities of her friends have bored, inconvenienced, and even embarrassed the author. It describes how she reacts to the actions of others.

1. It isn't easy leading an unhealthy life. Sometimes, in fact, it isn't worth the effort.

2. Take eating, for instance. The joy has practically gone out of it. Who needs to lunch or dine with friends who spend their time with you either lecturing on the finer points of nutrition and diet or stating categorically, but with infinite sorrow and regret, that your intestinal tract deserves better and that you are, all in all, a physical disaster. By the time the coffee arrives (make mine real coffee, please), instead of being happily satiated, you are convinced that you are probably a wreck and that if you live out the night, you're on bonus time.

3. It's true that there is more interest in good food these days than ever before in the country's history. It's certainly true that every second person is into gourmet recipes and that every second store is loaded with fresh coffee beans, spices, herbs and $12 olive oil. But what any rational person would like to know is, who is eating all that gourmet food, cooked with the $12 olive oil, and who is drinking the brew perked or dripped from those strong, caffeine-loaded coffee beans? No one in my vicinity.

4. Walk into any good restaurant on any given day and the sight is heartbreaking. Pathetic islands of boeuf bourguignon, roast potatoes and chocolate mousse are all but inundated by a sea of asparagus and poached fish. Be foolish enough to accept an invitation to a home-cooked meal and the hostess announces proudly that the meal about to be consumed is starch-free, carbohydrate-free, noncaloric, and hasn't been within 20 feet of a salt shaker. To anyone whose taste buds haven't completely atrophied, it's also inedible. Still, it's healthy—so they say.

5. Go up to the company cafeteria with colleagues, or to a luncheonette, and the situation becomes even worse. Sure, there are still places that serve pancakes dripping with syrup, mashed potatoes golden with butter and corned beef sandwiches with side orders of pickles and mayonnaise-soggy cole slaw. But try to eat any of them with any semblance of enjoyment. The person on one side of you is spooning yogurt as though it is the nectar of the gods; the person on the other side is chomping away on water-packed tuna on a lettuce leaf. And the third friend, or erstwhile friend, is—hard to believe but true—unpacking a little box of sprouts and tofu. Sometimes this delectable box of goodies has been assembled at home and sometimes it comes directly from the horse's mouth, so to speak. It has been lovingly prepared and dispensed by a nutritionist, a person who has become as indispensable to modern living as the psychiatrist and hairdresser.

6. None of this should come as a particular surprise to someone who has lived as long as I have. This preoccupation with diet is a replay of many periods in the past when my friends also went periodically berserk on peculiar diets. One year, they all lived on hard-boiled eggs; another year it was grapefruit, morning, noon and night. At yet another point in time, bananas were the thing. There was, too, another regimen, the exact details of which I have mercifully forgotten. What remains indelibly impressed on the memory are the gallons of water that had to be drunk as an accompaniment. As far as I could tell, the only useful thing that this accomplished for anyone was an intimate knowledge of every ladies' room in the city.

7. All this, however, was strictly a matter of weight, and, as eggs, grapefruit and water aren't the worst things in the world to look at, friendship was still possible. True, I would get the odd lecture as I gorged on hamburgers, french fries, licorice and cheese cake, which said, in effect, that I'd be sorry when I ended up looking like a tub of lard, especially when I saw my pals looking like sylphs. I thought then, and I still do, that it was poetic justice when all my french fries and cheese cake miraculously ended up on their hips and their scales, and the only thing that remained with me was the taste.

8. This time around, however, things are serious. There is a major difference. Friendships are being shot to pieces because the current objective is something more than slimness. It is flat stomachs and muscles and what is quaintly termed as "well-being."

9. For anyone who isn't into health, the thoughtlessness of friends who have succumbed to the fitness craze is absolutely galling. Havoc is being wreaked in perfectly innocent lives. For instance, there is no such thing as an early morning telephone chat anymore. Either there is no answer—the other party is off jogging around the reservoir—or the answer is impatient and breathless—the exercise instructor is at the apartment and you've interrupted the 79th push-up. There's no such thing as a drink after work because everyone is running off to aerobics. And at lunch, if it isn't tofu and yogurt, it's no one. They're all pedaling and rowing and running at health clubs or, for all I know, swimming to New Jersey.

10. Somehow, it seems necessary to say here that not being into fitness is quite a different thing from being against it. I am, in fact, all for health. Until all this stretching and jogging, wheat germ and tofu started, I actually thought my being was doing reasonably well. Now I'm not so sure. I get twinges of guilt as I recline on my bed watching 2 A.M. reruns of Mary Tyler Moore and munching a chocolate or two. Sometimes, little voices interrupt Mary and Rhoda and tell me that my system is being poisoned with sugar and that I should be sleeping so that I can get up at 5 A.M. and run somewhere. I'm trying to resist but I tell you, it's getting to me.

WORDS

What is the meaning of the italicized words in the following phrases?

1. "stating *categorically*" (par. 2)
2. "instead of being happily *satiated*" (par. 2)

3. "this *delectable* box of goodies" (par. 5)
4. "my pals looking like *sylphs*" (par. 7)
5. "thoughtlessness . . . is absolutely *galling*" (par. 9)

FORM AND CONTENT

1. This essay contains a kind of humor dependent, in part, on exaggeration or extreme overstatement. Find examples of this kind of statement in paragraph 2.
2. Find an example in the first three paragraphs of a rhetorical question—one that either requires no answer or is immediately answered by the writer herself.
3. What examples of hyperbole (overstatement or exaggeration) can you find in the first two sentences of paragraph 4?
4. How does the new interest in fitness differ from earlier concerns about losing weight (par. 8)?
5. What is the effect of the word *quaintly* as it is used in paragraph 8?

SUGGESTIONS FOR WRITING AND DISCUSSION

1. Using what you know about good nutrition, evaluate your own diet during the college term. Could it be improved without great expense or inconvenience?
2. If you are or have been markedly overweight or underweight, describe your efforts—successful or unsuccessful—to achieve a normal weight.
3. How can working men or women best organize their lives to give them adequate exercise?
4. One well-known educator said, "The only exercise I get is going to the funerals of friends who have exercised regularly." Attack or defend his point of view.
5. What fads in diet, dress, or life-style have you found interesting or attractive in recent years?

WHY

Reason and Argument

Why is a really healthful life not worth living? Why do some of our most sensitive and intelligent young people prepare for careers that may lead to job frustration and comparative poverty? Why do thousands of American families disrupt their way of life to support an organized activity that hurts, humiliates, or frightens many of their children? And why, after more than a decade of working to free themselves from traditional obligations and responsibilities, are many American women looking for new commitments? The articles in this section ask and answer these questions.

They are examples of a peculiarly important kind of exposition that ridicules, opposes, or supports particular kinds of actions or beliefs for individuals or whole communities. This kind of writing requires authors to examine the evidence, discarding what seems to be irrelevant, inappropriate, or inadequate, and explain what they believe to be important.

Writing in this way, they approach the level of persuasion and argument, attempting to lead the reader to accept their judgments and beliefs. They may, indeed, become advocates, sometimes ridiculing what they oppose, sometimes arguing strongly for what they believe to be necessary or true.

All of the articles in this section are examples of such writing. Each of them argues for a particular point of view, either using humor or presenting evidence and meeting possible objections. This kind of writing, which attempts to change the minds of its audience, is obviously important in any democratic society. It has, therefore, been the subject of special study ever since the greatest days of ancient Athens.

Farewell to Fitness

Mike Royko

Chicago based Mike Royko is one of America's foremost columnists and is known for witty, ironic commentaries on political and social subjects.

In the following piece, Royko offers some personal reasons for his opposition to the current American obsession with physical fitness. Using two well-known individuals to represent two conflicting points of view, the author sets up his argument by contrasting the pleasures of indulgence to the agony of keeping in shape. He works for laughs, but he also constructs his argument in such a way as to emerge the obvious winner. Using exaggerated contrast and carefully chosen examples, Royko convinces us that somehow pork shanks are superior to the "flesh of a dead chicken."

1. At least once a week, the office jock will stop me in the hall, bounce on the balls of his feet, plant his hands on his hips, flex his pectoral muscles and say: "How about it? I'll reserve a racquetball court. You can start working off some of that. . . ." And he'll jab a finger deep into my midsection.

2. It's been going on for months, but I've always had an excuse: "Next week, I've got a cold." "Next week, my back is sore." "Next week, I've got a pulled hamstring." "Next week, after the holidays."

3. But this is it. No more excuses. I made one New Year's resolution, which is that I will tell him the truth. And the truth is that I don't want to play racquetball or handball or tennis, or jog, or pump Nautilus machines, or do push-ups or sit-ups or isometrics, or ride a stationary bicycle, or pull on a rowing machine, or hit a softball, or run up a flight of steps, or engage in any other form of exercise more strenuous than rolling out of bed.

4. This may be unpatriotic, and it is surely out of step with our muscle-flexing times, but I am renouncing the physical-fitness craze.

5. Oh, I was part of it. Maybe not as fanatically as some. But about 15 years ago, when I was 32, someone talked me into taking up handball, the most punishing court game there is.

6. From then on it was four or five times a week—up at 6 A.M., on the handball court at 7, run, grunt, sweat, pant until 8:30, then in the office at 9. And I'd go around bouncing on the balls of my feet, flexing my pectoral muscles, poking friends in their soft guts, saying: "How about working some of that off? I'll reserve a court," and being obnoxious.

7. This went on for years. And for what? I'll tell you what it led to: I stopped eating pork shanks, that's what. It was inevitable. When you join the physical-fitness craze, you have to stop eating wonderful things like pork shanks because they are full of cholesterol. And you have to give up eggs benedict, smoked liverwurst, Italian sausage, butter-pecan ice cream, Polish sausage, goose-liver pate, Sara Lee cheesecake, Twinkies, potato chips, salami-and-Swiss-cheese sandwiches, double cheeseburgers with fries, Christian Brothers brandy with a Beck's chaser, and everything else that tastes good.

8. Instead, I ate broiled skinless chicken, broiled whitefish, grapefruit, steamed broccoli, steamed spinach, unbuttered toast, yogurt, eggplant, an apple for dessert and Perrier water to wash it down. Blahhhhh!

9. You do this for years, and what is your reward for panting and sweating around a handball-racquetball court, and eating yogurt and the skinned flesh of a dead chicken?

10. —You can take your pulse and find that it is slow. So what? Am I a clock?

11. —You buy pants with a narrower waistline. Big deal. The pants don't cost less than the ones with a big waistline.

12. —You get to admire yourself in the bathroom mirror for about 10 seconds a day after taking a shower. It takes five seconds to look at your flat stomach from the front, and five more seconds to look at your flat stomach from the side. If you're a real creep of a narcissist, you can add another 10 seconds for looking at your small behind with a mirror.

13. That's it.

14. Wait, I forgot something. You will live longer. I know that because my doctor told me so every time I took a physical. My fitness-conscious doctor was very slender—especially the last time I saw him, which was at his wake.

15. But I still believe him. Running around a handball court or jogging five miles a day, eating yogurt and guzzling Perrier will make you live longer.

16. So you live longer. Have you been in a typical nursing home lately? Have you walked around the low-rent neighborhoods where the geezers try to survive on Social Security?

17. If you think living longer is rough now, wait until the 1990s, when today's Me Generation potheads and coke sniffers begin taking care of the elderly (today's middle-aged joggers). It'll be: "Just take this little happy pill, gramps, and you'll wake up in heaven."

18. It's not worth giving up pork shanks and Sara Lee cheesecake.

19. Nor is it the way to age gracefully. Look around at all those middle-aged jogging chicken-eaters. Half of them tape hairpieces to their heads. That's what comes from having a flat stomach. You start thinking that you should also have hair. And after that comes a facelift. And that leads to jumping around a disco floor, pinching an airline stewardess and other bizarre behavior.

20. I prefer to age gracefully, the way men did when I was a boy. The only time a man over 40 ran was when the cops caught him burglarizing a warehouse. The idea of exercise was to walk to and from the corner tavern, mostly to. A well-rounded health-food diet included pork shanks, dumplings, Jim Beam and a beer chaser.

21. Anyone who was skinny was suspected of having TB or an ulcer. A fine figure of a man was one who could look down and not see his knees, his feet or anything else in that vicinity. What do you have to look for, anyway? You ought to know if anything is missing.

22. A few years ago I was in Bavaria, and I went to a German beer hall. It was a beautiful sight. Everybody was popping sausages and pork shanks and draining quart-sized steins of thick beer. Every so often they'd thump their magnificent bellies and smile happily at the booming sound that they made.

23. Compare that to the finish line of a marathon, with all those emaciated runners sprawled on the grass, tongues hanging out, wheezing, moaning, writhing, throwing up.

24. If that is the way to happiness and a long life, pass me the cheesecake.

25. May you get a hernia, Arnold Schwarzenegger. And here's to you, Orson Welles.

WORDS

What is the meaning of the italicized words in the following phrases?

1. "flex his *pectoral* muscles" (par. 1)
2. "a pulled *hamstring*" (par. 2)
3. "do . . . *isometrics*" (par. 3)
4. "being *obnoxious*" (par. 6)
5. "you're a real creep of a *narcissist*" (par. 12)
6. "those *emaciated* runners" (par. 23)

FORM AND CONTENT

1. Identify Arnold Schwarzenegger and Orson Welles (par. 25). How does one represent Royko's argument and the other an alternative to his argument?
2. What do Royko's opening four paragraphs have in common with paragraph 22?
3. Royko supports his intentionally exaggerated argument through the use of lists: elements in a series which illustrate his position. An example of this technique is paragraph 3. Cite three more instances of list making.
4. Paragraphs 22 and 23 develop a contrast of two ways of life. How do the modifiers of paragraph 22 make self-indulgence seem attractive? How do the verbals of paragraph 23 make strenuous exercise unattractive?
5. Explain Royko's use of "unpatriotic" (par. 4) and "Me Generation" (par. 17).

SUGGESTIONS FOR WRITING AND DISCUSSION

1. Attack or defend a follower of a current fad and describe such matters as his or her dress, attitudes, and behavior.
2. Make a strong argument for or against capital punishment.
3. Write a persuasive paper defending or attacking soap operas; explain how these dramas may differ from the real lives of their viewers.
4. Defend or justify the current fitness craze.
5. Argue for or against the use of vitamin-mineral food supplements, organic foods, or special diet programs.

Who Cares about the Renaissance?

Leslie S. P. Brown

Leslie S. P. Brown is an Annenberg Graduate Fellow at the University of Pennsylvania.

In this essay she argues to justify a career choice that others have condemned as unrealistic, impractical, and escapist. She concedes the truth of some of their criticisms, but then carefully details both the personal satisfactions and the benefits to society of the choice she has made. The essay is a good example of a straightforward, unpretentious explanation of personal motives and aspirations.

1. Last September, with the aid of an unusually generous fellowship, I enrolled in a doctoral program in Italian Renaissance art history. Although I had selected this particular career path as a college freshman and had never seriously considered any alternatives. I experienced severe doubts as I packed my bags and prepared to re-enter the academic life after a year away. For although my return to school elicited a few wistful wishes for happiness and success, it primarily provoked a chorus of lugubrious warnings about the "lack of relevance" of my chosen field and the uncertainty of my professional and financial future.

2. I coped easily with the tired jokes about Ph.D.'s driving cabs from the lawyers, doctors and M.B.A.'s of my acquaintance. But when a professor who had encouraged me to apply for graduate study sat me down and described in lurid detail his 20 years of frustration and comparative poverty as an academic, I began to be disturbed. And it was something of a shock to hear him say, as he leafed through the pages of his latest book, "I spent 10 years of my life on this thing, and what do I get? A thousand bucks and a pat on the back from a couple of colleagues. Sometimes I think it isn't worth it anymore."

3. Not surprisingly, there aren't many of us left, we young scholars of the past. Out of a total of 25 art-history majors at the college I attended, the vast majority went to law school. In these days of frantic attempts to gain admission to the best professional schools, the decision to pursue an advanced degree in literature, history, music or art is often viewed as a symptom of rapidly advancing lunacy—or, at least, as a sign of total disregard for the practical concerns of life. Media articles relentlessly describe the abysmal condition of the job market for Ph.D.'s in the humanities and the worry of department chairmen at universities where students are avoiding Chaucer and baroque music in favor of technical courses. Friends and family consider those of us who have chosen this course as aberrations. Some of us have been accused of being escapists, of refusing to face the constant changes of a technological society, of shutting ourselves up in ivory towers out of fear of competing with our pragmatic and computer-literate peers. In short, we hopeful scholars have had to accept the fact that we are considered anachronisms.

4. Why do we do it, then? Why have we, highly educated and raised, for the most part, by ambitious and upwardly mobile parents, turned our backs on the 20th century in order to bury our noses in dusty books and write articles that only our colleagues will read?

5. Well, in part we do it for love. Despite the gibes and jeers of our friends (and I might note that I have never once accused any of my lawyer friends of rampant materialism), we *are* realists. We are forced to be. We live in tiny, inexpensive apartments, take public transportation (or, more often, walk) and eat cheaply between long hours at the library. Many of us will be paying back huge educational loans for years and may never own a house or buy a new car. It is not a soft life, and sometimes we do complain. But usually we glory in it. We admire our contemporaries who are now making salaries that we only dream about, but we are secure in the knowledge that we have chosen to do what we love best. We have not relegated our joy in literature and art to the status of hobbies, and we can only hope that our passions will help us survive the lean years, the frustration and the occasional intellectual exhaustion.

6. Nor are we less competent or socially aware than our friends in more practical professions. Several of my teachers and classmates have verbal and analytical abilities that would make them gifted lawyers or product managers; a small contingent is making fascinating discoveries about medieval architecture by performing astounding arithmetical gymnastics—with the aid of a computer. Many of us love science —several of my most enjoyable hours have been spent with a telescope in a freezing observatory—and we pay close attention to political developments. And many of us are enthusiastic sports fans. In other words, we are not social cripples or intellectual snobs with no interests beyond our own esoteric and rarefied disciplines. We have chosen to endure the raised eyebrows and the despair of our families because we hope that, with hard work and dedication, we will never have to mourn a lost love of Botticelli or Bach while working in jobs that fail to touch our souls or feed our human hunger for beauty.

7. Not long ago, a bright 16-year-old girl—a mathematics prodigy—asked me who Michelangelo was. When I told her that he was one of the greatest artists who had ever lived, she asked me why she had never heard of him. Unfortunately, she is not alone. Universities today are wondering where they will find scholars of the humanities for new generations of students; perhaps it will be necessary to tell future freshmen that they cannot study literature, art, music or foreign languages because there is nobody to teach them.

8. So there is yet another—perhaps less selfish—reason that we persist. We are the men and women who prepare the museum exhibitions and keep the classics alive. We hold up the lessons of history before the world and try to ensure that they will not be forgotten, even if they go unlearned. We scramble for the funding and the grants—increasingly difficult to obtain these days—to save the deteriorating artworks, to publish new editions and translations of the great books, to give recitals of the loveliest music. In short, we fight to maintain the pockets of warmth and elegance that provide some relief to others who are tired and harried in a sometimes sterile and technological society. I am not a particularly altruistic person, but my studies have made me deeply sensitive to the alienation and coldness of our times. While I occasionally wish that I had a time machine to deposit me in the 16th century, where I would never have to worry about a bank card or a failed transmission, I believe that I can perform a certain service here and now. My work may go largely unappreciated by many, but a few will be grateful. And that is enough.

WORDS

What is the meaning of the italicized words in the following phrases?

1. "Italian *Renaissance* art history" (par. 1)
2. "my return . . . *elicited* a few wistful wishes" (par. 1)
3. "a chorus of *lugubrious* warnings" (par. 1)
4. "described in *lurid* detail" (par. 2)
5. "the *abysmal* condition of the job market" (par. 3)
6. "consider . . . us . . . as *aberrations"* (par. 3)
7. "our *pragmatic* and computer-literate peers" (par. 3)
8. "*relegated* our joy in literature" (par. 5)
9. "our own *esoteric* and rarified disciplines" (par. 6)
10. "a sometimes *sterile* . . . society" (par. 8)

FORM AND CONTENT

1. The first three paragraphs of the essay outline almost all of the objections to preparation for a career in the humanities. What one objection does the author *not* answer in the rest of the essay?
2. The author says, "I occasionally wish that I had a time machine to deposit me in the 16th century, where I would never have to worry about a bank card or a failed transmission." Considering, among other things, that her life expectancy in the 16th century would be half that in the 20th, that her life would be dirtier, more dangerous, and much harder than now, can you share her desire? Explain.
3. The essay suggests that you must take a Ph.D degree in the humanities to maintain a love of works by Michelangelo, Botticelli, or Bach? Can this assertion be refuted? Explain.
4. The author's studies have made her "deeply sensitive to the alienation and coldness of our times." What evidence, if any, is there to suggest that our times are more alienated and colder than any earlier period?
5. Consider the last two sentences of the essay. Is the gratitude of a few enough to reward a life of hard work and genteel poverty? Or are these sentences youthfully and extravagantly sentimental?

SUGGESTIONS FOR DISCUSSION AND WRITING

1. A prominent educator once remarked that education should prepare you for living a full life rather than for merely doing a job. Defend or attack this opinion.
2. Do you believe that an increasing number of students will find themselves overeducated for today's job market? Explain.
3. If you could live in another time and place—New York City in the 1920's, London in Shakespeare's time, or the Wild West of Billy the Kid—which would you choose? Defend your choice.
4. "Many people live rich and rewarding lives without ever seeing great art or hearing great music." Do you agree or disagree? Explain.
5. High school and college guidance counselors often come under attack for being uninterested and ill-informed. Criticize or defend the counseling program at your high school or college.

Strike Out Little League

Robin Roberts

Robin Roberts was a professional baseball player with the Philadelphia Phillies and has a secure place in the National Baseball Hall of Fame.

But in this essay the former major leaguer argues against the present organization and practices of Little League baseball. His own experience and reputation give his argument authority: he knows the game and its problems. And he recognizes that merely to point out faults of a popular program is not enough; he must—and he does—propose an alternative. And his argument is rhetorically effective; notice particularly how his last two paragraphs echo and reinforce the statements of his first paragraph.

1. In 1939, Little League baseball was organized by Bert and George Bebble and Carl Stotz of Williamsport, Pa. What they had in mind in organizing this kids' baseball program, I'll never know. But I'm sure they never visualized the monster it would grow into.

2. At least 25,000 teams, in about 5,000 leagues, compete for a chance to go to the Little League World Series in Williamsport each summer. These leagues are in more than fifteen countries, although recently the Little League organization has voted to restrict the competition to teams in the United States. If you judge the success of a program by the number of participants, it would appear that Little League has been a tremendous success. More than 600,000 boys from 8 to 12 are involved. But I say Little League is wrong—and I'll try to explain why.

3. If I told you and your family that I want you to help me with a project from the middle of May until the end of July, one that would totally disrupt your dinner schedule and pay nothing, you would probably tell me to get lost. That's what Little League does. Mothers or fathers or both spend four or five nights a week taking children to Little League, watching the game, coming home around 8 or 8:30 and sitting down to a late dinner.

4. These games are played at this hour because the adults are running the programs and this is the only time they have available. These same adults are in most cases unqualified as instructors and do not have the emotional stability to work with children of this age. The dedication and sincerity of these instructors cannot be questioned, but the purpose of this dedication should be. Youngsters eligible for Little League are of the age when their concentration lasts, at most, for five seconds—and without sustained concentration organized athletic programs are a farce.

5. Most instructors will never understand this. As a result there is a lot of pressure on these young people to do something that is unnatural for their age—so there will always be hollering and tremendous disappointment for most of these players. For acting their age, they are made to feel incompetent. This is a basic fault of Little League.

6. If you watch a Little League game, in most cases the pitchers are the most mature. They throw harder, and if they throw strikes very few batters can hit the ball. Consequently, it makes good baseball sense for most hitters to take the pitch. Don't swing. Hope for a walk. That could be a player's instruction for four years. The fun is in hitting the ball; the coach says don't swing. That may be sound baseball, but it does nothing to help a young player develop his hitting. What would seem like a basic training ground for baseball often turns out to be a program of negative thoughts that only retards a young player.

7. I believe more good young athletes are turned off by the pressure of organized Little League than are helped. Little Leagues have no value as a training ground for baseball fundamentals. The instruction at that age, under the pressure of an organized league program, creates more doubt and eliminates the naturalness that is most important.

8. If I'm going to criticize such a popular program as Little League, I'd better have some thoughts on what changes I would like to see.

9. First of all, I wouldn't start any programs until the school year is over. Any young student has enough of a schedule during the school year to keep busy.

10. These programs should be played in the afternoon—with a softball. Kids have a natural fear of a baseball; it hurts when it hits you. A softball is bigger, easier to see and easier to hit. You get to run the bases more and there isn't as much danger of injury if one gets hit with the ball. Boys and girls could play together. Different teams would be chosen every day. The instructors would be young adults home from college, or high-school graduates. The instructor could be the pitcher and the umpire at the same time. These programs could be run on public playgrounds or in schoolyards.

11. I guarantee that their dinner would be at the same time every night. The fathers could come home after work and relax; most of all, the kids would have a good time playing ball in a program in which hitting the ball and running the bases are the big things.

12. When you start talking about young people playing baseball at 13 to 15, you may have something. Organize them a little, but be careful; they are still young. But from 16 and on, work them really hard. Discipline them, organize the leagues, strive to win championships, travel all over. Give this age all the time and attention you can.

13. I believe Little League has done just the opposite. We've worked hard with the 8- to 12-year-olds. We overorganize them, put them under pressure they can't handle and make playing baseball seem important. When our young people reach 16 they would appreciate the attention and help from the parents, and that's when our present programs almost stop.

14. The whole idea of Little League baseball is wrong. There are alternatives available for more sensible programs. With the same dedication that has made the Little League such a major part of many of our lives, I'm sure we'll find the answer.

15. I still don't know what those three gentlemen in Williamsport had in mind when they organized Little League baseball. I'm sure they didn't want parents arguing with their children about kids' games. I'm sure they didn't want to have family meals disrupted for three months every year. I'm sure they didn't want young athletes hurting their arms pitching under pressure at such a young age. I'm sure they didn't want young boys who don't have much athletic ability made to feel that something is wrong with them because they can't play baseball. I'm sure they didn't want a group of coaches drafting the players each year for different teams. I'm sure they didn't want unqualified men working with the young players.

I'm sure they didn't realize how normal it is for an 8-year-old boy to be scared of a thrown or batted baseball.

16. For the life of me, I can't figure out what they had in mind.

WORDS

What is the meaning of the italicized words in the following phrases?

1. "without *sustained* concentration" (par. 4)
2. "athletic programs are a *farce*" (par. 4)
3. "they are made to feel *incompetent*" (par. 5)
4. "a program . . . that only *retards*" (par. 6)
5. "There are *alternatives* available" (par. 14)

FORM AND CONTENT

1. One common way of ending an essay is to echo the beginning or answer a question raised in the beginning. How does the author use this way of ending this essay?
2. In condemning Little League baseball, the author makes a number of assumptions. Which of them could you challenge if you were to try to defend Little League?
3. Do paragraphs 8 through 13 strengthen the author's criticism of Little League baseball? Why, or why not?
4. What is the rhetorical value of all the numbers in paragraph 2?
5. Why is the long series of negative statements in paragraph 15 not only diplomatic but also peculiarly effective as an argument?

SUGGESTIONS FOR WRITING AND DISCUSSION

1. Should parents put extreme pressure on their children to excel in sports, school, art? Drawing from your own experience or observation, answer this question.
2. If you or a member of your family have participated in Little League, write a response to answer Roberts's argument.
3. Many women complain today that they are "football widows." Do you think that American devotion to spectator sports is excessive? Explain.
4. Many children in years past have lived lives of completely unsupervised leisure outside of school: they fished, roamed the woods, played spontaneous games. Do you believe that this kind of childhood is desirable? Defend your opinion.
5. Good old Charlie Brown once remarked, "Winning isn't everything but losing is nothing." From your personal experience, agree or disagree with Charlie's observation.

A Comeback for Commitment

Linda Bird Francke

Linda Bird Francke, who has been an advertising copywriter, journalist, and author of several books, is also an editor of Newsweek.

In this essay she gives reasons for changes of attitudes and expectations experienced by her and her friends during the last two decades. She is not making an argument or advancing a proposal. She is, instead, looking for reasons for changing feelings about human relationships and commitments. She finds them in the comments of her friends and in her own experiences. She states them rather tentatively, but is perhaps the more persuasive because she is never dogmatic.

1. The envelope looked innocent enough lying amid my morning batch of mail, but its contents sent me reeling. It was the wedding announcement of a 38-year-old publishing mogul friend of mine (female) to a correspondingly distinguished 45-year-old publisher (male). The afternoon brought an even greater shock. As we were chatting over our Tab cans, an old friend of mine from Saint Louis, who has been single for 12 years, suddenly blushed and announced that she, too, was getting married in the fall.

2. *M-m-m-married?* The word stuttered from my throat even as my palms grew moist. We'd all been married before. And we'd all been unmarried, too. We all had successful enough careers, were more than lip-service feminists, and had spent many tortuous hours discussing men and the hopelessness of marriage. And here they both were, altar-opting again. Could it be age, a sort of last gasp before terminal wrinkles set in? Or was it something I hadn't caught up with yet? I investigated.

3. The result jolted me. According to the U.S. Department of Commerce, the rate of marriage has taken its first upswing since it began to decline back in 1974. And although the divorce rate continues at two out of every five couples who promised lots of things they couldn't live up to, the majority make those same promises again—to someone else. Four out of every five divorced people remarry, and the glue of experience keeps 60 per cent of these marriages together. Not terrific odds, but enough to bring a gleam of hope to eyes that had been clouded with marital cynicism.

4. Commitment is in the air again, the kind of commitment that goes along with double-ring ceremonies and bedroom suites. Whereas in the 1960s and 1970s commitment ran more to causes than coupling, now the pendulum is swinging back. My friend from Saint Louis explained it this way: "First I worked for Bobby Kennedy and then I got into the antiwar movement. I marched and lobbied and used all my emotional energy on stopping the war. When the war ended, I got into the environmental movement and lay down in front of a lot of bulldozers. And then one morning I got tired of waking up alone. I was issued out. What I really wanted was someone to share French toast with."

5. But why marriage, when so many couples are living together without ministerial or legal blessing? Another friend had an answer for that one. "I think people are tired of treading water in relationships," she said, admiring her new engagement ring. "There is a yearning for a sense of permanence, of continuity, after all these years of trends coming and going."

6. None of this is really so surprising when you look back over the social course many of my contemporaries have followed in the last ten years or so. Writer and pop sociologist Tom Wolfe pseudonamed the period the Me Decade, a time that embraced every form of self-expanding zealotry from *est* and TM to Gestalt therapy and the teachings of Sun Myung Moon. The phrase "I'm going to find myself" became an acceptable tag line for what was in fact a full-blown case of national hedonism. And the women's movement did its share by urging its followers to place their own happiness and potential ahead of male and family demands. The very use of the word *we* became almost reactionary.

7. So it seems inevitable that the newest wrinkle is the oldest—to try people again. It got sort of lonely out there always doing your own thing, wallowing in self-analysis, and mouthing such buzz words as *independent, self-fulfillment,* and *assertive.* Nowhere was there any mention of the heart. It was a period of separativeness (and probably a necessary one) during which women, especially, tried to analyze their feelings and their goals instead of just lurching through life on traditional societal momentum. But now, finally, many people appear to be coming out on the far side of all this "I can do it by myselfism" and trying to reconnect, albeit with new strengths.

8. As trends go, this is a lovely one to be caught up in. Romance rather than guarded hostility wafts through the air. Women's hair has gone curly, their no-nonsense jeans have turned to flowery skirts, and the most resolute anti-make-up types are at least painting their toenails.

9. Such whimsy turns dead serious for those who are plunging into the ranks of the newly committed, however. Where marriage was once thought of as a life sentence of—perish the thought—dependence, now some think of it as liberating. "I don't have time to be single," states one writer friend of mine. "It takes too much energy." Even the bearing of children has taken a tiny upswing as women who had postponed motherhood to remain free for cause or career now realize that childbearing is not a personal handicap or an act of submission to men, but a uniquely female joy (and one that those of us in our thirties cannot postpone indefinitely). "It was time," remarks a journalist friend of mine who is expecting her first child at the age of 39. "I've accomplished more than I ever thought I would. Now I can relax."

10. Just as I see the stirring of the new commitment all around me, I can feel a twinge of it in myself. I have lived alone for the past year with my three children, supporting us all in a style that is perhaps not the dream of the upwardly mobile, but is not all that deprived, either. I was excited that I could do without a steady man, without commitment, without a future laid out till death do us part. And I'm still excited about it. But my king-size bed for two, which for so long seemed to be adequately filled by me, has begun to feel half-empty. And the independence that caused me elation while putting up the storm windows or arriving at parties alone has begun to be a burden. I'm surely not ready for *m-m-marriage* again. But I am ready at least to take a baby step toward commitment. We all know that he or she who travels alone travels fastest. But many people seem to be deciding these days that traveling fastest may not necessarily be traveling best.

WORDS

What is the meaning of the italicized words in the following phrases?

1. "publishing *mogul* friend of mine" (par. 1)
2. "more than *lip-service* feminists" (par. 2)
3. "spent many *tortuous* hours" (par. 2)
4. "clouded with marital *cynicism*" (par. 3)
5. "Tom Wolfe *pseudonamed* the period" (par. 6)
6. "every form of self-expanding *zealotry* (par. 6)
7. "case of national *hedonism*" (par. 6)
8. "guarded *hostility* wafts through the air" (par. 8)
9. "the dream of the upwardly *mobile*" (par. 10)
10. "independence that caused me *elation*" (par. 10)

FORM AND CONTENT

1. (1) Combining words or (2) modifying their form or function helps to create an informal, conversational tone. Which of these has been done with *altar-opting* (par. 2), *pseudonamed* (par. 6), and *myselfism* (par. 7)?
2. Compare "As we were chatting over Tab cans" (par. 1) with "As we were having tea" or "As we were having some refreshments." Which is more informal? Which tells you more about the conversationalists?
3. What is *alliteration?* Find an example of it in paragraph 4.
4. What is a *paradox?* What statement in paragraph 7 seems paradoxical?
5. Find a transition between two paragraphs that is made by use of a pronoun. One made by beginning a paragraph with a coordinating conjunction.

SUGGESTIONS FOR WRITING AND DISCUSSION

1. What are some good reasons for getting married and what are poor reasons? Explain the differences.
2. Do you advocate a large family, a small family, or a childless family? What are the advantages and disadvantages of your preference?
3. Some people have such great commitments to art, religion or politics—Joan of Arc, Florence Nightingale, Vincent van Gogh—that they seem to have little time for commitments to other individuals. Explain why you would or would not want to live such a life.
4. Argue for or against joint custody after divorce, that is, sharing the parenting responsibilities equally.
5. In what ways have you experienced a sense of personal isolation? Have you found a way of combatting it?

PART TWO

How to Write in College

To succeed in any college work, you must learn to write clearly and correctly. You must begin by working to a achieve mastery of spelling and an understanding of sentence structure, for without these you cannot prepare acceptable papers for any college class. You must learn to understand the differences between the informal usage of casual conversation and the relatively formal usage of written English. You must learn to organize and develop your ideas in logical order, in effective paragraphs, and in complete essays and reports. If you do these things, then—whether you go on to practice engineering or law, to teach history or chemistry, to manage a home or a business—you will have one skill required of every educated person.

1

Spelling

WHEN YOU BEGIN TO STUDY or review the principles of good writing, you begin with the study of words. The first section of this book, therefore, deals with how words are spelled, when they are capitalized, and how they are commonly used in sentences.

If you are a poor speller, the improvement of your writing must begin with the improvement of your spelling. For poor spelling is the most conspicuous of all the faults of poor writing. Everyone notices it and ridicules it: whenever schools and colleges hear complaints about the writing of their graduates, nine out of ten of these complaints are about bad spelling.

You should of course know how to use a dictionary to find the correct spellings of the uncommon or difficult words you use. But you should not use the dictionary as a crutch, stopping to look up common words like *recommend* and *receive* every time you write a letter or a theme. You should know words like these, and you should be able to write them as correctly and as effortlessly as you write your own name.

The 250 words most commonly misspelled by students beginning college work are printed on the following pages. These words are used so frequently that you should begin your review of spelling by learning to spell them correctly.

To study the spelling of a word, do these things:

1. Look at the word carefully, noticing how it is built. Does it have a common prefix (*un*necessary, *un*interesting; *dis*appointed, *dis*satisfied) or a common suffix (exist*ence,* differ*ence;* perform*ance,* attend*ance*)?

2. Pronounce the word correctly. Many students misspell words like *government, candidate,* and *library* because they have always mispronounced them.

3. Pronounce the word by syllables: AC-COM-MO-DATE, REC-OM-MEND.

4. Notice the hard spots: persEverance, sepArate. Students who misspell words almost always misspell them in the same places.
5. Use any memory device ("letters are written on stationery") or spelling rule ("i before e, except after c") that you find helpful.

Write the words you are studying over and over, and practice them until the correct spelling is habitual. Learn them any way you can, but *learn* them.

1a .... The Basic List

First Group

absence
acquire
a lot
article
buried
certain
chief
destroy
eighth
entrance
finally
friend
let's
opinion
paid
perform
proving
receive
scene
sincerely
speech
surely
till
tries
village

Second Group

across
all right
appearance
athlete
becoming
carrying
control
dealt
excellent
experience
forty
fundamental
grammar
hoping
knowledge
library
ninth
original
pleasant
professor
shining
tragedy
until
usually
writing

Third Group

achievement
apparent
attendance
coming
continually
dining
disease
divided
extremely
independent
leisure
meant
merely
possess
preference
presence
recognize
relieve
sense
stopping
surprise
thorough
used
valuable
written

Fourth Group

accommodate
aggravate
argument
beginning
bulletin
completely
conscious
definite
equipped
explanation
guard
interesting
necessary
occurred
parallel
prejudiced
prominent
religious
separate
similar
studying
truly
unusual
using
Wednesday

Fifth Group

accomplish
adequate
analyze
candidate
condemn
decision
desperate
existence
fourth
government
humorous
interrupt
nevertheless
persuade
preceding
psychology
reference
restaurant
safety
source
succeed
unnecessary
varieties
villain
weird

Sixth Group

advisable
awkward
cemetery
convenience
emphasize
foreign
imagination
legitimate
neighbor
ninety
omitted
opportunity
optimistic
particularly
perceive
permanent
planned
possible
professional
quizzes
sacrifice
secretary
specimen
successful
twelfth

Seventh Group

acquaintance
believing
calendar
competitive
deceive
description
disappoint
dissatisfied
environment
exaggerated
February
grateful
incidentally
interpreted
license
marriage
noticeable
persistent
preferred
procedure
quitting
seized
sophomore
sufficiently
superintendent

Eighth Group

accessible
business
changeable
consistent
dependent
disappeared
efficiency
eliminated
especially
exhausted
fortunately
immediately
interfere
irrelevant
maintenance
mysterious
occasion
practically
probably
quantity
receipt
repetition
significant
supplement
temperament

Ninth Group

amateur
bureau
committee
conscience
courtesy
curiosity
desirable
discipline
embarrassed
familiar
height
inevitable
intelligence
laboratory
mischievous
occurrence
outrageous
paralyzed
preparation
pronunciation
recommend
referred
ridiculous
synonym
temporary

Tenth Group

apologizing
benefited
comparatively
conceivable
conscientious
criticism
despair
disastrous
eligible
fascination
guarantee
hindrance
ingredients
loneliness
mathematics
omission
perseverance
privilege
proceed
pursuing
rhythm
schedule
strength
transferred
unanimous

REVIEW 1a

EXERCISE 1

Underline the correctly spelled word in each of the following sets. Then compare your answers with those in the back of the book.

1. (a) amateur (b) amature
2. (a) comming (b) coming
3. (a) dining (b) dinning
4. (a) disastrous (b) disasterous

5. (a) eligable (b) eligible

6. (a) existence (b) existance

7. (a) foriegn (b) foreign

8. (a) fourty (b) forty

9. (a) greatful (b) grateful

10. (a) humerous (b) humorous

11. (a) inevitible (b) inevitable

12. (a) leisure (b) liesure

13. (a) loneliness (b) lonliness

14. (a) mischievous (b) mischievious

15. (a) optomistic (b) optimistic

16. (a) paralel (b) parallel

17. (a) prejudiced (b) predjudiced

18. (a) proffesor (b) professor

19. (a) recieve (b) receive

20. (a) rhythm (b) rythm

EXERCISE 2

Underline the correctly spelled word in each of the following sets. Then compare your answers with those in the back of the book.

1. (a) privilege (b) priviledge

2. (a) grammar (b) grammer

3. (a) accommodate (b) accomodate

4. (a) seperate (b) separate

5. (a) ridiculous (b) rediculous

6. (a) proceed (b) procede

7. (a) relegious (b) religious

8. (a) consistant (b) consistent

9. (a) athlete (b) athelete

10. (a) villain (b) villian
11. (a) truely (b) truly
12. (a) speach (b) speech
13. (a) dispair (b) despair
14. (a) courtesy (b) curtesy
15. (a) burried (b) buried
16. (a) temperment (b) temperament
17. (a) occurence (b) occurrence
19. (a) license (b) licence
20. (a) restaurant (b) restarant

EXERCISE 3

Underline the misspelled word in each of the following sentences. Then compare your answers with those in the back of the book.

1. The *courtesy* of the *canidate* was *immediately apparent.*
2. A *conscientious amateur* was *becomming* less *awkward.*
3. The *labortory* is *equipped* to *perform fundamental* tasks.
4. A *competitive environment* will not *distroy* a good *business.*
5. His *curiosity* about the *calendar* in the *bulletin* was not a *critisism.*
6. A *noticeable occurence interrupted* the *beginning* of the play.
7. A *sophmore* will *receive* a *similar privilege.*
8. *Lets* plan the *preparation* of a *particularly pleasant* meal.
9. A *professional secretary* was *payed* an *unusual* wage.
10. After *stopping* at the *village,* he *usually trys* to rest.
11. *Alot* of women are *coming* to a *definite decision.*
12. *Across* from the *entrance* of the *dinning* room, he *finally* saw her.
13. My *friend* and his *acquaintance* had a *disasterous argument.*
14. The *guard* kept *believing* that she had an *intresting opportunity.*
15. *Fortunately* the *goverment* did not *condemn* the *original* mistake.

16. He was *hoping* that his *grateful speach* would save his *marriage.*
17. *Height* is no *hinderance* to *achievement* on this *occasion.*
18. My *mysterious neighbor exagerated* her *foreign* accent.
19. The *chief* found the *explanation extremely familar.*
20. The *fourth proffessor* was *probably prejudiced.*

EXERCISE 4

Underline the misspelled word in each of the following sentences. Then compare your answers with those in the back of the book.

1. He is *sufficiently sucessful* to *relieve* himself of *unnecessary* work.
2. *Believing* that *knowlege* is a *privilege,* she *tries* hard.
3. He *benefited* from hiding the *appropriate source* in the *libary.*
4. Her *livelihood* was *dependant* on her *noticeable strength.*
5. We are *studing grammar* in a *competitive environment.*
6. As a *foreign volunteer,* he is *equipped* to do *exellent* work.
7. Is it *neccessary* to *proceed* with this *ridiculous criticism?*
8. A *seperate quantity* is *coming* within *forty* days.
9. The *rhythm* was *truly pleasant,* if a little *wierd.*
10. The *bulletin continually* warned them to be *conscious* of *safty.*
11. She *usually* shows a *preference* for *writting* about *familiar* people.
12. The *speech* may *persuade* him to *suprise* his *neighbor.*
13. The *preceeding scene embarrassed* the *religious* leader.
14. In *February,* we can *accomodate practically ninety* guests.
15. The *guard* was *probably buried* in the *cemetary.*
16. The continued *existance* of *certain diseases* must *disappoint* her.
17. The *exhausted superintendant* was *particularly awkward.*
18. The *apparent villian* was *completely eliminated.*
19. On *Wednesday,* the *sophomore* took two *quizes* in *mathematics.*
20. The *psychology professor seized* the sleeping *athelete.*

ADDITIONS

On this page write additional words dictated by your instructor or marked in your essays.

1b ....Words Commonly Confused

SOME WORDS SOUND THE SAME or look the same, although they have different meanings. Study the words in the following lists, paying particular attention to the way they are used in the sentences. Then, if you have any remaining questions about what they mean, look them up in your dictionary.

1.	*a*	Last year they bought *a* new car, *a* yacht, and *a* horse.
	an	We photographed *an* eagle, *an* umbrella, and *an* honest man.
2.	*accept*	I will not *accept* your bribe.
	except	Everyone was given a gift *except* me.
3.	*advice*	My *advice* was not accepted.
	advise	I *advise* you to run for mayor.
4.	*affect*	The warm weather will *affect* the growth of corn.
	effect	The president will *effect* a change in his cabinet and one *effect* of his action will be greater efficiency.
5.	*all ready*	We are *all ready* to support your cause.
	already	They had *already* left for the concert.
6.	*are*	The vegetables *are* overcooked.
	or	Do you want peas *or* lima beans?
	our	We were served *our* favorite foods.
7.	*brake*	I *brake* for animals. My car needs a *brake* adjustment.
	break	She will *break* her neck if she is not careful.
8.	*breath*	On a cold morning you can see your *breath.*
	breathe	I want to *breathe* fresh air.
9.	*capital*	The corporation does not have enough *capital.* Begin each word with a *capital* letter. Boston is the *capital* of Massachusetts.
	capitol	Senator Gray's office is in the state *capitol,* a famous building.
10.	*choose*	Tomorrow we will *choose* a new leader.
	chose	Last week we *chose* a new treasurer.
11.	*cloths*	Linens are *cloths* woven from flax yarns.
	clothes	My *clothes* need laundering.
12.	*coarse*	This cement contains *coarse* gravel.
	course	You know, of *course,* that English is a required *course.*

13.	*complement*	A good sauce will *complement* the flavor of the meat.
	compliment	He paid you a sincere *compliment.*
14.	*desert*	Do not *desert* your post during the *desert* maneuvers.
	dessert	My favorite *dessert* is strawberry shortcake.
15.	*do*	*Do* unto others as you would have them *do* unto you.
	due	Turn in your assignments when they are *due.* The mistake was *due* to carelessness.
16.	*forth*	The warriors went *forth* to destroy the enemy.
	fourth	This is the *fourth* time that he has been late.
17.	*have*	She could *have* been a fine actress.
	of	She is one *of* my best friends.
18.	*hear*	We could *hear* the distant thunder.
	here	Summer will be *here* soon.
19.	*its*	The committee has published *its* report.
	it's	*It's* the end of the year. *It's* been a pleasure to work with you.
20.	*know*	We all *know* what you did.
	no	Under *no* circumstances will we agree.
21.	*lead*	She will *lead* you to the old *lead* mine.
	led	The general *led* his troops into battle.
22.	*loose*	Wear *loose* clothing in hot weather.
	lose	Please don't *lose* my jacket.
23.	*moral*	There is a *moral* to this story. She has high *moral* character.
	morale	The *morale* of the employees was low.
24.	*passed*	We *passed* our examinations. The car *passed* us going at a reckless speed.
	past	In the *past* we had been friends, and his *past* deeds will be long remembered.
25.	*peace*	The President advocates *peace* in our time.
	piece	Please have another *piece* of pie.
26.	*personal*	His *personal* life is a mystery.
	personnel	Report to the *personnel* office at once!
27.	*plain*	I lived on the *plains* of Nebraska. She always told the *plain* truth.
	plane	I want to study *plane* geometry and learn to fly a *plane.*
28.	*principal*	A high school *principal* has been fired. His *principal* problem is alcohol.
	principle	As a matter of *principle* we quit the club. I am studying the *principles* of economics.

29.	*quiet*	A library should be a *quiet* place.
	quite	A few condors are living, but the dodo is *quite* extinct.
30.	*right*	This *right* is guaranteed. You must turn *right.*
	write	You *write* clearly and correctly.
	rite	Human sacrifice was a religious *rite* in that culture.
31.	*stationary*	He was *stationary,* but the train was moving fast.
	stationery	Did you receive a letter written on pink *stationery?*
32.	*than*	He likes steak more *than* fish.
	then	If you are hungry, *then* you should eat.
33.	*threw*	She *threw* my ring in the river.
	through	He flew *through* the air. I am *through* with my work.
34.	*their*	They have completed *their* work.
	there	*There* are three planes on the landing strip.
	they're	We know where *they're* going.
35.	*to*	We went *to* town *to* buy supplies.
	too	The coffee is *too* hot. May I come *too?*
	two	Do you want one or *two* cubes of sugar?
36.	*weather*	The *weather* is cold and windy.
	whether	I do not know *whether* to go to work or stay at home.
37.	*were*	Where *were* you last night?
	where	Were you *where* you said you would be?
38.	*whose*	Tell me *whose* car this is.
	who's	He is a man *who's* always prompt.
39.	*woman*	She is a *woman* I will never forget.
	women	She is one of many *women* I dearly love.
40.	*your*	Tell me *your* exact age.
	you're	Are you sure *you're* in the right place.

REVIEW 1b

EXERCISE 1

Underline the correct word (or words) in each of the following sentences. Then compare your answers with those in the back of the book.

1. For *(desert, dessert)* we had apple pie.
2. An honest politician will not *(accept, except)* a bribe.
3. The President's policy assured the *(peace, piece)* of the world.

4. The victim was hit by a *(lead, led)* pipe.
5. Oslo is the *(capital, capitol)* of Norway.
6. Tonight the candidate will *(choose, chose)* his running mate.
7. *(Its, It's)* a long, long way to San Jose.
8. A good lawyer will *(advice, advise)* you to settle out of court.
9. Loyal fans will never *(desert, dessert)* their favorite team.
10. The black cat arched *(its, it's)* back.
11. *(Its, It's)* obvious that the mayor will *(loose, lose)* the election.
12. The tour guide *(lead, led)* us to the senator's office in the *(capital, capitol)* building.
13. *(Accept, Except)* for Jim, we all took Grandfather's *(advice, advise).*
14. After the jury gave *(its, it's)* decision, we could *(hear, here)* shouts of approval.
15. We *(choose, chose)* to spend our last vacation camping in the *(desert, dessert).*
16. In the *(forth, fourth)* quarter, we lost the *(lead, led)* to our opponents.
17. If our star player had been *(hear, here),* we could *(have, of)* won the game.
18. Take my *(advice, advise)* and pack lots of warm *(clothes, cloths).*
19. There will be no *(brake, break)* in our *(coarse, course)* of action.
20. She has *(all ready, already)* finished the report that is *(do, due)* on Monday.

EXERCISE 2

Underline the correct word (or words) in each of the following sentences. Then compare your answers with those in the back of the book.

1. The *(moral, morale)* of the troops was inspiring.
2. We will leave at dawn, *(weather, whether)* permitting.
3. The night was *(quiet, quite)* and warm.
4. Somehow the puppies got *(loose, lose).*
5. We were *(to, too, two)* tired to finish our mathematics problems.

6. It is my *(personal, personnel)* feeling that we have won this election.
7. Does anyone know *(who's, whose)* books these are?
8. Carol is a more talented actress *(than, then)* Jennifer.
9. The truck went *(passed, past)* us on the wrong side of the street.
10. *(There, Their, They're)* summer plans include a visit to Washington, D.C.
11. The *(plain, plane)* truth about Alice and Bob is that *(there, their, they're)* engaged.
12. Call early and tell me *(weather, whether) (your, you're)* going or not.
13. Did your secretary select the *(right, write) (stationary, stationery)?*
14. *(Whose, Who's)* a better tennis player *(than, then)* I am?
15. Which of the *(woman, women) (passed, past)* the bar examination?
16. Her *(piece, peace)* of advice was both *(plain, plane)* and direct.
17. Tell me *(your, you're) (personal, personnel)* feelings about Professor Johnson.
18. Are you *(quiet, quite)* sure *(were, where)* you left your car?
19. My *(moral, morale)* has been low during the *(passed, past)* few months.
20. We walked *(threw, through)* the small town and found only *(to, too, two)* stores open.

EXERCISE 3

Underline the correct word in the following sentences. Then compare your answers with those in the back of the book.

1. She refused to pay him a *(complement, compliment).*
2. This is *(a, an)* exception to the rule.
3. Take my *(advice, advise)* and move to Kansas.
4. We were *(all ready, already)* to leave for Kansas.
5. Does the rain *(affect, effect)* your moods?
6. Balancing the budget was the *(principal, principle)* goal of the governor.
7. Scrappy is *(a, an)* ugly dog.

8. The building with the gold dome is the state *(capital, capitol).*
9. Your *(principal, principle)* defect is unreliability.
10. Imitation is a most sincere form of *(complement, compliment).*
11. What will be the overall *(affect, effect)* of his conviction?
12. The old library is *(a, an)* eyesore.
13. Do not *(desert, dessert)* your post or you will be court martialed.
14. A bullet whistled *(passed, past)* my head.
15. Please tell the officer *(whose, who's)* car this is.
16. As a matter of *(principal, principle)* we signed the petition.
17. The accident was *(do, due)* to reckless driving.
18. The letter was written on official White House *(stationary, stationery).*
19. She is a *(woman, women)* I truly respect.
20. His suffering does not *(affect, effect)* his cheerful attitude.

1c ....Useful Spelling Rules

You learn to spell by studying and practicing one word at a time, and you may find that some spelling rules are more confusing than helpful. But because rules describe the spelling of hundreds of words, they may help you to avoid many common difficulties. Here are four useful rules.

Rule 1. If a word ends with a *y* preceded by a consonant *(study, try),* change the *y* to an *i* before every suffix except *-ing.*

copy + es = copies
worry + ed = worried
try + ed = tried
lady + es = ladies

copy + ing = copying
worry + ing = worrying
try + ing = trying

If the *y* is preceded by a vowel, do not change it *(valley, valleys; portray, portrayed).*

Rule 2.

Write *i* before *e,* except after *c*
Or when sounded as *a,*
As in *neighbor* or *weigh.*

Examples of *i* before *e: brief, piece, belief, chief.*
Examples of *e* before *i: receive, ceiling, deceive, freight, weight, sleigh.*
Exceptions to the rule: *either, neither, seize, leisure, weird.*

Rule 3. If a word ends with a single consonant preceded by a single vowel *(stop, begin),* and you add a suffix beginning with a vowel *(-ed, -ance, -ing),* double the final consonant if

1. the word has only one syllable:

stop + ed = stopped
rub + ed = rubbed

trip + ed = tripped
drop + ed = dropped

2. the word is accented on the last syllable:

occur + ed = occurred
begin + ing = beginning

confer + ing = conferring
omit + ed = omitted

Do not double the final consonant if the accent is not on the last syllable (BENEfited, PROFited, EXHIBited).

Rule 4. If a word ends with a silent *e (bite, use),* and you add a suffix,

1. drop the *e* if the suffix begins with a vowel:

bite + ing = biting
desire + able = desirable

use + able = usable

2. keep the *e* if the suffix begins with a consonant:

use + full = useful	achieve + ment = achievement
love + ly = lovely	hope + less = hopeless

This rule has two sets of exceptions: words like *noticeable* and *courageous* in which the *e* is retained to keep the *c* or *g* sound soft, and words like *truly* and *argument* in which the silent *e* following a vowel is always dropped.

2

Capital Letters and Apostrophes

IN ORDER TO PREPARE a good paper, you must learn how to use capital letters and apostrophes. If you do not use them properly, you will either mislead or annoy your reader.

2a.........When to Use Capital Letters

HERE IS A VERY SIMPLE one-sentence rule for using capital letters: Capitalize all the important words in a title, the first word of every sentence or direct quotation, and the names of particular persons, places, or things. More specifically, here are ten detailed rules:

1. *Capitalize* the first word and all other words in a title except *an* and *the* and one-syllable linking words like *in, of,* and *or.*

   Instead of reading *The Decline and Fall of the Roman Empire,* Ann read *U.S. News and World Report.*

2. *Capitalize* the first word in any sentence or direct quotation.

   The coach arrived and said, "There will be no game today."

3. *Capitalize* the name of a person, city, state, or nation, as well as of a river, mountain, or well-defined geographical area.

   Mary Williams lives in Omaha, Nebraska. Robert Andrews will visit France, Germany, and Holland before he tours the Middle East. The pioneers crossed the Mississippi River and the Rocky Mountains.

4. *Capitalize* the particular name of a ship, plane, bridge, street, or building.

   The battleship *Missouri* and the plane *Spirit of St. Louis* have important places in history. Is Dexter Hall on Campus Street? All the passengers came on deck when the ship passed under the Golden Gate Bridge.

5. *Capitalize* the name of a language or of a particular governmental body, political party, religious group, or racial group, as well as a word identifying a member of such a group.

   The United States is a democratic nation with a republican form of government. Its two biggest political parties are the Republican Party and the Democratic Party. The Democratic candidate is a Methodist. Many of the services of the Catholic Church are conducted in English.

6. *Capitalize* the name of a business, school, or college, but capitalize a word like *company* or *school* only when it is a part of the name.

   Fred left high school to take a job with Southwestern Electronics, Inc. I came to Fordham University directly from Westchester High School. The company I work for is only slightly smaller than the General Electric Company.

7. *Capitalize* a person's title only when it is used with a name or in place of a name.

The reason that Professor Johnson is teaching this course is that the professor who taught it last year has retired. Well, Professor, what comes next? Louie wants to be a captain. All right, Captain, relax.

8. *Capitalize* a term of relationship *(father, mother, uncle)* only when it is used with a name or in place of a name.

   Your uncle is not larger than my Uncle Joe. Where are Father and Mother? Where are my father and mother? Please, Dad, send money!

9. *Capitalize* the name of a course only if it is followed by a number. Remember, however, always to capitalize the name of a language (rule 5).

   He was majoring in history and I in English. We met in Geology 1B. He gave me my ring in philosophy class, and we were married during the zoology field trip.

10. *Capitalize* the name of a day of the week or a month of the year, but *not* the name of a season.

    During the fall semester we shall meet on the second Thursday in September. This is the last Sunday in March, and I am sick of winter.

REVIEW 2a

EXERCISE 1

Underline any words that require capitals in the following sentences. Then compare your answers with those in the back of the book.

1. Our professor once taught spanish and algebra on the high school level.
2. Did your father pick Dealer's Choice to win the Kentucky derby?
3. In New York, Columbus day is always a holiday.
4. Is Uncle Ned inviting dad to the Elks Club weekly dinner?
5. The settlers traveled down the ohio river on their way to the west.
6. By the time I graduate from college, I will have taken four american literature courses.
7. My mother's favorite season of the year is autumn, particularly late october.

8. The social security act was once administered by the Department of Health, Education, and Welfare.
9. The meeting will be conducted by chief of police Williams.
10. Uncle Archie was once a major in the salvation army.
11. The grand canyon is in arizona, not too far from phoenix.
12. On monday, we went to Madison Square Garden and watched the lakers beat the knicks.
13. I suggested that mother buy a mercury cougar.
14. Did you know that professor Gordon was once a shakespearean actor?
15. I was amazed when the senator voted against her democratic colleagues.
16. A violent wind out of the northeast ruined dad's first birthday barbeque.
17. John's brother, after reading *the american way of death* decided to become an undertaker.
18. Jane's letter began, "we will not be able to see one another until new year's eve."
19. We camped at mammoth falls, a few miles south of mount everett.
20. After father left, mother carried on the family business.

EXERCISE 2

Underline any error (lack of capitalization or unnecessary capitalization) in the following sentences. Then compare your answers with those in the back of the book.

1. In my senior year in High School, we studied two of Shakespeare's Roman plays.
2. When she registered for Physics, Jenny was told that she would first have to take Algebra 20.
3. During the summer, we visited Hannibal, a small missouri city on the banks of the Mississippi river.

4. Major Jones, United States army, is a catholic chaplain stationed at Fort Benning, Georgia.

5. Jenny was born in a small iowa farming community and now lives in an apartment on Fifth avenue.

6. The annual Christmas party was highlighted by a Hawaiian Dance that Alice Foley had learned in her modern dance class.

7. We never realized how much Mother cared about her Father.

8. There has never been a coach at this College like Coach Riley.

9. As the son of a U.S. air force general, captain Berger had always wanted to be a military man.

10. British and american fans of Science Fiction will long remember *2001: A Space Odyssey.*

11. Students at Carver College are required to study french, german, or spanish.

12. The new high school in our town makes Fairfield high school look small and out of date.

13. The reporter asked, "well, mayor, will you support her for Governor?"

14. The President chose senator Kelley to be his representative at the conference in belgium.

15. Because he didn't believe in a republican form of government, Jim became a polish citizen.

16. In the spring, Father will become a Professor of hebrew at a small Ohio university.

17. Nathaniel Hawthorne, the american novelist, was born in Salem, Massachusetts, a city north of Boston.

18. The old Boston and Maine railroad used to cross Main Street and then go south to the town of Silver creek.

19. On Memorial day we heard Mr. Dilby, a retired Colonel, recite "The Charge of the light Brigade."

20. The Dallas public library has a fine collection of books on buddhism.

Using Editing Skills

EXERCISE 3

Underline any word that requires a capital letter in the following exercise. You should find seven errors.

Dear uncle Joe,

I have been here at Chambers University since late september, and college life is surely different from my high school days. To begin with, my schedule requires that I attend classes six days a week, even on saturday mornings! My classes include English, biology, music, sociology and french. I am living in Fairchild hall, the oldest dormitory on campus, and have two roommates. One is from Boston and the other is a foreign student from the Middle East. The weather has been cold, and we expect snow by thanksgiving. Well, I had better get back to my studies. I have to finish reading *A Tale of Two Cities* for tomorrow's English class. Thanks for your letter. If you see dad, tell him to send money! Give my best to Aunt Sue.

Regards,
Jerry

2b.........When to Use Apostrophes

YOU USE APOSTROPHES to do three things: (1) to indicate possession with nouns *(woman's, doctor's)* and indefinite pronouns *(everybody's, someone's);* (2) to indicate omission of letters in contractions *(don't, they'll);* and (3) to indicate the plurals of letters and numbers (two *n's,* the *1980's*).

TO INDICATE POSSESSION

Here are four simples rules for using apostrophes to indicate possession.

1. Use an apostrophe plus an *s* with a noun which does not already end in an *s.*

   We met at *Harry's* office (the office of *Harry*).
   This is Bill *Wilson's* car (the car of Bill *Wilson*).
   She fought for *women's* rights (rights of *women*).

2. Use an apostrophe plus an *s* with an indefinite pronoun.

   Anyone's guess is as good as mine (guess of *anyone*).
   He did *everybody's* work (work of *everybody*).

   Never use an apostrophe with the other pronouns: *its, his, hers, yours, ours, theirs, whose.*

3. Use an apostrophe alone to form the possessive of a plural noun which ends in an *s.*

   She attends a fashionable *girls'* boarding school (a school of *girls*).
   The *students'* goals were well-defined (the goals of the *students*).

4. Use either an apostrophe alone or an apostrophe plus an *s* to form the possessive of singular nouns ending in *s.*

   Jones' or *Jones's* house
   Burns' or *Burns's* poetry

TO INDICATE OMISSION OF LETTERS

Use apostrophes to indicate the omission of letters or numbers in contractions.

I *haven't* (have not) any money.
It *isn't* (is not) ten *o'clock* (of the clock) yet.
It's (it is) her birthday, and so *I'll* (I shall) call her.
He's (he is) the president of the class of *'86* (1986).

TO INDICATE PLURALS OF LETTERS, NUMBERS, AND WORDS

Use an apostrophe plus an *s* to form the plural of a letter, a number, or a word.

> How many *2's* are there in your Social Security number?
> How many *t's* are there in the word *benefited?*
> His speech included too many *you know's* and *sort of's.*

But do not use an apostrophe in ordinary plurals.

> The *Williamses* bought two *cows* and three *pigs.*
> We invited the *Scotts* and the *Marshes.*

REVIEW 2b

EXERCISE 1

Underline and correct the word that needs an apostrophe in each of the following sentences. Then compare your answers with those in the back of the book.

1. Can you borrow Jennys car?
2. The childrens toys were scattered on the lawn.
3. I sing tenor in the mens choir.
4. This year the staffs morale is excellent.
5. The managers assistants want to have her fired.
6. Someones car is blocking my driveway.
7. Audreys clothing copies the latest French fashions.
8. The mayors enemies tried to defeat him.
9. Your problem is nobodys problem but your own.
10. The two reporters versions were exaggerated.
11. Word processors have been put in the three managers offices.
12. The four waiters tips were shared with the busboys.
13. Larry felt that he was no ones friend.
14. Three soldiers rifles were found on the parade ground.
15. The womens team was undefeated.

EXERCISE 2

Underline and correct the word that needs an apostrophe in each of the following sentences. Then compare your answers with those in the back of the book.

1. You cant be serious about marrying him.
2. The phone call shouldnt take more than a few minutes.
3. Here come your friends, and theyre an hour early!
4. At five oclock we left for work.
5. Tell Clarence that hes one in a million.
6. Its too early to plant corn.
7. Dont stay too long at the fair.
8. My uncle doesnt know the meaning of manual labor.
9. You shouldnt worry about paying this month's rent.
10. Tell the boss that Ill be late for work.
11. The class of 66 is having its twentieth reunion.
12. Wont you come home, Bill Bailey?
13. In the spring well have many roses.
14. Havent you heard the latest gossip about your friends?
15. Well be where we said we would be.

EXERCISE 3

Underline and correct any words, letters, or numbers that need apostrophes in the following sentences. Then compare your answers with those in the back of the book.

1. You must remember to dot your is and cross your ts.
2. I think my mother was a hippie in the 1960s.
3. How many 3s are there on your license plate?
4. Monty's last name is spelled with two gs and two ms.
5. Your speech had too many ers and ahs.
6. The shoe department is overstocked in some sizes, particularly 9s and 10s.

7. How many As and Bs did you earn in college?
8. The decade of the 1970s was called the "Me Generation."
9. He has trouble pronouncing his rs and as.
10. There should be just two 2s in your answer.

EXERCISE 4

Underline and correct the words that require apostrophes in the following sentences. Then compare your answers with those in the back of the book.

1. Womens fashions are much more exaggerated this year, and I cant find a thing that appeals to me.
2. Theyre all guilty of extortion, and its a wonder they werent caught sooner.
3. We met at Charles house and later swam in Cindys pool.
4. Franks car is faster than Richards, and its sure to win the Daytona 500.
5. If the boys expect to pass the test, theyd better read *Gullivers Travels.*
6. His youngest brothers business cant last another month without your help.
7. The senators wife announced that hed have a press conference at 9 oclock.
8. We were all sick of Wandas attitudes, Harriets gestures, and Boris moods.
9. Let's tell Wanda how many rs there are in *embarrass.*
10. The waitresses wages arent very good at Donalds Diner.
11. Its too late to attend Mary Holmes party, so lets go home.
12. A two weeks stay at Henrys Health Spa will give you a years worth of energy and serenity.
13. Everyone elses house was damaged except the Wilsons.
14. The womens page in the local newspaper features a weekly column written by Everetts mother.
15. Lets go to Sams Fish House, for I love both the food and the atmosphere.
16. Didnt you buy this lettuce at Robertas Roadside Market?
17. Jeffs life was spared when the jury announced its verdict at nine oclock this morning.

18. Vicky Harris political views arent shared by her relatives or her friends.
19. I can't tolerate your friends wife, for her speech relies too much on nices, neats, and for sures.
20. Uncle Curts memoirs contained vivid descriptions of President Kennedys assassination, the Mets World Series victory, and the blizzard of 71.

3

Parts of Speech: A Brief Review

ANY WORD THAT IS EXCLAIMED by itself, not to give an order or command, but just to express a strong or sudden feeling, is called an interjection. *Wow!* and *Damn!*—as well as a number of words that cannot be printed here—are called interjections.

In written English, however, words ordinarily appear in sentences. In a sentence, each word has a function that you can describe by saying that the word is a particular part of speech—noun, pronoun, verb, adjective, adverb, preposition, or conjunction. In different sentences, the same word may have different functions:

> He had a dirty *face.* (a noun)
> Now *face* the music. (a verb)

Remember, then, that when you say that a word is a particular part of speech, you are describing its function in a particular sentence.

3a.........Nouns

A NOUN IS A WORD that names a person, place, thing, idea, or action. If it names a particular person, place, or thing, it is capitalized. If it names any of a group or class, it is not capitalized unless it is the first word in the sentence.

Persons:	*John* introduced *Mary* to his *mother.* *Professor Jones* met *Georgia Smith,* the *lawyer.*
Places:	*Lake Annesquam* is in *Massachusetts.* The big *lake* is behind the *mountain.*
Things:	The *Hope Diamond* is a famous *jewel.* Our *house* has a new *roof.*
Ideas:	*Love* is *bliss,* and *envy* is *agony.*
Actions:	The *demonstration* was followed by a *riot.*

3b.........Pronouns

A PRONOUN IS A WORD that takes the place of a noun. Personal pronouns take the place of nouns already known to the reader: *I, you, he, she, it, we, they.* Indefinite pronouns may take the place of the names of all the people in the world, of any one person, or of no person at all: *everybody, anybody, anyone, somebody, someone, nobody.* Pronouns like *who* and *which* can be used in questions; the reader must decide what nouns they stand for. And, finally, *who, which,* and *that* can be used not only to stand for nouns but also to link two statements (You met my mother, *who* is visiting me).

3c ....Verbs

A VERB MAKES AN ASSERTION. It says that someone or something *does something, is something, should be* or *do something,* or *has something done to it.* For example,

> Mary *writes* long letters.
> This letter *is* long.
> *Write* another long letter.
> This letter *was written* by Mary.
> Mary *must have written* this letter.

3d ....Adjectives

AN ADJECTIVE IS A WORD used to modify (limit or describe) a noun or a pronoun. It ordinarily answers one of these questions: Which one? How many? What kind?

The very common little words *a, an,* and *the* help by modification to answer the question *which one?* So do such words as *every, any,* and *each.* So do noun and pronoun forms used as adjectives: *her* book, *that* man, *Bill's* car.

Other adjectives answer the question *how many?* Here are examples: the *three* sisters, the *several* arguments, the *many* accidents, the *one* exception.

Most adjectives, however, answer the question *what kind?* Thus the kind of car you drive may be an *expensive, powerful* car, or it may be a *small, cheap* car. Here are other examples: *brass* doorknob, *old* man, *innocent* child.

3e ....Adverbs

An adverb is a word used to modify a verb, an adjective, or another adverb.

Modifier of a verb:	They played *badly.*
Modifier of an adjective:	She is a *very* happy girl.
Modifier of an adverb:	He speaks *rather* slowly.

An adverb usually answers one of these questions: Where? When? How? To what extent?

Where?	It happened *here.*
When?	It happened *yesterday.*
How?	It happened *slowly.*
To what extent?	He is *extremely* talented.

3f ....Prepositions

A preposition is a word used with a noun or pronoun (ordinarily called *the object of the preposition*) to form a phrase that modifies another word in the sentence. Here are a number of examples:

This is a book ABOUT *Mexico.*	(modifies *book*)
The acrobats worked ABOVE *the audience.*	(modifies *worked*)
The wall stands BETWEEN *us.*	(modifies *stands*)
The man was red IN *the face.*	(modifies *red*)

3g ....Conjunctions

A conjunction is a word that connects two parts of a sentence.

A *coordinating conjunction* links equal or similar words, phrases, or sentences. There are seven coordinating conjunctions: *and, but, or, nor, for, yet,* and *so.* Of these, the first three are commonly used to link similar words and phrases.

> This executive is rich *and* powerful.
> I hunt in the fall *and* in the spring.
> She works rapidly *but* carefully.
> I shall go in June *or* July.

All of them are used to link statements that can be written separately as complete sentences.

> My sister became a doctor, *and* my brother became a lawyer.
> My sister is a doctor, *but* my brother is a lawyer.
> You may go to the party, *or* you may stay home.
> He will be a good lawyer, *for* he has a fine mind.
> She will not remain silent, *nor* will she lie.
> He is a poor man, *yet* he drives an expensive car.
> She was ill, *so* she could not come.

In these examples, the two statements are of equal importance; neither is subordinate to the other. The second half of the sentence, even when it is introduced by the coordinating conjunction, could stand alone as a complete sentence. (Any review of contemporary writing will show many sentences beginning with *And* or *But,* as well as somewhat fewer sentences beginning with the other coordinating conjunctions.)

Some coordinating conjunctions are paired with other words to form *correlative conjunctions.* The most common of these are *either . . . or, neither . . . nor, both . . . and,* and *not only . . . but also.*

> She will be *either* a great public servant *or* a discredited politician.
>
> The child can *neither* read *nor* write.
>
> *Both* Ralph *and* George have been hired.
>
> *Not only* is he the wealthiest man in town, *but* he is *also* the mayor.

A *subordinating conjunction,* as its name implies, is used to make an otherwise complete statement subordinate to another. A statement so subordinated becomes merely a noun substitute or a modifier in a larger sentence. Among words most commonly used as subordinating conjunctions are *after, although, as, as if, if, in order that, since, so that, than, that, though, till, unless, until, when, where, whereas, whether,* and *while.*

> The team went to the bus *after* the game was over.
> She could solve the problem *if* she had a computer.
> He knew *that* the battle was lost.

3h.........Conjunctive Adverbs

CONJUNCTIVE ADVERBS ARE USED to show logical relationships. A conjunctive adverb, which may appear almost anywhere in a statement, shows the meaningful connection between that statement and the one immediately preceding.

She is hungry; *consequently,* she will order dinner early.
She is hungry; she will not, *however,* eat anything.
She is hungry. *Therefore,* she is asking for food.
She is hungry, and she is ill, *moreover.*

REVIEW 3a

EXERCISE 1

Underline the noun (or nouns) in the following sentences. Then compare your answers with those in the back of the book.

1. Aspen is a town in the Rocky Mountains.
2. The vote of the electorate pleased my father.
3. Basketball is a sport that requires stamina and intelligence.
4. My uncle was once the sheriff of this county.
5. In the fall we toured three states and part of Canada.
6. We enjoyed our vacation in Sussex and Cornwall.
7. The boxer was too tired to answer the bell for the final round.
8. From the mountain we could see the village and the surrounding farmland.
9. She watches little television, only an occasional newscast.
10. The bandits, grim and desperate, barked their demands in harsh, vulgar tones.

REVIEW 3b

EXERCISE 1

Underline the pronoun (or pronouns) in the following sentences. Then compare your answers with those in the back of the book.

1. The woman whom you met was an old friend.
2. We shall visit an elderly aunt who lives in Omaha.
3. Someone tell us when the game is about to begin.
4. Which of the teams do you and Jim favor?
5. Mary and Joe are the members who deserve our admiration.
6. Anyone as popular as she is should succeed in the insurance business.
7. Have they met all of the Russian scientists?
8. Everyone cheered as the candidate entered the party headquarters.
9. I saw Comstock's latest film, which is now playing at the Rialto.
10. Nobody knew anybody, and the party was a failure.

REVIEW 3c

EXERCISE 1

Underline the verb (or verbs) in the following sentences. Then compare your answers with those in the back of the book.

1. We regret that the rumor annoyed you.
2. If he is in the office, tell him that I went home.
3. Your visit cheered our spirits and warmed our hearts.
4. None of them, we thought, deserved our support.
5. I must repeat the course next quarter.
6. Fires have been reported in the foothills.
7. When we arrived, they had finished dinner.
8. Pass me the paper, and pour me some coffee.

9. We had been walking for hours before help arrived.
10. Faith and trust are required of a successful banker.

REVIEW 3d

EXERCISE 1

Underline the adjective (or adjectives) in the following sentences. Then compare your answers with those in the back of the book.

1. The dense forest is a dark and lonely place.
2. "I am old and sick," the poor woman said.
3. Three muscular men led the young man away.
4. The German professor is formal and polite.
5. Many poor students do not study until the night before the final examination.
6. How flat and stale this foreign beer tastes!
7. She is rarely found at home, for she spends much time in the new library.
8. The beautiful bookstore was an unprofitable business.
9. He wears English clothes and handsome shoes from Scotland.
10. Robert was the chief villain in the despicable plot.

REVIEW 3e

EXERCISE 1

Underline the adverb (or adverbs) in the following sentences. Then compare your answers with those in the back of the book.

1. To do this job properly, work slowly and carefully.
2. It is very pretty, but it is much too expensive.
3. She always spoke clearly and rapidly.
4. He speaks the language poorly, but he communicates well.
5. Do nothing tomorrow without consulting me.

6. I am truly sorry that I accidentally destroyed your car.
7. The cat is hissing angrily at a rather large dog.
8. He will surely regret having spoken thoughtlessly.
9. She is a friendly person, but she is easily bored.
10. One delicate red rose usually carries a symbolic message.

REVIEW 3f

EXERCISE 1

Underline the preposition (or prepositions) in the following sentences. Then compare your answers with those in the back of the book.

1. She was born in the early nineteenth century.
2. He lives at the edge of the lake.
3. They had a nostalgic talk about the good old days.
4. The lost child was hiding behind the red barn.
5. We found it difficult choosing between the two candidates.
6. They live outside the town and beyond the county line.
7. She lived in Maui during the winter months.
8. After the game, the crowd rushed for the goalposts.
9. He felt better after talking with the coach.
10. At the border, we parked our van in a large field.

REVIEW 3g

EXERCISE 1

Underline the conjunction (or conjunctions) in the following sentences. Then compare your answers with those in the back of the book.

1. They were late, so we left without them.
2. She will go either to London or to Cairo.

3. The mayor was defeated, although she had waged a vigorous campaign.
4. His car was stolen yesterday, yet he didn't miss our appointment.
5. Not only are you arrogant, but you are also insincere.
6. We parked on the street so that you could use our driveway.
7. Either close the door or go out into the storm.
8. Please feed me, for I haven't eaten for three days.
9. We were sure that you would be reelected.
10. She will neither give us her address nor sign the complaint.

REVIEW 3h

EXERCISE 1

Underline the conjunctive adverb in each of the following sentences. Then compare your answers with those in the back of the book.

1. We shall not, however, become smug and self-satisfied.
2. We have, therefore, dismissed the clerk.
3. Thus he demonstrated his skill.
4. Unfortunately, we are not able to come.
5. The President, moreover, will veto the bill.
6. The doctor, furthermore, has done everything she could.
7. He was mentally ill, and hence he was not responsible.
8. Dr. Sprague decided to operate immediately; consequently, the patient stayed in the hospital.
9. I shall, consequently, stay in New York for five days.
10. The epidemic, nevertheless, grew even worse during the days that followed.

4

How Sentences Are Made

THE SIMPLEST WAY TO DEFINE a written sentence is to say that it is a group of words beginning with a capital letter and ending with a period, a question mark, or an exclamation mark. Such a definition will include all the patterns of informal speech, all the parts of a conversation like this:

> "Going to the game?"
> "I can't. Got to write a term paper."
> "Too bad. See you later."
> "So long."

The definition will comprehend special sentence patterns rather sparingly used in college writing, including expressions of strong or sudden feeling like "My God!" or "Ouch!" It will also include words and phrases used for transition ("So much for his arguments.") or for emphasis ("She was a great woman. *A truly great woman.*"). And, finally, it will include the great majority of written sentences—those that make statements, ask questions, or give directions. It is these sentences that are studied in this book.

A sentence is also defined as a group of words expressing a complete thought.

In a command or instruction, a single verb may be a sentence (no subject is needed):

> *Stop.*
> *March.*
> *Begin.*

Other sentences must have at least one subject and one verb.

A complete sentence may contain only two words, a subject and a verb:

> (S) *Cats* (V) *fight.*
> (S) *Babies* (V) *smile.*

A sentence may contain two or more subjects (a compound subject):

(S) *Cats* and *dogs* (V) fight.
(S) *Cats, dogs,* and *boys* (V) fight.

A sentence may contain two or more verbs (a compound verb):

(S) Cats (V) *fight* and *howl.*
(S) Cats (V) *bite, scratch,* and *howl.*

A single verb may be one word, or it may be two, three, or even four words:

(S) Cats (V) *fight.*
(S) Cats (V) *are fighting.*
(S) Cats (V) *had been fighting.*
(S) Cats (V) *may have been fighting.*

A verb may require an object to complete the meaning of the sentence:

(S) Cats (V) fight (O) *dogs.*
(S) Babies (V) drink (O) *milk.*
(S) Jack (V) is eating (O) *steak.*

A verb may require an object and an indirect object to complete the meaning of the sentence:

(S) She (V) gave (IO) *me* (O) money.
(S) John (V) is bringing (IO) *you* (O) food.

A verb may require an object and an objective complement (a word that names or describes the object) to complete the meaning of the sentence:

(S) They (V) elected (O) him (OC) *president.*
(S) We (V) considered (O) her (OC) *honest.*

A verb may require a subjective complement (a word that names or describes the subject) to complete the meaning of the sentence:

(S) Father (V) is (SC) a *doctor.*
(S) Candy (V) tastes (SC) *good.*

A verb may be modified by an adverb, several adverbs, or groups of words acting as adverbs:

(S) Cats (V) were fighting *savagely.*
Yesterday (S) cats (V) were fighting *underneath my window.*

A subject, an object, or a complement may be modified by an adjective, several adjectives, or groups of words acting as adjectives:

The alley (S) cats (V) are fighting.
The old (S) cats *in the barn* (V) are fighting.
(S) I (V) hate *sour* (O) apples.

4a.........Subject and Verb

YOU CAN UNDERSTAND THE STRUCTURE of English statements only if you can identify the subject (or subjects) and the verb (or verbs). What every sentence talks about is the subject, and the heart of what the sentence says is the verb. The relationship between subject and verb is so close that frequently the form of the verb changes if the subject changes:

> I *am eating* spinach.
> You *are eating* spinach.
> He *is eating* spinach.

Only the subject has any effect on the form of the verb; the object can change drastically without affecting the verb at all:

> I *am eating* spinach.
> I *am eating* beets and lettuce.
> I *am eating* everything but ground glass.

The verb agrees with the subject, and only with the subject.

In most English sentences the subject comes before the verb: (S) subject (V) verb. And frequently this order is your only indication of which word is the subject of the sentence. "John hates Mary" obviously means something quite different from "Mary hates John": *John* is the subject of the first sentence, and *Mary* is the subject of the second. Similarly, you may say, "The worst *feature* of the road *is* the deep ruts," but you may also say, "The deep *ruts are* the worst feature of the road." Here the two sentences mean the same thing, but the word *feature* is the subject of the first sentence, and the word *ruts* is the subject of the second. And the change of subject results in a change of the form of the verb.

The (S-V) subject-verb order is very common, but it is sometimes reversed. Consider this sentence:

> The (S) *house* (V) *is* behind the trees.

The normal order of the sentence may be reversed:

> Behind the trees (V) *is* the (S) *house.*
> There (V) *is* the (S) *house* behind the trees.
> (V) *Is* there a (S) *house* behind the trees?

Notice that normal order may be reversed by putting a modifying group of words at the beginning of the sentence, by changing the sentence into a question, or by using the word *there* to signal a change of order. The word *there* is never the subject of a sentence. Compare:

> There *is* one new *student* in the room.
> There *are* three new *students* in the room.

To identify the subject of a sentence, first find the verb. Remember that the verb may be one word *(stands)* or a phrase of three or four words *(must have been standing).* Remember, too, that parts of the verb may be separated by adverbs *(must* certainly *have been standing).* Once you have found the complete verb, ask *who* or *what* stands or must have been standing. The answer will be the subject.

There *stands* the old man.
(Who stands? *Man.*)

Through the gate *marched* the army.
(What marched? Not the gate. The *army.*)

The man with big ears *wears* a cap.
(Who wears a cap? The *man,* not the ears.)

Remember, too, that the sentence may have a compound subject (two or more subjects joined by *and*):

Men and *women* are working together.
The *students, teachers,* and *parents* met at the picnic.

Or the sentence may have a compound verb:

The students *shouted, danced,* and *sang.*
He *ignored* or *insulted* all the people at the party.

Only in orders or directions will you find no expressed subject. *You* (meaning the reader or listener) is said to be the implied subject:

[*You*] Go home!
[*You*] Turn the page.

REVIEW 4a

EXERCISE 1

Each of the following sentences has one subject and one verb. Underline the verb with a single line and underline the subject with a double line. Then compare your answers with those in the back of the book.

1. The library buys books directly from publishers.
2. I attend a small college in Michigan.
3. The tree fell on the garage during the storm.
4. My friend's mother sells stocks and bonds.
5. In the spring a young man's fancy lightly turns to thoughts of love.

6. The mayor of the town owns a turkey ranch.
7. After a long search the men found the oasis.
8. My father built a house in Palm Desert.
9. After a long deliberation the jury returned with its verdict.
10. Everybody in the city voted in the last election.
11. The man in the moon leads a lonely life.
12. The famous chef wrote a book about the preparation of unusual salads.
13. There are only a few women on the golf course today.
14. Under the palm tree sat three bearded men.
15. His development of calculus revealed Newton's genius.

EXERCISE 2

Each of the following sentences has one subject and one verb. But the verb may be one word or a group of two, three, or four words. Underline the complete verb with one line and underline the subject with a double line.

1. The cadets in the police academy were beginning the first week of training.
2. All of the candidates had been told the requirements of the job.
3. The captain is standing on the bridge of the ship.
4. At that moment Edward must have known the truth about the conspiracy.
5. In science fiction some authors have predicted future events rather accurately.
6. Next March we shall have been married for ten years.
7. The engineer in the purchasing department is preparing an estimate of the additional costs.
8. The most important person in the company has been traveling in Europe.
9. The artistry of the actor can be seen in the film now at the Nuart Theater.
10. Only in show business can a person be paid large sums of money for a ridiculous performance.
11. The carpenter on the job should have been paid more money.

12. Finally he awoke from his stupor.
13. This painting might have been done by a student in the master's studio.
14. In the conspiracy they may have been plotting against us five weeks before the election.
15. The most idealistic member of the group has been hoping for a change in the behavior of politicians.

EXERCISE 3

The following sentences may contain two or more subjects and two or more verbs. Underline the complete verb or verbs with one line and underline the subject or subjects with a double line. Then compare your answers with those in the back of the book.

1. In the forest we have been watching a group of monkeys.
2. My father and mother are leaving tonight and will arrive tomorrow.
3. The cats and dogs ruined the furniture and soiled the carpets.
4. In our country a corporation may be a single person or a company with thousands of employees.
5. His clothes, his shoes, and his hats had been purchased in England.
6. Tom, Dick, and Harry go to all the games and cheer for the home team.
7. She will begin the project, work long hours, and be responsible for all costs.
8. The statue of General Lee and his staff dominates the Courthouse Square and dwarfs the old men on the benches.
9. I attend every class, take many notes, and study at least two hours every night.
10. The clerk of the court and the bailiff assist the judge, record the proceedings, and maintain order in the court.
11. A teacher, a lawyer, or an actor must speak clearly and avoid annoying mannerisms.
12. Near the Rodin Museum is a restaurant with a fine reputation.
13. Its canals, bridges, and fine old buildings make Amsterdam the Venice of Northern Europe.

14. The new patrolman has been walking up and down both sides of the street and has checked the locks on every door.

15. His athletic trophies, his army medals, and his framed citations are standing on the mantel, displayed in two glass cases, and hung on the walls of his study.

4b.........Phrases

A PHRASE IS A GROUP of related words used in a sentence as though it were a single word. Unlike the sentence itself, it does not contain both a subject and a complete verb, and it does not make a complete statement. Learning the structure and function of various kinds of phrases will help you in writing and revising your papers.

PREPOSITIONAL PHRASES

A prepositional phrase is a preposition followed by a noun or pronoun—its object. *In the house* and *on the floor* are prepositional phrases. The phrase may be longer if the object has modifiers: *in the beautiful old house* and *on the cold marble floor.*

Prepositional phrases are almost always used as adjectives or adverbs.

The news *of the raid* spread quickly.
(Here the phrase is an adjective modifying the subject, *news.*)

Hartford is a city *in Connecticut.*
(Here the phrase is an adjective modifying the subjective complement, *city.*)

He ordered a hamburger *with onions.*
(Here the phrase is an adjective modifying the object of the verb, *hamburger.*)

The couple danced *across the floor.*
(Here the phrase is an adverb modifying the verb *danced.*)

She was sure *of herself.*
(Here the phrase is an adverb modifying the adjective *sure.*)

VERBAL PHRASES

Some verb forms are used not only as parts of verbs but also as adjectives, adverbs, or nouns. Participles, gerunds, and infinitives function accordingly in verbal phrases.

Participial Phrases

A past participle *(written, spoken, decided)* is used as a part of the verb in sentences like "He *had written* the letter" and "The letter *was written* yesterday." But when it appears without auxiliary words like *is, was,* or *has,* it is used as an adjective.

He left *written* orders.
(Here the participle *written* is an adjective modifying *orders.*)

News *written yesterday* is history today.
(The participial phrase *written yesterday* is an adjective modifying *News.*)

The present participle *writing* may similarly be a part of a verb (he *is writing, was writing, had been writing*). But used by itself, without auxiliary words, it is either an adjective or a noun.

The man *writing letters* is my father.
(The participial phrase *writing letters* is used as an adjective modifying *man.*)

Writing to her friend, the woman explained everything.
(The phrase *writing to her friend* is an adjective modifying *woman.*)

Gerund Phrases

When the present participle form is used as a noun, it is called a gerund.

Writing is hard work.
(The gerund *writing* is the subject of the sentence.)

I enjoy *writing poetry.*
(The gerund phrase *writing poetry* is the object of the verb *enjoy.*)

Infinitive Phrases

Although the infinitive *(to write)* can be used as a part of a verb, it is usually used as an adjective, an adverb, or a noun.

He has a letter *to write.*
(The infinitive *to write* is used as an adjective modifying *letter.*)

The letter is hard *to write.*
(The infinitive is used as an adverb modifying *hard.*)

I want *to write.*
(The infinitive is used as a noun, the object of *want.*)

An infinitive phrase, the infinitive plus its subject, objects, complements, or modifiers, is used in the same way.

I want *him to write me a letter.*
(Here the whole infinitive phrase—(S) *him to write* (IO) *me* (O) *a letter*— is used as a noun, the object of *want.*)

To write good poetry is her ambition.
(The infinitive phrase is used as a noun, the subject of the sentence.)

REVIEW 4b

EXERCISE 1

Underline the prepositional phrase (or phrases) in each of the following sentences. Then compare your answers with those in the back of the book.

1. The big department store is in the middle of the next block.
2. Behind the podium sat the members of the faculty.
3. In this election I do not like any of the candidates.
4. After he slipped the letter under the door, he looked through the keyhole.
5. She told us many stories about her adventures in the South Seas.
6. The roast duck is one of the best dishes on the menu.
7. Without any doubt she will be the new senator from this state.
8. At the end of the play there were four bodies on the stage.
9. He moved his troops quickly across the river and into the forest.
10. This is a government of the people, by the people, and for the people.
11. Take the bus to the park and then walk into the zoo.
12. If you understand this part of the economic theory, you must have some knowledge of statistics.
13. During the recession he made many mistakes in the management of the corporation.
14. She lives in a house by the side of the road.
15. Above the pond and immediately under the cliff is a large corral for our horses.

EXERCISE 2

Underline the verbal phrase (or phrases) in each of the following sentences. Then compare your answers with those in the back of the book.

1. He always wanted to visit Paris.
2. Whistling a happy tune, Amanda painted the fence.

3. Learning modern Greek requires a great deal of time.
4. A majority of the legislature wanted him to be the speaker.
5. The mayor of this town is a woman to be admired.
6. They caught him breaking into an empty mountain cabin.
7. Her favorite sport is running in the Boston Marathon.
8. I plan to spend many hours in London's Tate Gallery.
9. Edward Herron was the best interpreter helping the prime minister.
10. Dancing the samba requires knowledge of Latin rhythms.
11. To understand this contract, you must be able to read German.
12. We asked him to go home immediately.
13. I have always enjoyed her singing and dancing.
14. Robert recognized the farmer leading the white horse.
15. Visiting European friends occupied most of her time last year.

EXERCISE 3

Each of the following sentences contains a verbal phrase used as a noun. Underline it. Then compare your answers with those in the back of the book.

1. He wanted to join us.
2. She enjoys studying unusual foreign languages.
3. Eating shellfish can be dangerous in some parts of the world.
4. Only his religion kept him from committing suicide.
5. Keeping a budget requires careful work.
6. To sing popular songs well requires unusual talents.
7. When I finish my project, I shall enjoy visiting you.
8. To spend that much money is ridiculous.
9. The old farmer believed that stealing watermelons was her only crime.
10. He was punished for cheating the local merchants.

EXERCISE 4

Each of the following sentences contains a prepositional phrase or a verbal phrase used as an adjective. Find it and underline it. Then compare your answers with those in the back of the book.

1. The woman in the picture is wearing a police uniform.
2. The man to see is the beauty shop manager.
3. Wearing a black dress, Edna walked slowly through the cemetery.
4. In this neighborhood you can usually see Sam watering his lawn.
5. Criticizing your host's art collection is definitely not the thing to do.
6. His brief note, written rapidly, explained his attitude.
7. Crossing the finish line, George was stumbling and gasping for breath.
8. In this theater's balcony one can hear even a line whispered very softly.
9. I looked angrily at the dog chewing my slipper.
10. The woman wearing a surgical gown has been my doctor for many years.

EXERCISE 5

Each of the following sentences contains a prepositional phrase or a verbal phrase used as an adverb. Find it and underline it. Then compare your answers with those in the back of the book.

1. Laying bricks is work that is very hard to do.
2. He walked into the room and confronted his frightened enemy.
3. The fire curtain was quickly lowered when the smoke blew on the stage.
4. He is quick to criticize the work of any other dentist.
5. I am willing to work every day of the week.
6. Although it rained very hard, we stayed dry because we stood under the bridge.
7. The villain burst into the saloon and ordered a drink.
8. We were lucky to find the little boy who had been lost.
9. Walking in the rain is one of her favorite sports.
10. All of us had a merry tailgate lunch before the football game between USC and UCLA.

4c ....Clauses

A CLAUSE IS ANY GROUP of words containing a subject and a complete verb. Because the following groups of words lack either a subject or a complete verb or both, they are not clauses:

was running a race	(lacks a subject)
the man to see	(lacks a complete verb)
in the middle of the town	(lacks both subject and verb)

The following groups of words, on the other hand, are clauses:

> the (S) *man* (V) *died* yesterday
> (S) *which* (V) *made* me unhappy
> because (S) *she* (V) *studied* French

To understand the structure of sentences, you must learn to distinguish clauses from phrases, and you must learn to distinguish between *independent clauses* and *dependent clauses.*

INDEPENDENT CLAUSES

An independent clause can stand alone. It then is a complete sentence. Such a clause may contain only two words:

> (S) Robins (V) fly.

If you add modifying words and phrases to it, it may be much longer:

> Before the first hard frost of the winter, the (S) robins (V) fly south to make their winter homes in warmer climate.

But no matter how long or how short, every English sentence must contain at least one independent clause.

DEPENDENT CLAUSES

A dependent clause cannot stand alone. It cannot be a complete sentence. It functions like a single word (an adjective, adverb, or noun) in the main clause. Compare these sentences:

Single Word	*Dependent Clause*
He is an *honest* man.	He is a man *who is honest.*
I came *early.*	I came *before the class started.*
She knows the *theorem.*	She knows *that the square of the hypotenuse is equal to the sum of the squares of the other two sides.*

In the sentences to the left, single words—an adjective, an adverb, and a noun—are italicized. In those to the right, corresponding clauses are italicized—adjective clause, adverb clause, and noun clause.

Adjective Clauses

An adjective clause modifies a noun or pronoun, and it is usually introduced by one of the relative pronouns *who, whom, which,* or *that.*

Harry T. Miller, *who lives in this city,* is a lawyer.
(The adjective clause modifies *Harry T. Miller.*)

Is he the man *of whom you spoke?*
(The adjective clause modifies *man.*)

Music is an art form *that we all love.*
(The adjective clause modifies *form.*)

My older car, *which is ten years old,* is a Ford.
(The adjective clause modifies *car.*)

Sometimes, however, adjective clauses are introduced by subordinating conjunctions.

I can remember a time *when he had no money.* (modifies *time*)
This is the place *where Lincoln spoke.* (modifies *place*)

Adverb Clauses

An adverb clause modifies a verb, adjective, or adverb. It is usually introduced by a subordinating conjunction like *since, although, that,* or *as if.*

His health has improved *since he left the Arctic.*
(The dependent clause tells *when* his health *has improved.*)

Although we arrived late, we were seated in the first row.
(The adverb clause tells *under what conditions* we *were seated.*)

I am sorry *that she is ill.*
(The adverb clause modifies *sorry.*)

The beach was so crowded *that we could hardly see* the water.
(The adverb clause modifies the adverb *so.*)

Noun Clauses

A noun clause functions like a noun or pronoun and becomes a subject, object, or complement in a larger clause. Here are three sentences showing the same noun clause performing these three different functions:

That he was not a candidate was made quite clear.
(The noun clause is the subject of the sentence.)

They knew *that he was not a candidate.*
(The noun clause is the object of the verb *knew.*)

The truth is *that he was not a candidate.*
(The noun clause is a subjective complement, linked to *truth.*)

REVIEW 4c

EXERCISE 1

Each of the following sentences contains only one independent clause. Find it and underline it. Then compare your answers with those in the back of the book.

1. When I first saw her leading the chorus, she was dressed in a white robe that reflected some of the colored light from the stained glass windows.
2. After driving for more than five hours, we finally came to the river that we had been searching for.
3. I am the woman who drew up the plans and carried them to a successful completion.
4. If he thinks that we have failed, he will tell us.
5. After boring everybody at the party with long stories about his work as a mail clerk, he went home.
6. When the sun rose, he walked until he was exhausted.
7. Although he may have won a fortune playing poker, I doubt it.
8. I came after he had gone to the old house that he had inherited.
9. Although he admitted that he needed a job, he refused to accept charity.
10. I want to find an electrician who can understand the peculiar wiring in this house.
11. When I saw her, I ran to meet her.
12. We need a car that can stand the punishment of being driven rapidly over rough, unpaved desert roads.
13. While the rest of the men were working, Ralph wandered off into the forest.
14. She left the theater after the first act, while much of the audience was standing in the crowded lobby.

15. Because she had experience that no other candidate could match, we hired her.

EXERCISE 2

Each of the following sentences contains a dependent clause used as an adjective. Find it and underline it. Then compare your answers with those in the back of the book.

1. This job will be filled by someone who is extraordinarily intelligent.
2. The man that I saw was dressed in black.
3. I shall make a detour to visit my oldest sister, who lives in North Dakota.
4. The election of Franklin Roosevelt, which took place in 1932, marked the beginning of a new era in American politics.
5. The woman whom you saw was the president of the biggest corporation in this city.
6. Nocturnal animals, which move about only at night, are difficult to display in a zoo.
7. The work that she did will never be equaled by any other writer.
8. Although he was the president of the company, a position that had many important duties, he was not the company's chief executive officer.
9. Municipal bonds are frequently desirable investments for a person who has a large income.
10. The state of Oregon, which receives heavy rainfall near the coast, also has some very dry inland areas.

EXERCISE 3

Each of the following sentences contains one dependent clause used as an adverb. Find it and underline it. Then compare your answers with those in the back of the book.

1. Ruth Haglitt has accomplished much since she was elected mayor.
2. Before he goes, he will leave his proxy with the company's secretary.

3. This country, while he was President, experienced great prosperity.
4. I am delighted that you could come to dinner.
5. If he does not complete the assignment, he will not pass the course.
6. Although he was an engineer, he could not solve the problem he had been given.
7. Your coach will turn into a pumpkin when the clock strikes midnight.
8. Since his illness he has looked as if he were a very old man.
9. I know that you will do the work because you enjoy solving problems that are difficult.
10. This mutual fund, although it has had a good record, is now under new management with very little investment experience.

EXERCISE 4

Each of the following sentences contains one dependent clause used as a noun. Find it and underline it. Then compare your answers with those in the back of the book.

1. We believed that she would succeed if she tried hard.
2. What he wants can be found in Idaho or California.
3. His opinion, which we sought, was that the contract could not be enforced.
4. He said that he would serve if he was elected.
5. That you can make an omelette without breaking any eggs is very unlikely.
6. She knew when she was very young that she would be a millionaire before she was forty.
7. My belief is that the church can survive this financial crisis.
8. If you can do it, no one will ask how you did it.
9. If you continue to practice on those drums, I know that I shall lose my mind.
10. What you are doing may be profitable, but it is illegal and immoral.

5

How Sentences Should Not Be Made

THE RATHER FORMAL WRITING you will do in either college or business should not contain sentences that are awkwardly incomplete or jumbled together. If you write incomplete sentences, you will sound incoherent and breathless—a little like a person who is exhausted or drunk:

> I tried to write the paper. Tried hard. Even read a lot of books. Which took a lot of time. Because I'm a slow reader. Very slow. Didn't do me any good. The reason being that I couldn't find anything on the subject.

If you jumble sentences together without clearly separating statements or showing the relationship between them, the effect will be similar:

> I tried to write the paper, I tried very hard I went to the library and read a lot of books, that took me a long time, I'm a slow reader. Reading the books didn't do me any good, I couldn't find anything on the subject.

In attempting to improve your writing, you should begin by taking care to write complete and properly related sentences.

5a ....Fragments

A FRAGMENT IS A PHRASE or a dependent clause standing alone as if it were a sentence. In student writing, the repeated use of fragments is ordinarily a sign of carelessness or ignorance. Fragments distract the reader's attention from what is being said, and they make the writer's work seem incoherent and slovenly.

One common kind of careless fragment is a verbal phrase written as a sentence:

> We came too late to see Mary. *Her plane having left at seven o'clock.*
> This is my most precious possession. *A letter written by Abraham Lincoln.*
> We agreed that I was to do the dishes during the week. *My brother to do them on Saturdays and Sundays.*

Another kind of fragment is a dependent clause written as a sentence:

> I saw Howard last Saturday. *While we were shopping.*
> He is driving a powerful sports car. *Which must have cost thousands of dollars.*
> My father once met Alice Walker. *Who is a famous American author.*

The above fragments have all been carelessly separated from the sentences that precede them. They should be put back where they belong:

> We came too late to see Mary, *her train having left at seven o'clock.*
> This is my most precious possession, *a letter written by Abraham Lincoln.*
> We agreed that I was to do the dishes during the week *and that my brother was to do them on Saturdays and Sundays.*
> I saw Howard last Saturday *while we were shopping.*
> He is driving a powerful sports car *that must have cost thousands of dollars.*
> My father once met Alice Walker, *who is a famous American author.*

A less common kind of fragment is a group of introductory phrases and clauses so complicated that the writer loses his way and never completes his statement:

> *My father, having been educated at MIT, an institution famous for the quality of its technical education.* He is an engineer.

If awkward fragments have appeared in your own writing, learn to read carefully what you have written. Find and correct any constructions that are grammatically or logically incomplete.

REVIEW 5a

EXERCISE 1

Each of the following paragraphs contains four complete sentences and one fragment. Underline the number of the fragment. Then compare your answers with those in the back of the book.

1. (1) During the summer of 1984, I worked for the U.S. Olympic Committee in Los Angeles. (2) My job was guarding the weightlifting equipment. (3) As if anyone would try to steal anything so heavy. (4) I met many famous athletes from around the world. (5) My favorites were the weightlifters from Rumania.

2. (1) My brother is a dedicated physical fitness enthusiast. (2) He jogs 4 miles each morning before breakfast. (3) Then he's off to the spa for a sauna and massage. (4) He also watches his diet carefully. (5) Avoiding fatty meat, especially pork and lamb.

3. (1) We started the climb early in the morning. (2) Eager for the chance to scale the rugged face of Mount Garfield. (3) However, we should have waited for a weather report. (4) It took four hours to reach the 5,000-foot level. (5) A wet snow had been falling all night.

4. (1) Leonard was tried and convicted. (2) The jury, however, recommended that his sentence be suspended. (3) He had never broken the law before. (4) The judge agreed that imprisonment would not be a wise idea. (5) Because of Leonard's age.

5. (1) Macy's is having its annual clearance sale. (2) A sale that we have all been waiting for. (3) Every item of men's and women's clothing has been reduced by 40 percent. (4) Buy a suit or a dress and you will receive a free pair of shoes. (5) Doors will open promptly at 9:00 A.M.

6. (1) When I was 4 years old, we moved to Dallas, Texas. (2) My parents had recently divorced, and Mother and I had gone to live with Grandmother Evans. (3) She was a wonderful person. (4) As well as a marvelous cook. (5) I shall always cherish those Dallas memories.

7. (1) Uncle Ben was a fabulous storyteller. (2) He had been a successful car dealer and had retired at the age of 40. (3) Once a year he visited us.

(4) Usually in either July or August. (5) I loved to hear his tales of shady business deals.

8. (1) We asked the boss to reconsider our request. (2) The changes we wished to institute were perfectly fair. (3) Since they didn't violate any existing company policy. (4) But he wouldn't listen to us. (5) He said that we must do things according to his regulations.

9. (1) The police have arrested George Thomas for taking a bribe. (2) Old Mr. Thomas, the most respected man on the city council. (3) As it turned out, however, two other council members were the guilty ones. (4) Mr. Thomas' good reputation has been saved. (5) He will run for mayor in November.

10. (1) We attended the lecture on Wednesday night. (2) A speaker talked on the history of the national park system. (3) She was an employee of the Department of the Interior. (4) Her speech was well received. (5) Getting a standing ovation from an audience that agreed with her conservationist philosophy.

EXERCISE 2

Each of the following paragraphs contains four complete sentences and one fragment. Underline the number of the fragment. Then compare your answers with those in the back of the book.

1. (1) Wanting a happy, carefree life. (2) I would love to live in Hawaii, on the island of Maui. (3) During the day, I would lie on the warm sand. (4) At night I would meet friends and play till dawn. (5) Now, unfortunately, I have to leave for work at the steel mill.

2. (1) Mr. Breen, our neighbor, certainly doesn't look like a war hero. (2) Therefore, we were astonished to learn that he had won the Medal of Honor in Vietnam. (3) Alone on patrol, he had encountered an enemy stronghold. (4) He stormed the position, taking the enemy by surprise. (5) Killing six and taking many prisoners.

3. (1) McDonald's offered me a job last month. (2) At first, I hesitated. (3) In spite of the fact that I needed the money badly. (4) I wasn't afraid of the work. (5) But I felt I couldn't work for such a large organization.

4. (1) Talking too much and making too many promises. (2) That is the picture too many people have of contemporary politicians. (3) But this assess-

ment is not really fair. (4) A great many of these men and women are honest and dedicated. (5) And those that are not are seldom elected.

5. (1) Did Beth tell you about the man she met at the beach? (2) She was immediately attracted to him. (3) He had good looks and appeared to have money. (4) But, as it turned out, absolutely no brains at all. (5) After talking with him awhile, she suddenly remembered another engagement.

6. (1) Great Grandfather was a very lucky man. (2) He went to Alaska in 1881. (3) Years after the gold rush was over. (4) Within 6 months he found a rock deposit of ore that the others had overlooked. (5) He will always be remembered as the founder of our family's fortune.

7. (1) My friend was arrested for selling stolen watches. (2) He argued that he didn't know they were stolen. (3) You see, he had bought them at a swap meet. (4) But the judge found him guilty. (5) Because ignorance of the law is no excuse.

8. (1) Linda is a very talented young woman. (2) Her paintings have earned her over $4000. (3) She is a published poet and short story writer. (4) She has the lead in an amateur theater production. (5) And still finds time to be a dedicated wife and mother.

9. (1) His order had been perfectly clear. (2) To return the money I had borrowed by October 1. (3) However, I found it difficult earning such a large sum. (4) My repayment was a month late. (5) As a result, I had to pay a 15 percent late charge.

10. (1) At first we didn't believe the story about Mr. Birdwell. (2) Known to all as the most "up-tight" member of the personnel department. (3) But the rumor was true. (4) He had once been an exotic dancer in a Las Vegas revue. (5) After we learned this fact, we smiled every time he passed by.

EXERCISE 3

Four of the following items are fragments. Identify them and underline their numbers. Then compare your answers with those in the back of the book.

1. My father spent his youth on a small farm near Huron, South Dakota.
2. A part of the country where only strong-willed people survive.
3. An area hard hit by both terrible drought and devastating wind.

4. When he was 13, however, his family all moved to San Francisco.
5. There they settled in a poor but honest neighborhood.
6. And Dad quickly adapted to the soft city life.
7. He especially loved roaming around the Embarcadero.
8. That being the famous waterfront section of the city.
9. From his bedroom window he could see both the Golden Gate Bridge and Alcatraz Island.
10. Two of San Francisco's most famous landmarks.

EXERCISE 4

Four of the following are fragments. Identify them by underlining their numbers. Then compare your answers with those in the back of the book.

1. Mark Twain wrote about his California experiences in a book called *Roughing It.*
2. He discussed the stagecoach ride across the plains and mountains of the West.
3. Twain was particularly amused by the little rivers he found in Nevada.
4. The Carson River, for example, which tumbles down from the High Sierra and then meanders around the desert.
5. Because he had once been a steamboat pilot on the Mississippi, he thought the Carson River was pitifully small.
6. It turned and twisted, he said, because it was afraid that someone would come along and drink it.
7. A joke that he later used to describe the Humboldt.
8. But Twain enjoyed his life in Nevada and California.
9. Realizing his first success as a humorist and lecturer in those two states.
10. Going on to become one of America's best-loved writers and literary comedians.

5b .... Run-Together Sentences

A RUN-TOGETHER SENTENCE is produced when two or more sentences are written as one sentence, without adequate coordination or separation between them. The more conspicuous—the clearly illiterate—form of this error is sometimes called a *fused* sentence:

> Mary is studying for final examinations that is why she has not written.
> It snowed for three hours yesterday the skiing was perfect today.

The more common form of this error is sometimes called a *comma splice*. Here statements are separated, but separated inadequately by commas:

> Mary is studying for final examinations, that is why she has not written.
> It snowed for three hours yesterday, the skiing was perfect today.

If no words are added, the two statements in each of the above sentences must be separated either by a period or by a semicolon (a weak period):

> Mary is studying for final examinations. That is why she has not written.
> It snowed for three hours yesterday; the skiing was perfect today.

If a conjunction joins the two statements, a comma is an adequate mark of separation:

> Mary is studying for final examinations, *and* that is why she has not written.
> *Because* it snowed for three hours yesterday, the skiing was perfect today.

Here, in summary form, are the kinds of run-together sentences and the ways they may be corrected:

	RUN-TOGETHER SENTENCES
Fused sentence:	His father is an engineer his mother is a doctor.
Comma splice:	His father is an engineer, his mother is a doctor.
	CORRECTED SENTENCES
Separated by a period:	His father is an engineer. His mother is a doctor.
Separated by a semicolon:	His father is an engineer; his mother is a doctor.
Joined by a coordinating conjunction:	His father is an engineer, *and* his mother is a doctor.
Joined by a subordinating conjunction:	*Although* his father is an engineer, his mother is a doctor.

Remember that the conjunctive adverbs, which show logical relationships, are not conjunctions. The addition of a conjunctive adverb to a run-together sentence, consequently, will not correct the error. Compare these sentences:

Run-together sentence: His father is an engineer, his mother is a doctor.
Run-together sentence: His father is an engineer, *however,* his mother is a doctor.
Correct sentence: His father is an engineer; his mother is a doctor.
Correct sentence: His father is an engineer; however, his mother is a doctor.

When a conjunctive adverb is added to one of two statements, it does not affect the punctuation required to separate the statements.

It is easy to distinguish between conjunctions (*and, but, because, while,* and so forth) and conjunctive adverbs (*however, therefore, moreover, consequently, nevertheless,* and so forth). Conjunctions make sense only at the beginning of a clause:

Sense: His father is an engineer, *but* his mother is a doctor.
Nonsense: His father is an engineer, his mother, *but,* is a doctor.
Nonsense: His father is an engineer, his mother is a doctor, *but.*

Conjunctive adverbs, on the other hand, may appear at the beginning, in the middle, or at the end of a clause:

Sense: His father is an engineer; *however,* his mother is a doctor.
Sense: His father is an engineer; his mother, *however,* is a doctor.
Sense: His father is an engineer; his mother is a doctor, *however.*

Any word that can be moved like this is an adverb or conjunctive adverb; merely adding such a word to a run-together sentence will not correct the error.

REVIEW 5b

EXERCISE 1

Each of the following paragraphs contains one run-together sentence. Underline its number. Then compare your answers with those in the back of the book.

1. (1) I am tired of working for a living, I really mean it. (2) My job is delivering the morning edition of the *Times.* (3) My alarm, the noisy beast, goes off at 4:00 A.M. (4) It takes me about four hours to complete my route, and by then I'm exhausted. (5) Oh, how I would love to retire and spend my days in Hawaii.

2. (1) My favorite class is Cinema 100. (2) It is taught by Professor Dante, who truly loves classic films. (3) His favorite is *Casablanca,* it stars Humphrey Bogart. (4) Professor Dante always weeps during the final scene. (5) When the lights go on, his eyes are red and moist.

3. (1) "Please come to my office, then we can discuss your work habits." (2) Those words were spoken by my boss, a man I truly despise. (3) His name is Clancy, and he runs the Penguin restaurant. (4) It is a coffee shop on Maple Street. (5) The food is terrible, and so is the service.

4. (1) Not all bargains are really worth the money. (2) Last year I bought a used car from Honest Dan. (3) He assured me that I would find the car reliable and economical. (4) Two days after I made the purchase, the engine threw a rod. (5) I had it towed to Dan's lot, he only laughed.

5. (1) My supervisor is a person whom I greatly admire. (2) Her name is Lucy, she is from Vietnam. (3) She lost her entire family during the civil war in her country. (4) She first visited the United States in 1975 and then decided to make her home here. (5) Lucy is an ideal boss, both friendly and caring.

6. (1) Virginia Woolf wrote many short stories, almost all of them classic. (2) Hers was a powerful, perhaps too powerful, imagination. (3) Her last days were troubled, for she was subject to both depression and mental breakdowns. (4) Some of her most powerful stories were written after her breakdowns. (5) Woolf was a troubled woman, she was also a literary genius.

7. (1) My father, usually an honest man, has one character flaw. (2) He cheats on his income tax. (3) There are only three people in our family, he claims four dependents. (4) He also claims many nonexistent business expenses. (5) Sometime next year his return will probably be audited.

8. (1) Our neighbor, Mr. Carey, was once a famous jockey. (2) In 1977, he rode in the Kentucky Derby, in fact, his horse came in first. (3) Although riding is dangerous, Mr. Carey was never injured. (4) He is quite a celebrity around town. (5) People wave to him as he rides past them on his bicycle.

9. (1) Mayor Wilkins was re-elected, she won by a 2 to 1 margin. (2) Her opponent was Oscar Turner, a two-term congressman. (3) Turner's cam-

paign was both vicious and slanderous. (4) He even attacked Mayor Wilkins' husband. (5) After Wilkins is inaugurated, she will sue Turner for defamation of character.

10. (1) The tire was flat, and we had no spare. (2) We were 3 miles from Topsfield, therefore, we decided to walk to town. (3) When we arrived at Donkin's Garage, the doors were locked and the lights out. (4) There was only one option open to us. (5) We called a taxi and arrived home in style.

EXERCISE 2

Each of the following paragraphs contains one run-together sentence. Find it and circle its number. Then compare your answers with those in the back of the book.

1. (1) This summer Alfred plans to make his first trip to Europe. (2) He will take a charter plane to England, it will land at Gatwick Airport. (3) His British cousin will meet him there after he has been passed by immigration and customs officials. (4) Then they will take the train to London, where his cousin has a house off Bayswater Road. (5) He will spend two weeks in London before flying on to Paris, where he hopes to find an apartment on the Left Bank, somewhere near the Sorbonne.

2. (1) Harriet was a remarkable student, one of the best I have ever known. (2) She earned high grades all the way through high school. (3) Naturally, she won a scholarship, it was for $10,000. (4) Her college record was also remarkable, and she was offered several fellowships. (5) She is now doing graduate work and will earn a Ph.D. in physics.

3. (1) The rented car, which had no chains, skidded on the icy turn. (2) Norton slammed on the brakes, the worst thing he could have done. (3) Still going much too fast, the car slid completely off the road. (4) It was not damaged very much, it nosed into a large snowbank. (5) As usual, Norton had been very lucky and had made a soft landing.

4. (1) She was supposed to be one of the best chefs in all of the Midwest. (2) She had been honored by many awards and much praise from food editors and travel guides. (3) But her desserts were failures, often you found that they were sickeningly sweet. (4) For many years, no one could account for

this serious flaw in her work. (5) Then it was discovered that a jealous rival regularly adulterated her sugar supply with a powerful artificial sweetener.

5. (1) Let's go to Aspen, it's only a four-hour trip. (2) We can stay in my uncle's condominium, which is empty when he is in Europe. (3) While I am skiing, you will enjoy shopping in one of America's most charming resorts. (4) You will find stores selling everything from primitive art to expensive furs. (5) Your vacation, I fear, will be much more expensive than mine.

6. (1) For some reason our last foreign sales promotion was not an outstanding success. (2) Five of us planned the program, designed the packaging, and worked on the sales campaign. (3) The vodka we were selling was the best our distillery has ever produced. (4) But we did not realize that an Islamic culture frowns on drinking alcohol. (5) So, except for a few cases bought by several embassies, we sold no product, I am sorry to have to make this report.

7. (1) Please accept this letter as my application for the position you have advertised. (2) I have sold to department store buyers before, unfortunately, my experience has been in selling women's dresses, not men's wear. (3) My other qualifications, however, are exactly those you specified. (4) If the position is still open, I should like to show you why I believe I can serve your company well. (5) I shall, therefore, call your office on Tuesday morning to request an appointment for an interview.

8. (1) Our family owns three dogs, one of them being a basset hound named Humphrey. (2) This dog is the most independent animal I have ever known. (3) Humphrey obeys no one, in fact, he walks away when he is told to lie down. (4) He is so lazy that he slept through an earthquake and a hurricane. (5) It is little wonder that Mother loves poodles.

9. (1) Clancy is the best tennis player at our club. (2) He is also its most conceited member. (3) Last February someone sent him an anonymous Valentine card. (4) Clancy checked the handwriting of several club members, hoping to identify the secret admirer. (5) Characters like him are amusing for a time, then they become pitiful.

10. (1) During my sophomore year in college, I played bridge at least six hours a day. (2) Consequently, my grades were barely passing, and my self-

esteem was shattered. (3) I made an appointment to see a counselor, who cured me of my "bridge addiction." (4) Then I hired a tutor, she worked with me for three hours a day. (5) I am now off probation and am staying clear of the bridge tables.

EXERCISE 3

Five of the following sentences are run-together. Find them and circle their numbers. Then compare your answers with those in the back of the book.

1. Because he worked late last night, Miles was late for his 8:00 A.M. appointment.
2. Do not ask for special treatment, you cannot really expect any more favors.
3. For years I have been looking forward to visiting South America, and now my opportunity has arrived.
4. I shall never write another run-together sentence, Mr. Billings, I know it would be unacceptable.
5. We must reach the Mexican border by noon, no matter how tired and thirsty we are.
6. Tired and hungry, we reached our campground, where we pitched tents and prepared dinner.
7. My apartment is quite small, it consists of two rooms and a bath.
8. The old man walked casually into the bank, unaware that a holdup was in progress.
9. We have always loved Florida, in fact, Miami Beach is our favorite vacation spot.
10. Don't release this information to the White House reporters, they cannot be trusted.

EXERCISE 4

Five of the following sentences are run-together. Find them and circle their numbers. Then compare your answers with those in the back of the book.

1. I stood at the podium and surveyed the audience, not one face looked relaxed and friendly.
2. Although we arrived five minutes late, we still did not miss any of Senator Tandy's acceptance speech.
3. The speaker laughed, she was amused by the audience's negative response.
4. Get the police, and tell them our predicament.
5. After completing her courses in business management, she bought a hamburger franchise, an investment that made her a wealthy woman.
6. I read slowly, not realizing that the teacher was testing my reading speed, then I was surprised when he told me that I had done badly.
7. The company was very profitable, and it showed a steady improvement that pleased the stockholders.
8. Although the incoming plane was spotted by radar, it could not be identified, consequently, three fighter planes were sent to intercept it.
9. He was educated at Eton and Oxford, and after earning his degree, he joined a provincial acting company to begin his career in the theater.
10. You have lost ten pounds, your blood pressure is high, and your hands tremble, therefore, you should take a long vacation.

REVIEW 5ab

Using Editing Skills

EXERCISE 1

Find and underline the fragments and run-together sentences in the following paragraph. Then compare your answers with those in the back of the book.

Our summer vacation was nearly over. My youngest sister, Jenny, and I were traveling the last leg of our journey, a lonely stretch of highway between Middleton and Victor's Ferry. The latter being our hometown. A steady rain, which had begun to fall around noon, was now pouring, making the road dangerous and visibility poor. Jenny, always a cautious driver, reduced speed and stayed in the right lane. In the distance we could barely make out a sign announcing that Victor's Ferry was only four miles away. Suddenly the engine began to sputter, then it let out a noisy cough and died. We pushed it to the side of the road, locked the doors securely, and waited for the storm to pass over. In a few minutes the rain stopped, and the sun came out. Jennifer then tried to start the car. To our surprise, it purred smoothly. Once on the road again, we headed for home. Singing a silly child's song as we rolled merrily along. Soon we arrived at our house, it felt good to unpack and tell the family about all the good times we had shared. Never mentioning the brief interlude with the coughing engine.

EXERCISE 2

Find and underline the fragments and run-together sentences in the following paragraph. Then compare your answers with those in the back of the book.

One of the greatest novels in English literature is Jane Austen's *Pride and Prejudice,* first published in 1813. Its heroine, Elizabeth Bennet, is both lively and intelligent, but unfortunately she is prejudiced against the hero at their first meeting. Particularly by his proud and haughty manner. Later her prejudice is increased by a false report of the hero's mistreatment of a young soldier. Other plot developments also strengthen her dislike of the hero, consequently, she refuses his unexpected proposal of marriage. Speaking, as she does so, angrily and bitterly about his conduct. Later, however, she learns that she has made at least one mistake. The young soldier has lied, he is really a villain, as he later proves. Elizabeth comes to regret her prejudice, and the hero eventually explains and apologizes for his proud speeches and actions. Jane Austen handles a complicated plot skillfully as she develops her novel and brings it to a happy ending.

6

Parts of Sentences That Should Agree

IF ENGLISH IS YOUR NATIVE LANGUAGE, you know that your verbs should agree with your subjects; you would not say "I *are* going home" or "he *were* my friend." And you know that your pronouns should agree with the nouns they stand for; you would not say "I like my brother; *they* are a nice boy." Consequently, if you always know what you are writing about and know whether it is singular or plural, your verbs will agree with your subjects, and your pronouns will agree with the nouns they stand for.

6a.........Verbs with Subjects

To BE SURE THAT YOUR VERB agrees with your subject, be sure you know what your subject is. Here are five reminders:

1. Don't confuse the subject with its modifiers.

   A *line* of hungry, ragged people IS at the gate.
   The *men* in the other car ARE hungry. (The *men* are hungry, not the car.)
   One of the three women IS here. (Only *one* is here.)

2. Don't confuse the subject with its complement.

   My favorite *food* IS peanut butter sandwiches. (The subject is *food.*)
   Peanut butter *sandwiches* ARE my favorite food. (Now the subject is *sandwiches.*)

3. Don't be confused by inverted sentence order.

   There ARE three *women* on the committee.
   There IS one *woman* on the committee. (Remember that the word *there* is never the subject of a verb.)
   Under the palm trees SITS an old *man.* (The palm trees aren't sitting.)

4. Recognize compound subjects joined by *and.*

   My *brother* and my *sister* ARE coming. (Two singular subjects joined by *and* make a plural.)
   My *brother,* as well as my sister, IS coming. (Only *brother* is now the subject; sister got tucked into a modifying phrase.)

5. Know what *who, which,* or *that* refers to.

   There is the *man who* IS on the city council. (*Who* refers to *man.*)
   There is one of the three *men who* ARE on the city council. (*Who* refers to *men;* there are three of them.)
   This is one of the *products that* ARE in the catalog. (*That* refers to *products.*)

After you find the subject, decide whether it is singular or plural. Here are five more reminders:

1. Indefinite pronouns like *each, any, anybody, everybody, either,* and *neither* are always singular.

   Everybody in the crowd IS excited.
   Each of these men IS ready to volunteer.
   Neither of my parents IS at home.

2. If two singular subjects are linked by *or* or *nor,* the subject is singular.

   Either the *student* or the *teacher* IS wrong.

If one subject is singular and the other is plural, the verb agrees with the one that is closer.

Either the students or the *teacher* IS wrong.
Either the teacher or the *students* ARE wrong.

3. Collective nouns (words like *team, committee,* and *jury*) are usually *singular.*

The *committee* IS meeting now.
The *team* IS flying to Chicago.
The *jury* IS out.

But when collective nouns are used to refer to the group as a number of individuals, they may be plural.

The *committee* ARE working separately.
The *jury* ARE disagreeing among themselves.

(This usage sounds awkward, however, and most writers prefer to write *the members of the committee* or *the members of the jury.*)

4. Words like *all* and *some,* as well as fractions and percentages, are plural if their modifiers are plural (ALL *of the men* ARE here) but singular if their modifiers are singular (ALL *of the butter* IS rancid).

Half of the students ARE coming.
Half of the summer IS gone.
Ten percent of the women ARE employed.
Ten percent of the money IS mine.

5. Some words that look plural are singular, and some words that look singular are plural.

No *news* IS good news. (Did you ever read a *new?*)
Physics IS a science.
The *data* ARE being processed.
The *phenomena* ARE being observed.

REVIEW 6a

EXERCISE 1

Underline the correct verb form in each of the following sentences. Then compare your answers with those in the back of the book.

1. Near the center of town *(was, were)* three parking lots.

2. Statistics *(is, are)* a difficult subject for many people.

3. There *(is, are)* several different ways to skin a cat.
4. A line of eager shoppers *(was, were)* stretched over three blocks.
5. Neither of the twins *(is, are)* employed in this building.
6. My entire library, including two dictionaries and an encyclopedia, *(was, were)* stolen by the burglar.
7. One of Shakespeare's famous plays *(is, are)* being staged at the college.
8. At the end of a long row of cyprus trees *(stand, stands)* the tomb.
9. Neither of the plays submitted for the contest *(is, are)* worthy of the prize.
10. Both Edward and Nicholas *(sing, sings)* in the operetta.
11. Newton, not to mention several of his contemporaries, *(was, were)* interested in optics.
12. This fine collection of recipes *(was, were)* made by my aunt.
13. On the cricket field *(was, were)* several men in white flannel trousers waiting for their teammates.
14. There *(is, are)* a professor and one of her students in the law library.
15. Only two-thirds of the sugar *(has, have)* been used by the cook.

EXERCISE 2

Underline the correct verb form in each of the following sentences. Then compare your answers with those in the back of the book.

1. When *(was, were)* you going to call your mother?
2. Is it true that one of the passengers *(was, were)* killed?
3. The lights in the recreation center *(is, are)* turned off at midnight.
4. The distance *(is, are)* too great for us to walk.
5. The younger members of the jury *(want, wants)* to disbelieve the witness.
6. The general managers of all the houseware departments *(has, have)* a special responsibility.
7. The pilot, in addition to the rest of the crew, *(has, have)* our comfort and safety in mind.

8. *(Is, Are)* the final reports due this week or next?
9. The sale of the new calendars *(has, have)* been disappointing.
10. Few of the employees *(know, knows)* the general manager.
11. Here *(come, comes)* one of my friends and his wife.
12. The mayor, as well as the committee members, *(is, are)* ready to report to the electorate.
13. Neither Joy nor her sister *(was, were)* aware of the robbery.
14. Neither the firefighters nor their chief *(was, were)* mentioned by the press.
15. The weakest of the roles in this presentation *(is, are)* that of butler.

6b .... Pronouns with the Words They Stand for

WHEN YOU USE A PRONOUN that stands for another word (its *antecedent*), be sure that it agrees with that word in person, gender, and number.

AGREEMENT IN PERSON

Failure to maintain agreement in person between a pronoun and its antecedent is a sure sign that you have forgotten what you are talking about:

> A *person* who comes to college soon finds that *you* spend more money than *you* did in high school.
>
> As a student of dentistry, *I* know it is important to brush *his* teeth every morning.

AGREEMENT IN GENDER

Only a person first learning English is likely to say or write something like this:

> My pen is gone, and I cannot find him anywhere.

But you may occasionally be confused by reference to an antecedent that can be either masculine or feminine. For such a reference, it has long been common practice to use the masculine pronoun. Increasingly, however, many writers use *his* or *her;* others rewrite sentences, using plural antecedents and plural pronouns.

> *Correct:* *Everybody* has finished *his* work.
> *Correct, but awkward:* *Everybody* has finished *his* or *her* work.
> *Correct:* *All* the students have finished *their* work.

If the reference, however, is to a noun or pronoun which is necessarily feminine, use a feminine pronoun:

> *Correct:* *Each member* of the sorority was asked to name *her* favorite sport.

You may also use a feminine pronoun for an affectionate reference to a country or a college, and common usage demands that you always use a feminine pronoun to refer to a ship:

> *Correct:* England expects *her* sons to do their duty.
> *Correct:* Antioch College sends *her* students to jobs in all parts of the country.

Correct: While the Queen Elizabeth II was in New York, *her* captain entertained the press.

AGREEMENT IN NUMBER

To be sure that your pronoun agrees with its antecedent in number, always remember how many things or people you are writing about. Do not write sentences like these:

A person walking here must watch *their* step.
A Volkswagen is a good car, but *they* are too small.

Such sentences are obviously illogical.

Remember that a demonstrative pronoun used as an adjective should always agree with the word it modifies:

Correct: *That kind* (not *Those kind*) of gifts is popular.
Correct: *This sort* (not *These sort*) of men succeeds.

Remember, too, that in reasonably formal English the indefinite pronouns like *one, anybody, somebody, each,* and *everybody* take singular pronouns.

Correct: *Everybody* has done *his* or *her* (not *their*) work well.
Correct: *Nobody* knew what *he* or *she* (not *they*) was doing.

When *either* and *neither* are used as pronouns, they also take singular pronouns:

Correct: *Neither* of the singers performed *his* or *her* part well.

When two or more antecedents are joined by *and,* they take a plural pronoun:

Correct: Mary and John have lost *their* way.

But when two singular antecedents are joined by *or* or *nor,* they take a singular pronoun:

Correct: Neither Tom nor Bill lost *his* head.

If one of the two antecedents joined by *or* or *nor* is singular and the other is plural, the pronoun agrees with the nearer:

Correct: Neither the old man nor the two women have finished *their* work.
Correct but awkward: Neither the two women nor the old man has finished *his work.* (Most careful writers avoid this kind of sentence construction.)

Finally, remember that you must be consistent in your use of collective nouns. If the collective noun stands for a group taken as a unit, refer to it with a singular pronoun:

Correct: The basketball team has won *its* fifth game.

But if the collective noun stands for a number of individuals, refer to it with a plural pronoun:

Correct: The committee could not agree, and *they* argued all afternoon.

REVIEW 6b

EXERCISE 1

Underline the correct form of the pronouns in each of the following sentences. Then compare your answers with those in the back of the book.

1. *Time* magazine decided to send one of *(its, their)* editors to the exhibition.
2. *(This, These)* kind of article will never be printed in our paper.
3. Some of the members of the Faculty Women's Club *(has her, have their)* committee meetings in the library.
4. Neither the police chief nor his two deputies had done *(his, their)* jobs.
5. Both of the shoemakers had learned *(his, their)* trades in the penetentiary.
6. I have always disliked *(this, these)* kind of violent scenes in motion pictures.
7. If anybody wants a copy of my book, I wish *(he or she, they)* would buy it at the bookstore.
8. Each of the women entering the church found it necessary to cover *(her head, their heads).*
9. Nobody who cares about *(his or her, their)* reputation would steal spoons from the club.
10. Both the manager and the chef do what *(she, they)* can to make the restaurant a success.
11. Any member of the football team must turn in *(his, their)* uniform if the coach asks for it.
12. Each of our wives has *(her, their)* own way of asking favors or giving orders.
13. Anyone who thinks that being a lifeguard is easy should try it *(himself or herself, themselves).*
14. The class always shows *(its, their)* irritation by muttering and moving restlessly.

15. Neither Reginald nor Mortimer ever left town without being accompanied by *(his, their)* house servants.

EXERCISE 2

Underline the correct form of the pronoun in each of the following sentences. Then compare your answers with those in the back of the book.

1. The track team has *(its, their)* new uniforms.
2. Every Boy Scout who participated in the drive was complimented on *(his, their)* cooperation.
3. No farmer who really cared about *(his, their)* livestock would overfeed them.
4. It is a mistake for the banker to try being *(her, their)* own lawyer.
5. Everyone in the organization is busy working on *(his or her, their)* own project.
6. Every one of the women brought *(her, their)* own plans for the new building.
7. One member of the men's choir has left *(his, their)* car lights on.
8. Not one of the soldiers expected to see *(his, their)* home again.
9. Either Bob or Bill will let us borrow *(his, their)* car.
10. Someone has left *(his or her, their)* briefcase on the plane.
11. Because the jury were unable to agree on *(its, their)* verdict, the judge dismissed the case.
12. Professor Nancy Ross, along with four other faculty members, has taken *(her, their)* place in the reception line.
13. Everyone on the committee has done *(his or her, their)* work well.
14. The Smithsonian Institution is where Lindbergh's *Spirit of St. Louis* makes *(her, its)* permanent home.
15. More often than not, *(these, this)* kinds of movies are depressing.

REVIEW 6ab

Using Editing Skills

EXERCISE 1

Each of the following paragraphs contains one sentence which is incorrect because of faulty verb or pronoun agreement. Find the incorrect sentence and underline its number. Then compare your answers with those in the back of the book.

1. (1) Neither of the Wilson brothers have a very good reputation. (2) They were expelled from high school for both academic reasons and bad conduct. (3) Frank, who is a year older than Larry, was dishonorably discharged from the Marine Corps after only six months of training. (4) Larry volunteered for every branch of the service, but was accepted by none. (5) His arrest and conviction record has made him ineligible for military service.

2. (1) Our next door neighbors decided to build a homemade swimming pool. (2) The plan received our unanimous vote of approval. (3) Every one of us was willing to offer their expert advice on the pool's size, shape, and location. (4) But the planning stage was as far as we got. (5) Not one of us was willing to do the digging, hauling, and framing.

3. (1) Today's company election was very hotly contested. (2) Four candidates were nominated for the position of social director. (3) Each of the candidates had an enthusiastic group of loyal supporters. (4) By now, the votes of every department in the company has been counted. (5) Within a few minutes the winner of the election will be announced.

4. (1) Many people who live in the Northeast spend their winter vacations on one of the many islands of the Caribbean. (2) They can hardly wait for the day when they will leave the snow and wind behind and fly to the warm sunshine. (3) There they will enjoy a quiet, relaxing life-style, forgetting business pressures and threatening weather reports. (4) But after a few weeks, business will call them back to Boston or New York or Philadelphia. (5) The sad part of the vacation is that he must leave the sun and sand to go back to the ice and snow.

5. The city manager appointed a commission to study Middletown's traffic problems. (2) The commission conducted a thorough study and agreed that traffic conditions were, indeed, terrible. (3) Then the commission

recommended that all streets be made one-way thoroughfares, but this plan did not prove successful. (4) Next the commission requested that several patrol cars be added to the traffic detail, but these cars only added to the congestion. (5) Finally, having failed in their purpose, the commission was disbanded.

EXERCISE 2

Each of the following paragraphs contains one sentence which is incorrect because of faulty verb or pronoun agreement. Find the incorrect sentence and underline its number. Then compare your answers with those in the back of the book.

1. (1) The pleasures of our annual family reunion are already beginning. (2) We are sorry that our grandparents could not come. (3) Although George, as well as his brother and sister, have not yet arrived, almost everybody else is here. (4) Sometimes it seems as if everybody is talking at once. (5) All of us enjoy the annual reunion each year and look forward to seeing relatives who have come together from far and near.

2. (1) Paleontology is one of the most fascinating of the natural sciences. (2) It studies the remains of the plants and animals that lived during the various ages of the earth. (3) Each of the stages of the earth's development have their own typical fossils. (4) Merely by looking at a prehistoric footprint, a trained paleontologist is able to describe the animal that made it. (5) The earth possesses a graphic record of millions of years of its history.

3. (1) Neither Henry Durant nor William Hammond are going to be elected to the city council. (2) Durant lives in a remote suburb, and he and his wife rarely attend public functions. (3) Durant is little known, consequently, and has very little public support. (4) Hammond, on the other hand, has become notorious for leading many crusades for lost causes (like banishing junk foods from all city properties). (5) Both men, for quite different reasons, are unlikely to succeed in politics.

4. (1) The governor's investigating committee is studying all of the recent activities of the state university trustees. (2) The committee has found that the trustees have been very indecisive and slow to move. (3) The committee has recommended that the board of trustees should decide on its program and make up their minds to act. (4) But nothing, in my opin-

ion, has been done to implement these recommendations. (5) The governor, with the help of some of our legislators, is going to have to force the trustees into action.

5. (1) A person who comes to college in later years, particularly after spending some time working in business or government, is likely to find that they have no interest in some college activities. (2) One who has been responsible for directing construction projects or personnel recruitment is rarely going to want to be a cheer leader. (3) He or she may not spend much time riding in homecoming parades or attending pep rallies. (4) But such a person can find intellectual challenges in classrooms and libraries, as well as companionship with serious students of all ages. (5) The quality of college life has been improved in recent years by the attendance of increasing numbers of mature students.

7

How to Write Clear Sentences

TO WRITE CLEAR SENTENCES, you must learn to avoid constructions that are ambiguous, misleading, or illogical. Of these, the most common are the ones containing faulty pronoun reference, misrelated modifiers, or faulty parallelism.

7a ....Avoid Faulty Pronoun Reference

In order to avoid awkward repetition, you must use pronouns in place of nouns. But you must be sure that your readers know what noun each pronoun replaces; if they do not, your writing may be confusing or ridiculous. And it may be both of these if you use a pronoun that refers to more than one antecedent, to a hidden antecedent, or to no antecedent at all.

MORE THAN ONE ANTECEDENT

Do not use a pronoun in such a way that it might refer to either of two (or more) antecedents. If you do, your sentence will be ambiguous.

Ruth told Helen that *she* was gaining weight.
(Who needs the diet, Ruth or Helen?)
The teachers always tell the students that *they* are doing a good job.
(Are the teachers boasting, or are they complimenting the students?)

Even if your meaning is obvious, your sentence may be ridiculous.

Because my cat likes scraps of liver, I eat *it* once a week.
(Your cat lives well, but you write badly.)

A HIDDEN ANTECEDENT

Do not use a pronoun to refer to a noun that is "hidden" because it is used as a modifier.

Faulty: When I stepped on the dog's tail, *it* growled.
Clear: When I stepped on its tail, *the dog* growled.

Faulty: Jane's aunt died when *she* was 25.
(Who was 25, Jane or her aunt?)
Clear: When Jane was twenty-five, her aunt died.

Faulty: At every police station, *they* told us that Casey had not been found.
Clear: At every police station, *the police* told us that Casey had not been found.

NO ANTECEDENT AT ALL

Do not assume that your reader enjoys guessing what you mean. Although skillful writers occasionally use a pronoun to refer to a phrase, a clause, or a whole sentence, you can best avoid difficulty by making certain that each of your pronouns refers clearly to one word. Here are some typically confused and confusing sentences in which the pronouns have no antecedents at all:

Faulty: The fraternity is quiet after dinner because *they* are all studying.
Clear: The fraternity is quiet after dinner because *the members* are all studying.

Faulty: This university has many rules, but *they* don't obey all of them.
(*Who* doesn't?)
Clear: This university has many rules, but *the students* don't obey all of them.

Faulty: The professor forced her students to listen to her newest symphony, *which* annoyed them.
(What annoyed them? Being forced to listen? Listening? The symphony itself?)
Clear: The professor forced her students to listen to her newest symphony, *a requirement* that annoyed them.
Clear: The professor forced her students to listen to her newest symphony, *a collection of dissonances* that annoyed them.

REVIEW 7a

EXERCISE 1

Each of the following sentences contains a faulty pronoun reference. Find it and rewrite the sentence on a separate piece of paper. Then compare your answers with those in the back of the book.

1. My father is a geologist, but I am not interested in it.
2. The hounds chased the foxes until they were exhausted.
3. They say on the sports page that tonight's game has been postponed.
4. Jim called Jeff and told him that he had been awarded the prize.
5. I was very angry and had mislaid your phone number, which is the reason I didn't call.
6. Uncle Don has become disillusioned with professional football because they have become too violent.
7. We do our weekly shopping at Hardin's Market, for their produce is always fresh.

8. After Janis told Holly the sad news, she wept for an hour.
9. The clumsy waiter dropped the hot soup on the customer's new white suit, which embarrassed him very much.
10. I have received only one letter from Judy, which is depressing.
11. In Finland they have long, cold, depressing winters.
12. Todd went home, found the key in the car, and returned it to me.
13. My mother occasionally reads a detective novel or does a crossword puzzle but, as a rule, she considers it a waste of time.
14. Pamela told her mother that she was gaining too much weight.
15. The opera star smiled at Uncle Ted and gave him an autograph, which thrilled him immensely.

EXERCISE 2

Each of the following sentences contains a faulty pronoun reference. Find it and rewrite the sentence on a separate piece of paper. Then compare your answers with those in the back of the book.

1. Alfred enjoyed his tour of Germany, even though he could not understand them.
2. Stephanie made a dramatic entrance before she tripped over the dog, which all of us thought was amusing.
3. The next day Ralph told his brother that his books were still in the car.
4. Pamela says that she is unable to live in the dormitory because they serve too few fruits and vegetables.
5. Father showed us the outdoor spa that he had recently built, which delighted us.
6. Stephen says that his father died when he was 30.
7. Elizabeth has been studying chemistry for five years because she has always wanted to be one.
8. They say that New Zealand has the most varied scenery of any country in the world.

9. All of the graduate students gave Professor Scott a set of the New Oxford English Dictionary, which left her speechless.
10. The sales manager refused to let the salesmen lend the automobiles to customers, for she knew how careless they were.
11. The vice-president asked the plant manager if he knew how expensive his new plan would be.
12. Whenever you see a new gopher hole, poison it.
13. I went to the payroll office and told them that I was quitting.
14. Immediately after we heard the lion's roar, it charged at us.
15. Mr. Miller had a mild heart attack while he was climbing the mountain which frightened him very much.

EXERCISE 3

Each of the following sentences contains a faulty pronoun reference. Find it and rewrite the sentence on a separate piece of paper. Then compare your answers with those in the back of the book.

1. I agree that she is a talented artist, but it is difficult to make a living at it.
2. We visited Mexico during the summer, for we love their food and culture.
3. They say that the price of gas will be higher than it was last year.
4. I seldom watch television, for they usually put on shows that are either violent or silly.
5. If the children refuse to eat the raw vegetables, cut them up and make a soup.
6. My friend is taking courses in photography, for he has always wanted to be one.
7. In the almanac it says that this winter will be unusually cold.
8. The plumber we hired worked for two hours, but it continued to drip.
9. I am studying engineering, for I have always wanted to be one.
10. He went to the police station and told them that someone had stolen his truck.

11. In the opening chapter of this novel, it describes life in Victorian England.
12. Uncle Jim told his son that his hair was turning gray.
13. Take the antique statues off the shelves and dust them.
14. In Paris, they serve the world's finest food.
15. When the judge spoke to my father, he frowned.

EXERCISE 4

Some of the following sentences contain a faulty pronoun reference and some do not. Underline the number of any incorrectly written sentence. Then compare your answers with those in the back of the book.

1. When the settlers came west along the Oregon Trail, they were prepared for hostile Indian attacks.
2. She told us that her mother was married when she was 18.
3. When a young woman wants to become a lawyer, she must do well on the Legal Scholastic Aptitude Test.
4. Yesterday's editorial in our newspaper stated that taxes will have to be increased this year.
5. While conducting audits for the IRS, they are expected to be both accurate and polite.
6. If the dog will not eat the raw liver, cook it.
7. I saw your picture in yesterday's paper, but now I can't find it.
8. During the Thanksgiving weekend blizzard, the city came to a complete standstill because it was not prepared for such an early storm.
9. Hawaii is noted for their spectacular scenery, exotic foods, and hula dancers.
10. Our group met the senator at his office, and then he took us on a tour of the capitol.
11. My family takes all holidays seriously, for we are a group of rigid traditionalists.

12. The newspaper article stated that my brother had been arrested, which made me angry.
13. In my neighborhood, they all live in modest, single-family houses.
14. The men removed all the furniture from the recreation room and cleaned it.
15. Lucy loved to discuss acting theory but she had never been one.

7b ....Avoid Illogical Modification

TO ACHIEVE VARIETY AND EMPHASIS in your writing, you must learn to use many different kinds of modifying phrases and clauses. But remember that if the meaning of the modifier depends upon its association with a particular noun or pronoun, it must be attached clearly to the word to which it refers.

DANGLING MODIFIERS

A *dangling modifier* is a construction that expresses an illogical or ridiculous idea because it has been awkwardly separated from the word on which its meaning depends. Sometimes that word is not even in the sentence. Always, however, the separation is so drastic that mere rearrangement of the sentence —merely moving the modifier—will not cure the fault. Here, for example, are some sentences that contain dangling modifiers:

At the age of 10, Father retired from business and moved our family to Florida.
(Who was 10? Certainly not Father.)

After diving from the high tower into a small tank of water, the audience cheered.
(Who dived?)

Having been eaten by snails, John tried spreading poison bait around his plants.
(Poor John!)

The professor gave only two lectures during the semester, *caused by illness.*

Both prepositional phrases and a wide variety of verbal phrases can become dangling modifiers. Here are some more examples of dangling modifiers.

Written by Shakespeare, Snowden enjoyed reading *Hamlet.*
(Shakespeare did not write Snowden.)

After taking a shower, a large dog walked into my bathroom.
(*Who* took the shower?)

To be a doctor, anatomy is studied.
(A subject never becomes a doctor.)

After two years of college, my mother refused to increase my allowance.
(This sentence makes sense only if my mother is going to college.)

Only a little practice will give you skill in recognizing and identifying dangling modifiers. Although you can usually guess what the sentence was meant to say, what it says is usually something quite different.

One way to correct such a sentence is to leave the modifier as it is and to rewrite the rest of the sentence. Here are some examples:

Dangling: *After singing* Tosca, a large *meal* was what the soprano wanted.
Correct: *After singing* Tosca, the *soprano* wanted a large meal.

Dangling: *Frightened by the bull,* my *knees* were weak.
Correct: *Frightened by the bull,* I felt weak in the knees.

Another way to correct dangling modifiers is to expand the dangling phrases or elliptical clauses into complete dependent clauses:

Dangling: *Eating my dinner,* the *siren* sounded.
Correct: *While I was eating my dinner,* the siren sounded.

Dangling: *When only 7 years old,* my *mother* took me to a dancing class.
Correct: *When I was only 7 years old,* my mother took me to a dancing class.

MISPLACED MODIFIERS

MISPLACED MODIFIERS ARE LIKE dangling modifiers in that they result in illogical or ridiculous statements. But they are unlike dangling modifiers in that they can be corrected merely by moving the modifier to its proper place in the sentence.

Some modifiers, of course, can be placed almost anywhere in a sentence or clause without being misplaced. Modifiers of the verb or of the whole sentence are usually easy to move about. Here are two examples:

Verb modifier: *Slowly* the bus came down the hill.
The bus *slowly* came down the hill.
The bus came *slowly* down the hill.
The bus came down the hill *slowly.*

Sentence modifier: *Consequently,* the senator refused to vote.
The senator, *consequently,* refused to vote.
The senator refused to vote, *consequently.*

You can take advantage of this kind of flexibility to write sentences with the exact rhythm and emphasis you want.

But some words require exact placement. A word like *only, nearly,* or *almost,* for instance, can be moved about in a sentence, but the meaning of the sentence changes each time the word is moved. Observe the changes in meaning as the word *only* moves in the following sentences:

Only he told me that he liked my sister. (Nobody else told me.)
He *only told* me that he liked my sister. (That's all he did; he didn't show me.)
He told *only me* that he liked my sister. (He didn't tell anybody else.)

He told me *only that he liked my sister.* (He didn't tell me anything else.)
He told me that *only he* liked my sister. (He thought everybody else disliked her.)
He told me that he liked *only my sister.* (He didn't like anybody else.)
He told me that he liked my *only sister.* (I have no other sister.)

It is obvious that misplacing a word like *only, nearly,* or *almost* will result in your writing something you do not mean.

Almost any modifier can be misplaced if there are two or more words in the sentence that it might modify. Here are examples of misplaced phrases and clauses, together with suggested corrections:

Misplaced: John and Mary talked while I studied *in whispers.*
Correct: John and Mary talked *in whispers* while I studied.

Misplaced: The fire was extinguished before much damage had been done *by the brave firefighters.*
Correct: The fire was extinguished *by the brave firefighters* before much damage had been done.

Misplaced: We rented a cabin near the lake *that had two bedrooms.*
Correct: We rented a cabin *that was near the lake* and *that had two bedrooms.*

In revising your own writing, take particular care to correct a "squinting modifier": that is, a modifier so placed that it can modify either of two parts of the sentence.

Squinting: People who get drunk *frequently* disgrace themselves.
Correct: People who *frequently* get drunk disgrace themselves.
Correct: People who get drunk disgrace themselves *frequently.*

You will find that many people consider any modifier misplaced that appears between the parts of an infinitive (to *quickly* return, to *really* be understood). Although this opinion has no historical or logical justification, a decent regard for the harmless prejudices of others should lead you to split infinitives only when necessary. And certainly you should avoid awkwardly splitting an infinitive with a phrase or a clause.

Awkward: It is bad manners to, *when you are dancing,* step on your partner's toes.

REVIEW 7b

EXERCISE 1

Some of the following sentences contain misplaced modifiers and some do not. Underline the number of any illogically written sentence. Then compare your answers with those in the back of the book.

1. We served Sunday dinner to fifteen guests on expensive paper plates.
2. We walked up the street to the corner and entered a beautiful green park.
3. Surely you want to, if you possibly can, visit your grandfather in the hospital.
4. The supervisor told us on Friday we would have a paid holiday.
5. After eating a hearty dinner, we all went for a long walk along the deserted beach.
6. My friend wore a baseball cap on his head that was blue and white.
7. We saw the thief steal the diamond necklace with our own eyes.
8. Most people do not own cars that live in New York City.
9. The test pilot reported seeing a Martian spacecraft with a shaking voice.
10. I want to buy a computer that can not only prepare a payroll for 500 employees but also maintain the records of a large inventory of farm machinery.
11. We want to buy a house on a hill with three bedrooms.
12. She has bought a new car that has an air conditioner and an FM radio.
13. Roger said on Sunday he would entertain us all by showing a classic motion picture.
14. Yesterday I bought a new set of speakers from an old friend that can be played at high volume with little or no distortion.
15. The survey revealed that the average resident of this rich suburb has three cars and fewer than three children.

EXERCISE 2

Some of the following sentences contain dangling modifiers and some do not. Underline the number of any illogically written sentence. Then compare your answers with those in the back of the book.

1. Not being able to change the tire, the Automobile Club had to be called.
2. While wrapping all our gifts, we heard people outside singing Christmas carols.
3. To avoid being cheated, this unscrupulous antique dealer must be avoided.
4. Driving down the village road, a beautiful English garden caught my eye.
5. In filling out this application, you must print your name in capital letters.
6. After getting out of our sleeping bags, hot coffee and doughnuts tasted very good.
7. The author's style seemed very confusing when reading two of her books.
8. Staring at the cloudy sky, the solution to my problem seemed impossible to find.
9. While still in elementary school, my parents and I moved from Chicago to Sacramento.
10. Without realizing that he had made a serious mistake, Arthur continued his speech.
11. By simply replacing the spark plugs, our old car can be made to run like new.
12. Before buying a new home, one should have it inspected by an expert builder.
13. When drinking and driving, the accident occurred and injured an innocent bystander.
14. Since leaving New York, she has established a successful new business in Chicago.
15. Only a week out of the hospital, the scar was completely healed.

EXERCISE 3

Each of the following sentences contains an illogical modifier. Find it and rewrite the sentence on a separate piece of paper. Then compare your answers with those in the back of the book.

1. Standing at the curb, a crosstown bus splashed us with water.
2. When applying for a new job, neatness and courtesy are essential.
3. We bought a purebred Irish setter from a breeder that was thoroughly trained.
4. During their senior year at the university, Don asked Martha to marry him several times.
5. Looking north, the old O'Hara plantation can be seen in the distance.
6. After saving the company several thousand dollars, the boss gave me a generous raise in pay.
7. The manager said on Monday we would reevaluate our advertising campaign.
8. I bought a valuable antique guitar from a professional musician with steel strings.
9. Buried somewhere on the little island, the treasure hunters searched for the chest full of Spanish gold pieces.
10. Finishing her foreign policy address, the applause of the crowd pleased the senator.
11. To understand some modern poetry, each word must be studied carefully.
12. I borrowed a gas-powered mower from a friendly neighbor that was rusty and in need of repair.
13. After filling out my application form, the personnel director asked me to come to his office.
14. Upon graduating from college, my parents bought me a late-model used car.
15. My brother only wanted to borrow $50.

EXERCISE 4

Each of the following sentences contains an illogical modifier. Find it and rewrite the sentence on a separate piece of paper. Then compare your answers with those in the back of the book.

1. Our relatives are visiting at our house from Crawfordsville, Indiana.
2. I only have to rewrite the last chapter of my book.
3. The study group that I am attending now meets on Monday evenings.
4. After jogging for several miles, the cool glass of orange juice gave me welcome relief from the heat.
5. To register to vote, a permanent home address must be given.
6. While addressing the alumni association, my raincoat and umbrella were stolen.
7. Upon hearing the news of the mayor's defeat, a loud cheer filled the reception hall.
8. To receive the scholarship, a high grade-point average is necessary.
9. After meeting Mayor Kelley, my attitude toward him remained cautious and noncommittal.
10. We all want to, if all goes well, visit Niagara Falls in July.
11. Shortly before noon, we had almost prepared the entire Thanksgiving meal.
12. The hunter killed the grizzly bear that attacked him with a bow and arrow.
13. He was sitting in the front of the ski lodge with a bandage on his head and a cast on his leg that had just been put on by the orthopedist.
14. People who run marathons occasionally are injured.
15. While visiting London, the rich collections of the British Museum occupied most of Nancy's time.

7c ....Avoid Faulty Parallelism

When you want to express two or more ideas that are related and similar, you should give them the same grammatical forms. In this way you will use parallelism to make your ideas clear and emphatic.

AVOID A FAULTY SERIES

Whenever you list a series of things, actions, or ideas, they should be similarly expressed. If you express them in different ways, you will merely make your ideas harder to understand.

Faulty: We called the meeting *to elect new members, for raising money,* and *that we could plan for the conference.*

Correct: We called the meeting *to elect* new members, *to raise* money, and *to plan* for the conference.

Faulty: I want a *wrench,* a *hammer,* and *that you will get me a screwdriver.*

Correct: I want a *wrench,* a *hammer,* and a *screwdriver.*

Sometimes, of course, a difference in expression shows that you are trying to write a series that is not logical:

Faulty: The men ate *steak, potatoes,* and *drank* coffee.

The ideas in this sentence should not be expressed as a series, for no series is really intended.

Correct: The men *ate* steak and potatoes and *drank* coffee.

AVOID FAULTY COORDINATION

When two words or groups of words are linked by a coordinating conjunction, they must have the same grammatical function. Notice the similarity of words, phrases, and clauses linked by *and* in the following sentences:

He enjoys reading *plays* and *poetry. (two nouns)*
He *blocks* and *tackles* skillfully. *(two verbs)*
He looked *in the drawers* and *under the beds. (two prepositional phrases)*
She is a woman *who has worked hard* and *whom we all respect. (two dependent clauses)*
I shall return to Purdue, and *she will go to Smith. (two independent clauses)*

When the words, phrases, or clauses linked by *and* are not similar, they sound confusing and illogical:

She plays *volleyball* and *skillfully.*
He does his *homework* and *without mistakes.*
John is an *engineer* and *who works for my father.*
This is a *thermostat* and *which is very delicate.*

Perhaps the most common kind of faulty coordination in student writing is the *and who* or the *and which* sentence making an illogical link between a dependent and an independent clause:

Faulty: My mother is a lawyer *and who has been a judge.*
Correct: My mother is a lawyer who has been a judge.
or
My mother, *who is a lawyer* and *who has been a judge,* has retired.

Another kind of faulty coordination is the misuse of correlative conjunctions. These are conjunctions used in pairs (not only . . . but also; both . . . and; either . . . or; neither . . . nor) as particularly emphatic ways of comparing or contrasting similar things or ideas. Therefore the construction that follows the first half of the pair should be exactly balanced by the construction that follows the second half of the pair:

Faulty: The new book is not only *longer,* but also *it is more difficult.*
Correct: The new book is not only *longer* but also *more difficult.*
or
Not only *is the new book longer,* but *it is also more difficult.*

Faulty: He is either *a madman* or *he is a fool.*
Correct: He is either *a madman* or *a fool.*
or
Either *he is a madman,* or *he is a fool.*

AVOID FAULTY COMPARISON

When you make a comparison using the word *than* or *as,* be certain that the things you compare are similar logically as well as grammatically.

Faulty: The sunsets in Texas are more beautiful than California.

This sentence compares sunsets to a state, a comparison probably not intended. What the writer meant to say was that the sunsets in Texas are more beautiful than *the sunsets* in California.

REVIEW 7c

EXERCISE 1

Some of the following sentences contain faulty parallel structure and some do not. Underline the number of any sentence that is flawed by faulty parallelism. Then compare your answers with those in the back of the book.

1. In California, avocados are cheap, nutritious, and taste good.
2. The political satire of Jonathan Swift is similar to George Orwell.
3. His wife's hair is short, layered, and its color runs from mouse gray to dirty blonde.
4. We were told to study hard, write well, and that we must learn to use the library.
5. During the winter, I plan to visit Alaska, hike in the wilderness, trap fur-bearing animals, and speak to no human being for an entire month.
6. His monthly salary as a police officer is far better than either a teacher or a librarian.
7. The versatile chicken is excellent for baking, frying, and to boil.
8. In college we were asked to write legibly and that we should be concerned with spelling, punctuation, and mechanics.
9. The severe windstorm broke many branches, uprooted trees and with costly damage to power lines.
10. Credit cards encourage people to buy items they don't need, won't use, and can't afford.
11. The life in Coral Gables, Florida, is much more leisurely than either New York or Chicago.
12. My friend is a reference librarian and who is helpful for those doing research.
13. You are either a sore loser or you are a stubborn, uncaring idiot.
14. My yacht is 58 feet long and 18 feet wide.
15. Father's new pickup truck, a white Ford with four-wheel drive, is both a practical and a durable vehicle.

EXERCISE 2

Some of the following sentences contain faulty parallel structure and some do not. Underline the number of any sentence flawed by faulty parallelism. Then compare your answers with those in the back of the book.

1. I called the doctor's office, gave the nurse my symptoms, and made an appointment for the following day.
2. If you want to eat some good Italian food and listen to some good stories, drop by my apartment this evening.
3. My grandfather is not only a kind man but also is helpful, thoughtful, and understanding.
4. I have always enjoyed watching tennis matches, playing touch football, swimming, and to take long walks in the country.
5. Here are the three qualities I look for in a friend: loyalty, reliability, and honesty.
6. The humor of Richard Pryor is not at all similar to Eddie Murphy.
7. Grandmother loved the country life, the quiet surroundings, the friendly neighbors, and the beautiful sunsets.
8. Unfortunately, only a few male college students take courses in how to cook, nursing, and interior designing.
9. A sellout crowd jammed the amphitheater to hear the concert and to applaud the performers.
10. The office manager told me that my letters were disorganized, incoherent, and illiterate.
11. I wrote Father for a $100 loan and to see if he could give me some advice.
12. My supervisor told me to work harder and that I must stop taking half-hour breaks.
13. As a file clerk my salary was even smaller than a receptionist.
14. On my vacation I plan to read, relax, roller skate, and attending several parties.
15. The candidate pledged that she would accept the nomination, campaign vigorously, and win the November election.

EXERCISE 3

Rewrite the following sentences to correct faulty parallelism. Then compare your answers with those in the back of the book.

1. He could not decide whether he wanted to play professional baseball, become a teacher, or to join the U.S. Marine Corps.
2. A good driver is alert, skillful, and must be careful.
3. The old witch's teeth looked as long and sharp as a wolf.
4. Mayor Dellworth is a woman of legislative ability and who always speaks her mind.
5. The acceptance speech was tedious, rambling, and could not readily be understood.
6. We were told to report to the army base and that we had been placed on a 24-hour alert.
7. The house built by my grandfather, and which was designed by my father, was recently destroyed by fire.
8. My employer is not only kind, but she is also generous.
9. My brother has always enjoyed writing essays, short stories, one-act plays and writing newspaper articles.
10. I wrote Uncle Ted for a loan and to see if he could write me a letter of recommendation.
11. Tell the other climbers to walk in single file, to listen to instructions from the trail leader and that they should be aware of falling rocks.
12. Cousin Sue enjoyed going to movies and to write long love poems.
13. The wide receiver ran at top speed, leaped in the air, caught the ball in the end zone, and then he did a little victory dance.
14. The nurse told me that I should rest and not to get nervous about my many problems.
15. Yosemite has beautiful scenery, clean camp sites, friendly rangers, and it has half-tame bears.

EXERCISE 4

Rewrite the following sentences to correct faulty parallelism. Then compare your answers with those in the back of the book.

1. To get to Hollywood, an aspiring actress may travel by bus, by train, by plane, or drive her own car.
2. The hourly wage of a plumber or a carpenter is larger than a high school teacher.
3. There are three good reasons for owning your own business: (1) you keep the profits, (2) working your own hours, and (3) the tax advantages are in your favor.
4. The hobbies I really love are woodworking and to collect stamps.
5. Either you can repair the tire in the driveway or in the garage.
6. He wanted a full-time job and not to apply for unemployment.
7. Your instructions are clear, timely, and have given me many valuable ideas.
8. The movie was long, confusing, was boring, and was overacted.
9. My business failure was not only a financial disaster but caused damage to my ego.
10. She has worked as a dance instructor, tennis coach, and has served as a bank teller.
11. That television movie was exciting, dramatic and had an involved plot.
12. The commencement speaker concluded her address with a personal anecdote and then wishing the graduates success and prosperity.
13. They were shocked when they discovered one tire was flat and that the jack was missing.
14. During the summer, I learned to groom horses, to exercise them, and how to pick winners.
15. I was told to report to the police department and that my license would be revoked.

REVIEW 7abc

Using Editing Skills

EXERCISE 1

Each of the following paragraphs contains one sentence which is incorrect because of faulty pronoun reference, illogical modification, or faulty parallelism. Find the incorrect sentence and underline its number. Then compare your answers with those in the back of the book.

1. (1) Many people do not realize that national differences are greatly exaggerated. (2) They think that every Chinese is expressionless and inscrutable. (3) They think that every German is careful and thorough. (4) They think that in France they all drink wine for breakfast. (5) People forget that citizens of other nations may be very different from one another.

2. (1) You really must improve your schoolwork. (2) Your grades have been getting worse and worse during the past three months. (3) I have some suggestions, and I want you to take them seriously. (4) I want you to study more, take better notes, and why not give up playing on the football team? (5) If your grades do not improve, you will have to drop out of college at the end of the year.

3. (1) Because he was a social worker with no special training, Henry Dunning received a small salary. (2) Having a soft heart, he found it impossible to refuse any request for aid, even if he had to spend his own money. (3) Consequently, his wife soon found that he was giving away much more than he was bringing home. (4) Realizing that she had to protect her family and herself, Henry was surprised to find that she had arranged with his superiors to have his salary paid directly to her. (5) But, knowing that his charities had been ill advised, Henry made no complaint.

4. (1) Dr. Potter, who was a lover of fine food, arranged to have cheeses sent to him regularly from France and England. (2) Some of his cheeses, he found, developed undesirable flavors if stored at room temperature. (3) When he stored them for long times in his refrigerator, they developed molds that tasted like rancid butter. (4) Finally, out of desperation, he put some of his best cheeses in his home freezer. (5) When removed from the freezer three months later, the doctor found that the flavor of the cheeses was nearly perfectly preserved.

5. (1) Every college student must learn to use the library card catalog, an indispensable reference tool. (2) In it are listed all the books in the library, with at least three cards for every book. (3) One card is alphabetized by the author's last name, one by the subject, and the third is alphabetized by the title. (4) A student who knows either the author or title of a book can find the book quickly. (5) If he is interested in a particular subject, he can easily find all the books in the library that may contain the information he wants.

6. (1) People who enjoy professional wrestling say that they do not really hurt each other in wrestling matches. (2) The professionals pull their punches; they pretend to hit each other very hard, but they actually tap each other lightly. (3) Wrestlers also pretend to be injured when they are not. (4) They appear to kick and hit each other savagely. (5) But the whole performance is a show; if it were an honest sport, the wrestlers would kill each other.

7. (1) Frequently teachers and students do not fully understand one another. (2) They may assign tasks that they think are easy, but they do not know how hard they are for them. (3) Before teachers make assignments, they should plan carefully. (4) Students should read each assignment critically to be certain that they know what must be done. (5) If both teachers and students make sincere efforts, they will understand and respect one another.

8. (1) Mrs. Thompson cared for her husband throughout the long years of his last illness. (2) She was his companion, his cook, and his nurse, and she remained cheerful in spite of his constant complaints. (3) Then she returned to Iowa after the old man died to be with relatives. (4) There she found that her Uncle Gridley was bedridden. (5) So, after having come so far and done so much, she again had another bad-tempered invalid to care for.

9. (1) Among the advantages of a home built with cement blocks are its durability, you don't have to paint it, and it never is infested by termites. (2) Such a house stands almost forever, safe from fire or flood. (3) The blocks must be waterproofed, however, for they are extremely porous. (4) They must also be reinforced with steel and cement so that they can resist

earthquake tremors. (5) But they are still among the best materials that can be used in a low-cost house.

10. (1) My sister warned me to have a mechanic inspect the car before I bought it. (2) But I thought I could check the car myself by kicking the tires and running the engine for a few minutes. (3) As a result I took delivery of the car from a dishonest dealer with bad bearings. (4) It cost me more than $200 to make the necessary repairs. (5) The next time I buy a car, I shall take my sister's advice.

8

Common Errors You Must Avoid

In earlier sections of this book you have studied the construction of clear and logical sentences. Failure to remember and apply what you have learned would result in muddled and confused writing. Now, however, you are asked to review some of the common usage difficulties that can appear as blemishes even in clear, well-organized writing. These are matters merely of convention and tradition, but to ignore them in your writing would be as embarrassingly conspicuous as the wearing of tennis shoes to a formal wedding.

8a .... Wrong Pronoun Case

IN SIMPLE, UNCOMPLICATED SENTENCES, only children or adults first learning English choose the wrong pronoun case. Sentences like "me did it" or "him is my friend" are the mark of the child who has just learned to talk. Such a child soon learns to say "I did it" or "he likes me," automatically and effortlessly choosing the correct form of the pronoun.

Adults ordinarily have difficulty only with a few special constructions or a few difficult choices. Here they are:

"WE VOTERS, US VOTERS"

You have no difficulty in choosing the right form of the pronoun in sentences like "*We* want a change" or "She promised *us* prosperity." But you may have momentary difficulty when the pronoun is followed by a noun, as in "*We voters* want a change" or "She promised *us voters* prosperity." If so, read the sentence omitting the noun, and your ear will tell you which pronoun to use.

> The candidate promised *(we* or *us)* citizens a balanced budget.
> (The candidate promised *us* a balanced budget.)
>
> The candidate claims that *(we* or *us)* Americans are soft.
> (The candidate claims that *we* are soft.)

"JIM, HENRY, AND I OR ME"

Sometimes the function of the pronoun is obscured because it is one of a pair or a series. Then, although you would never say "Mary gave the prize to *I,*" you might write "Mary gave the prize to *John and I.*" To avoid this kind of error, listen to the sentence when the other parts of the pair or series are omitted; again your ear will give you the right answer.

> Jim, Henry, and *(I* or *me)* will go.
> (*I* will go.)
>
> Mary invited Bill and *(I* or *me).*
> (She invited *me.*)
>
> The class elected Mary, Ruth, and *(he* or *him).*
> (The class elected *him.*)

"BETWEEN YOU AND ME"

Remember that *between* is a preposition and that it ordinarily takes two objects.

There are no secrets between *him* and *me.*
This argument is between *them* and *us.*
There is no trouble between *John* and *her.*

"AS" AND "THAN"

Remember that *as* and *than* are conjunctions that introduce clauses, although these clauses may not be fully expressed:

My sister is older than *I.* *(than I am old.)*
His mother liked his sister more than *him.* *(than she liked him.)*
His mother liked his sister more than *he.* *(than he liked his sister.)*

Notice that in some sentences your choice of pronoun form will define what you mean.

"IT IS I"

If you knock on a friend's door and are greeted with the question, "Who's there?" you need not answer, "It is *I.*" Like most educated people, you will probably disregard formal grammar and say, "It's *me.*"

But in writing, you will follow the formal tradition which calls for a subject form of the pronoun after any form of the verb *to be.* Observe the form of the pronouns in the following sentences:

It was *he* who stole the jewels.
The victims of the theft were my mother and *I.*

"HIMSELF, HERSELF, THEMSELVES"

Words like *himself, herself,* and *themselves* are compound pronouns with only two proper uses. As intensive pronouns, they repeat and emphasize information already given by another noun or pronoun:

The *President himself* made the presentation.
I myself delivered the message.
This malfunction is in the *motor itself.*

As reflexive pronouns, these words show that the action of the verb (or verbs) returns to the subject:

I cut *myself.*
He hurt only *himself.*
Because of a short circuit, the *machine* destroyed *itself.*

In other constructions, however, these words should not be misused as substitutes for personal pronouns. Do not overemploy the compound pronouns in order to try to avoid making a choice between *I* and *me, he* and *him, she* and *her, we* and *us,* or *they* and *them.*

They gave the prize to Marie and *me* (not *myself*).
The captain and *he* (not *himself*) studied the maps.
The prize was divided between Jim and *her* (not *herself*).

"WHO" AND "WHOM"

You may have been confused by the perfectly truthful statement that the case of *who* or *whom* is determined by its grammatical function in its own dependent clause. The only difficulty with this statement is that it involves you in isolating the clause and analyzing its structure. Faced with these chores, many students despair.

You can dispense with grammatical analysis ordinarily, however, by using a simple test. Merely cover up all of the beginning of the sentence, including the *who* or *whom,* and read what is left, inserting *he* or *him* wherever you can. If *he* sounds right, use *who.* If *him* sounds right, use *whom.*

It was he *(who, whom)* we chose to be captain.
(We chose *him* to be captain; so use *whom.*)

It was he *(who, whom)* we thought would win the prize.
(We thought *he* would win the prize; so use *who.*)

Sometimes you will find that you cannot insert *he* or *him* in the sentence unless you also consider the word immediately before *who* or *whom.*

It was he in *(who, whom)* we had the greatest faith.
(We had the greatest faith *in him;* so use *whom.*)

It was they from *(who, whom)* we received the reward.
(We received the reward *from him;* so use *whom.*)

Use the same procedures to choose between *whoever* and *whomever:*

Give the telegram to *(whoever, whomever)* answers the telephone.
(He answers the telephone; so use *whoever.)*

They will give the prize to *(whoever, whomever)* we elect.
(We elect *him;* so use *whomever.*)

REVIEW 8a

EXERCISE 1

Underline the correct form of the pronoun in each of the following sentences. Then compare your answers with those in the back of the book.

1. Are you going to the concert with Beverly and *(I, me)?*
2. The doctor recommended flu shots be given to the teachers as well as to *(us, we)* students.

3. The inheritance must be divided between my sister and *(I, me).*
4. Both Beth and *(her, she)* are members of the church choir.
5. Father is a far better golfer than *(I, me).*
6. The grievance committee asked Wilbur and *(I, me)* to meet with them after work.
7. Sandwiches and hot coffee have been ordered for *(us, we)* workers.
8. Mother and *(her, she)* are responsible for the success of the party.
9. Not one of *(us, we)* loyal supporters was appointed to the governor's staff.
10. It was *(they, them)* who refused to sign the petition.
11. Have you had as much work experience as *(he, him)?*
12. There can be no secrets between you and *(I, me).*
13. I hired Bruno to dig the trench, for he is stronger than *(I, me).*
14. The delegates, Lisa and *(I, me),* were seated on the convention floor.
15. We had far more delegates than *(they, them).*

EXERCISE 2

Underline the correct form of the pronoun in each of the following sentences. Then compare your answers with those in the back of the book.

1. Just between you and *(I, me),* the chief's new plan won't work.
2. There was no reason for you to be hostile to Jane and *(I, me).*
3. *(Us, We)* staff members were planning the company picnic.
4. The boss claims that *(us, we)* employees are not working hard enough.
5. He fired Jim, Jack, Jane, and *(I, me).*
6. Except for you and *(I, me, myself),* no one wants to support Jim's candidacy.
7. The employees who worked the hardest were Jenny and *(I, me).*
8. The acting award was shared by Burt and *(I, me).*
9. Was it *(he, him)* who started that nasty rumor?
10. The committee was unfair to *(us, we)* disgruntled workers.
11. It must have been *(she, her)* who called during dinner.

12. Except for you and *(I, me, myself),* all the members are making a terrible mistake.
13. Just between you and *(I, me),* I dislike your attitude toward the nuclear freeze.
14. There was no love lost between Joan and *(her, she).*
15. It was *(they, them)* who organized the palace revolt.

EXERCISE 3

Some of the following sentences contain an error in pronoun case and some do not. Underline the number of any incorrectly written sentence. Then compare your answers with those in the back of the book.

1. The friendship between you and me has been an inspiration to others.
2. As Lisa is more intelligent than me, she will be awarded the promotion.
3. The committee will honor you as well as me.
4. Was it she who leaked the secrets to the press?
5. Many people were unimpressed by the performance of Michael and I.
6. No one was more serious about the work than her.
7. Please return the ballots to either Judy or I.
8. To Jim, Joe, and me, your decision was a great disappointment.
9. Your friends are people whom I truly despise.
10. There were no secrets between Carol and me.
11. Were there any letters for my brother and I?
12. Us employees have decided to go on strike.
13. My uncle drove Karen and I to the lake.
14. Please give my sister and me your total support in this matter.
15. It must have been he who was to blame.

EXERCISE 4

Underline the correct form of the pronoun in each of the following sentences. Then compare your answers with those in the back of the book.

1. Offer your support to *(whoever, whomever)* deserves it.
2. They are the friends *(who, whom)* we met during our vacation.
3. To *(who, whom)* should we address these envelopes?
4. The woman *(who, whom)* they appointed was my aunt.
5. He was one man *(who, whom)* I had never liked.
6. I am certain I know *(who, whom)* your choice is for mayor.
7. Greg wrote letters to *(whoever, whomever)* he felt would aid his candidacy.
8. He is the type of person *(who, whom)* is satisfied with his station in life.
9. The jockey *(who, whom)* I thought would win the race came in last.
10. The prize should be awarded to *(whoever, whomever)* writes the finest essay.

8b ....Wrong Verbs or Verb Forms

Some errors in the use of verbs are among the most conspicuous marks of uneducated speech or writing. Thus you are obviously using a substandard dialect of English if you say or write, "When I *seen* what she *done*, I *knowed* she was wrong." Rightly or wrongly, your listeners or readers will immediately assume that you lack education.

The verb *to see* presents typical problems. In standard English, three different forms of this verb are used to form various tenses:

Present tense:	I *see* her every day.
Past tense:	I *saw* her yesterday.
Perfect tenses:	I *have seen* her; *I had seen* her.

The present form, the past form, and the participle used in the perfect forms are called the principal parts of a verb; thus the principal parts of the verb *to see* are *see, saw, seen.*

In the speech and writing of uneducated people, the three most troublesome verbs are *see, do,* and *go.* These are their principal parts:

Present	*Past*	*Past Participle*
see	saw	seen
do	did	done
go	went	gone

And here are the three most common errors:

I *seen* him yesterday. (Instead of *saw*)
He *done* it yesterday. (Instead of *did*)
He had *went* there often. (Instead of *gone*)

There are some other verbs which may occasionally give you trouble. Unlike most verbs, which keep the same stem and merely add *-ed, -d,* or *-t* to form the past tense and past participle *(look, looked, looked; walk, walked, walked),* they are irregular verbs like *see, do,* and *go.* Here are 20 verbs occasionally troublesome in student writing:

Present	*Past*	*Past Participle*
bite	bit	bitten
break	broke	broken
bring	brought	brought
choose	chose	chosen
come	came	come
drink	drank	drunk
eat	ate	eaten
freeze	froze	frozen

Present	*Past*	*Past Participle*
give	gave	given
know	knew	known
ride	rode	ridden
ring	rang	rung
run	ran	run
speak	spoke	spoken
steal	stole	stolen
swim	swam	swum
take	took	taken
tear	tore	torn
throw	threw	thrown
write	wrote	written

Most other verbs, particularly those that form their past tense and past participle regularly, will give you little trouble so long as you remember to add the *-ed* in sentences like these:

He was *supposed* (not *suppose*) to give a speech.
He *used* (not *use*) to visit the hospital.
He was *prejudiced* (not *prejudice*) against other religions.

You should also take some care to avoid archaic or dialectical forms like *drownded* for *drowned* or *busted* for *burst.*

Six verbs are troublesome because you may confuse one of them with another which looks or sounds like it; these verbs are *lie* and *lay, sit* and *set, rise* and *raise.*

To lie is to recline or to stay in a given position; the principal parts of this verb are *lie, lay, lain.*

The boy's clothes *lie* where he dropped them.
The boy's clothes *lay* there yesterday.
They have lain there for more than a week.

This verb can never have an object; you cannot *recline* anything.

To lay something is to place it or put it in position; this verb, consequently, does take an object. Its principal parts are *lay, laid, laid.*

I *lay* my books on the table every day.
I *laid* them there yesterday.
I *had laid* them there the day before yesterday.

To sit is to assume or to hold a sitting position; the principal parts are *sit, sat, sat.*

I *sit* in this chair every day.
I *sat* in this chair yesterday.
I *have sat* here for an hour.

To set something is to fix or place it in position; the principal parts are *set, set, set.*

Every morning I *set* my traps.
Yesterday I *set* my traps.
During the past month I *have set* many traps.

Although this verb usually has an object, it does have a few special uses (the sun *sets;* a hen *sets*) in which it takes no object.

To rise is to get up or move up; the principal parts are *rise, rose, risen.*

I *rise* at seven o'clock every morning.
I *rose* at six o'clock yesterday morning.
By eight o'clock my whole family *had risen.*

To raise something is to lift it or increase it; the principal parts are *raise, raised, raised.*

They *raise* their hands when they want to speak.
The company *raised* my salary last year.
The school *has raised* its standards during the last year.

REVIEW 8b

EXERCISE 1

Underline the correct form of the verb in each of the following sentences. Then compare your answers with those in the back of the book.

1. The river *(raises, rises)* after every rain.
2. After John had *(ate, eaten)* breakfast, he went to work.
3. My toes were nearly *(froze, frozen)* when we came down from the top of the mountain.
4. I had *(swam, swum)* all the way across the bay.
5. All of the citizens *(use, used)* to attend the town meetings.
6. At the end of his term, he had *(chose, chosen)* to retire.
7. She had gone to a cafe, where she had *(drank, drunk)* mineral water.
8. He took a gun from the drawer and *(sat, set)* it on the table.
9. All of the speeches were *(suppose, supposed)* to be brief.
10. All of the church bells in the city have *(rang, rung)* to celebrate the coming of peace.

11. Because all the water pipes were *(broke, broken),* the irrigation system was useless.
12. The tread of the tire had come off and was *(tore, torn)* into small pieces.
13. We had lost the game because Mitch had *(throwed, thrown)* three intercepted passes.
14. Last Saturday she *(come, came)* to the office in the afternoon.
15. Our instructor *(use, used)* to be an army captain.

EXERCISE 2

Underline the correct form of the verb in each of the following sentences. Then compare your answers with those in the back of the book.

1. He is one who has *(bit, bitten)* off more than he can chew.
2. The officer wanted to know who had *(broke, broken)* the street light.
3. Joan reported that she *(saw, seen)* the man who committed the crime.
4. The committee has *(chose, chosen)* its winner.
5. Last night we *(drank, drunk)* too much coffee and couldn't sleep.
6. We were taught to speak when we were *(spoke, spoken)* to.
7. Charlie admitted that he had *(rang, rung)* the wrong alarm.
8. Our car was *(stole, stolen)* shortly after midnight.
9. We have *(knowed, known)* of your existence for many years.
10. The joggers were exhausted, for they had *(ran, run)* for over 10 miles.
11. She admitted that in 1984 she had *(swam, swum)* from the mainland to Dollar Island.
12. The violent storm had *(tore, torn)* the shutters loose from the house.
13. She was late for work because she had *(took, taken)* the wrong bus.
14. Because the heating equipment failed, we were nearly *(froze, frozen)* to death.
15. Once again our stockbroker has *(give, given)* us poor advice.

EXERCISE 3

Underline the correct form of the verb in each of the following sentences. Then compare your answers with those in the back of the book.

1. My grandparents *(use, used)* to own a corner grocery store in Chicago.
2. The Puritans were *(prejudice, prejudiced)* against the Quakers.
3. Weren't you *(suppose, supposed)* to be here at noon?
4. My college roommate has *(written, wrote)* a letter to the editor of the campus paper.
5. Tom has *(swam, swum)* competitively for the last four years.
6. The investors groaned when they learned that their financial bubble had *(burst, busted).*
7. Because the company liked my work, I was *(give, given)* a Christmas bonus.
8. I was unable to repair your car because my hydraulic lift was *(broke, broken).*
9. The hopelessly outclassed boxer was relieved when his manager *(threw, throwed)* in the towel.
10. After the accident we learned that all of the crew had *(drowned, drownded).*
11. When I was young I *(use, used)* to believe in Santa Claus.
12. Who was *(suppose, supposed)* to cook the Thanksgiving turkey?
13. My English teacher was *(prejudice, prejudiced)* against poor spellers.
14. The university will *(raise, rise)* its entrance requirements in the fall.
15. We *(use, used)* to visit Canada every summer of my childhood years.

EXERCISE 4

Underline the correct form of the verb in each of the following sentences. Then compare your answers with those in the back of the book.

1. I want you to *(lay, lie)* the box on the table.
2. The doctor asked me to *(lay, lie)* down on the examining table.
3. Don't just *(lay, lie)* there!

4. We *(laid, lay)* all of the broken parts on the floor of the garage.
5. Grandfather *(laid, lay)* all of the chess pieces on the board.
6. The animal just *(laid, lay)* still and played dead.
7. For three centuries the bones of the saint had *(laid, lain)* under the church floor.
8. The lazy fellow spent all his time *(laying, lying)* in the sun.
9. Two sleeping dogs *(laid, lay)* in front of the fireplace.
10. The old mason slowly picked up the brick and *(laid, lay)* it in place.

REVIEW 8ab

Using Editing Skills

EXERCISE 1

Find and underline the ten errors of pronoun case and verb form in the following paragraphs.

Lisa Aherne, who had always been friendly to my youngest brother Bob and I, called us last week. She invited us to join her in climbing Mount Kibo, the highest peak in this part of Alaska. She said that she was an experienced climber and use to belong to the University Outing Club.

We were joined by Greg White, who Lisa had known in college. Us adventurous souls drove by truck to the base of Kibo, where we began our climb. After three solid hours of traversing rocky switchbacks, we rested for ten minutes. We set down on an elevation marker; then we started out again.

Suddenly, Lisa became sick. She had drank water from her canteen too quickly. Greg, Bob, and myself decided to call off our climb and return home. The return ride found Greg at the wheel, Bob and I beside him in the cab, and Lisa laying ill in the bed of the truck. She was unable to raise her head. When we reached her house, Lisa's feet were nearly froze, but she soon recovered.

EXERCISE 2

Find and underline the eight errors of pronoun case and verb form in the following paragraph. Then compare your answers with those in the back of the book.

As a member of the Junior Chamber of Commerce, Mary Webster was very busy. She was the chairperson of several committees formed to plan future events, and no one ever worked harder than her. She come to be called "Ms. Fixitall" because she made almost all of the plans. At that time I was the president of the local athletic club, so she frequently use to talk with leaders of other civic groups and I about her plans and her occasional need to use our assembly rooms and other facilities. It was me, for instance, to whom she confided her plans for a Christmas party. She had chose me, as well as Pat Green, head of the Optimists, to find a good location for all of us Christmas revelers. She was herself suppose to send out invitations and plan the program. Thus all of we prominent citizens got letters from her and were reminded of her name and good works.

9

How to Use Commas

COMMAS ARE THE MOST COMMON marks of punctuation used inside sentences. They serve to clarify sentence structure and meaning, and they substitute for many of the subtle inflections and pauses of speech.

Although there are naturally some differences about commas and other punctuation among professional writers and editors, there are a number of commonly accepted punctuation conventions. These common rules are summarized in this book.

Commas have two kinds of uses: (1) to separate words, phrases, and clauses that need to be separated, and (2) to set off those parts of a sentence that might interrupt, confuse, or mislead a reader if they were not set off.

9a ....Commas to Separate

COMMAS ARE USED TO SEPARATE (1) independent clauses linked by coordinating conjunctions, (2) words, phrases, or clauses in series, (3) coordinate adjectives, and (4) any sentence elements that might be misunderstood if not separated.

TO SEPARATE INDEPENDENT CLAUSES

Independent clauses may stand alone as simple sentences. Or two independent clauses may be separated by a semicolon and be written as one sentence.

But when two independent clauses are linked by a coordinating conjunction, they are separated by a comma:

> The coaches chose the manager, *but* the team elected the captain.
> Mary prepared the dinner, *and* Greg washed the dishes.
> He will succeed in his new business, *for* he has made his plans carefully.

Remember, however, that a comma precedes a coordinating conjunction only when the conjunction links two independent clauses. No punctuation is used when the conjunction links two words, phrases, or dependent clauses:

> He stole money from the state treasury *and* speculated on the stock market.

In the above sentence the conjunction *and* links two verbs, *stole* and *speculated;* no comma is required.

> You will find him on the tennis court *or* in the swimming pool.

In this sentence the conjunction *or* links two phrases, *on the tennis court* and *in the swimming pool;* no comma is required.

> I know that he will win the election *and* that he will be a good mayor.

In this sentence the conjunction *and* links two dependent clauses, *that he will win the election* and *that he will be a good mayor;* no comma is required.

TO SEPARATE ELEMENTS IN A SERIES

A series is a group of three or more similar words, phrases, or clauses having the same function in a sentence:

> We shall invite *Tom, Dick,* or *Harry.* (nouns)
> He *wrote* the letter, *sealed* it, and *stamped* it. (verbs)
> She is *intelligent, charming, rich,* and *beautiful.* (adjectives)
> John knew *that his crime had been discovered, that the police were searching for him,* and *that he could not escape.* (dependent clauses)
> Horses *neigh,* dogs *bark,* and birds *sing.* (independent clauses)

Each element in a series is separated from the others by a comma: *Tom, Dick,* and *Harry.* (Although some writers and some publications omit the comma before the conjunction—*Tom, Dick* and *Harry*—it is usually retained in college and professional writing.) The punctuation is the same if the conjunction in a series is omitted:

> He hired three men—Tom, Dick, Harry.

But no commas are used if a conjunction is used between every two elements in a series:

> We invited *Tom* and *Dick* and *Harry.*
> He should *go to the corner* and *turn right* and *stop.*
> A restaurant should serve *bread* or *biscuits* or *muffins.*

TO SEPARATE COORDINATE ADJECTIVES

Coordinate adjectives are two or more adjectives that stand in the same relationship to the noun or pronoun they modify. Here are two examples of coordinate adjectives:

> an *intelligent, athletic* woman
> *happy, carefree* people

That these adjectives are coordinate can be shown by writing them with an *and* between them:

> an *intelligent and athletic* woman
> *happy and carefree* people

Compare these with some examples of adjectives that are not coordinate:

> a *fine French* restaurant
> an *expert electrical* engineer

That these adjectives are not coordinate can be shown by writing them with an *and* between them:

> a *fine and French* restaurant
> an *expert and electrical* engineer

They sound even more awkward if their order is reversed:

> a *French fine* restaurant
> an *electrical expert* engineer

Two or more adjectives that are not coordinate should be written without punctuation separating them; coordinate adjectives should be separated by commas.

TO SEPARATE SENTENCE ELEMENTS TO PREVENT MISUNDERSTANDING

Some sentences that might be perfectly clear if heard in conversation require the addition of commas to prevent possible misreading:

Ambiguous: By ten fifteen boy scouts were hiking up the trail.
Clear: By ten, fifteen boy scouts were hiking up the trail.

Ambiguous: When eating little children should not be entertained by television.
Clear: When eating, little children should not be entertained by television.

Awkward: All that she has has been pledged for the loan.
Clear: All that she has, has been pledged for the loan.

REVIEW 9a

EXERCISE 1

Insert the necessary commas in the following sentences. Some sentences require no commas. Then compare your answers with those in the back of the book.

1. Phoenix is the capital of Arizona and has the largest population of any state capital in the United States.
2. Montpelier is the capital of Vermont and has the smallest population of any state capital in the United States.
3. You must write your essays legibly for your teacher has poor eyesight.
4. The bill may not pass during this session but you can be certain it will pass soon.
5. The snow fell for two days and all our classes were cancelled.
6. I enjoyed reading your latest article and am anxious to read your forthcoming book.
7. Benjamin Franklin first met Tom Paine in 1774 and the two men became good friends.
8. Marguerite Young began writing *Miss MacIntosh, My Darling* in 1944 and finally completed the novel in 1962.
9. We are convinced that your comedy will be a success but you must rework the opening scene.

10. The President prepared carefully for his last press conference and greatly impressed those who saw him.
11. Williamsburg, Virginia, is the site of William and Mary College and is one of the most fascinating towns in America.
12. Kampala is Uganda's capital and is the country's social and economic center.
13. Warren Beatty might never have become an actor but a high school teacher encouraged him to seek a theatrical career.
14. Rita and Beverly were really close friends but their brothers were bitter enemies.
15. The budget was rejected by the legislature so the governor had to submit a new one.
16. I arrived at the concert an hour early and went backstage to speak with several of my favorite musicians.
17. We have not seen each other since our high school graduation nor has either of us ever revisited the school.
18. Coppola's latest movie was a financial success but the critics panned it unmercifully.
19. Boy Bob has a legion of fans yet in recent years he has produced nothing new or original.
20. Orwell's novel contains a terrifying look into what the future may hold in store for us.

EXERCISE 2

Insert the necessary commas in the following sentences. Some sentences require no commas. Then compare your answers with those in the back of the book.

1. The new comedy contained old material tired jokes and predictable situations.
2. One could see guests sitting in the den chatting in the rose garden and swimming in the pool.
3. French Spanish and Russian were spoken at the restaurant.

4. The bus driver slammed on the brakes swerved sharply to the left and plowed into the stalled truck.
5. The speaker's loud raspy voice made the audience nervous and hostile.
6. Raging winds whipped the trees knocked over billboards tore down electrical lines and blew the roofs off a few cabins.
7. The day of our graduation was warm sunny and cloudless.
8. Beethoven wrote symphonies quartets concertos and sonatas.
9. We have come to honor artists and architects and composers.
10. My parole officer wanted to know how long I would be gone what cities I would be visiting and how he could contact me quickly.
11. The settlers rose early ate a hearty breakfast saddled their horses and rode toward the Nevada border.
12. A popular college English teacher won last month's Massachusetts lottery.
13. The waiter wore a dirty tattered apron and spoke in harsh impatient tones.
14. Early Chinese music was enriched by foreign influences such as the importation of drums cymbals and harps.
15. We purchased tickets and took our seats in time to hear half of the warm-up act and the entire concert of the featured group.
16. Our popular mayor is a dedicated public servant and an effective administrator.
17. The operator thanked me dialed my number and asked me to deposit seventy-five cents.
18. During our vacation we plan to visit the national parks in Oregon Washington Utah and California.
19. We arrived in Dodge City on a hot humid July afternoon.
20. Football and baseball and basketball are the most popular sports on television.

EXERCISE 3

Insert the necessary commas in the following sentences. Some sentences require no commas. Then compare your answers with those in the back of the book.

1. We asked Jerry to come with us but Martha asked us to excuse him.
2. A baseball glove dirty clothing overdue library books and assorted magazines were piled on top of Jerry's desk.
3. The police must get here soon or we will all be in trouble.
4. It was a rainy windy night and we were late for the concert.
5. Groups of students were discussing the press conference and demanding the governor's resignation.
6. You had better start looking for a summer job or you will have to secure a government loan.
7. Loud noises were coming from the engine from the tail pipe and from the flat tire.
8. After twelve fifteen dangerous armed prisoners escaped.
9. Many of the tourists did not like Venice nor Paris nor London.
10. Rain must come soon or all our crops will die on the ground.
11. Once before the judge had warned the witness to be more specific.
12. The star witness walked into the crowded courtroom and was instructed to take the stand.
13. All major highways and city streets have been closed by the raging blizzard.
14. After painting Agatha cleaned her brushes capped her paints and took a long walk.
15. A large London bus arrived and took us for a tour of the city.

EXERCISE 4

Insert the necessary commas in the following sentences. Some sentences require no commas. Then compare your answers with those in the back of the book.

1. The guest star waved to the crowd shook hands with the host and took his seat on the platform.
2. My broker was ill and unable to advise me to sell my utility stocks.
3. I ordered bacon and eggs and toast with jelly.
4. Perched on a high ledge was a snarling mountain lion.
5. Outside the crowded auditorium was a group of hostile disappointed ticket-holders.
6. We liked all the candidates but one was really excellent.
7. Before waxing John swept and mopped the floor.
8. The arena resembled a violent free-for-all so we ran for safety in the street.
9. After washing and brushing the stray dog looked like a purebred.
10. Soon after she left the party and drove home alone.
11. To Mary Ann seemed angry and irritable.
12. The silver-haired distinguished-looking man was a swindler.
13. Though old Uncle Ben was in perfect physical condition.
14. The college was overcrowded but the high school had few students.
15. Your idealistic dedicated efforts to achieve world peace have not been in vain.

Using Editing Skills

EXERCISE 5

Insert the necessary commas in the following piece of writing. Seven commas are needed. Then compare your answers with those in the back of the book.

Some people like Sandra Warren for her rare charm and beauty but I most admire her quiet sense of humor. She is just 23 years of age and is well-known in America as a humorous writer. She was born in Texas spent twelve years on a farm near Odessa and then moved to a charming quiet neighborhood south of San Francisco. In her senior year at Hilton High School, she received good grades played guard on the basketball team and edited the yearbook. Some people thought she would become an actress or model or singer. But after two years at a local college, she decided to become a professional writer. When she was 20, two of her sketches were published in *Rolling Stone* and a year later her first novel appeared. Sandra now lives in San Francisco and owns her own home. Every time I read her work, I am amazed at how she can find funny things to say about almost any subject.

9b.........Commas to Set Off

SOME WORDS AND GROUPS OF WORDS must be set off from the rest of the sentence of which they are a part. If they are not set off, they may interrupt, confuse, or mislead a reader. If they appear at the beginning or end of a sentence, they can be set off by one comma:

______Sentence______, (words set off).
(Words set off), ______Sentence______.

If they appear in the middle of a sentence, they are set off by two commas:

Sentence begins______, (words set off), ______sentence ends.

Commas are used to set off (1) nonrestrictive modifiers and appositives, (2) sentence modifiers and contrasted sentence elements, (3) introductory elements, and (4) words and phrases that slow the movement of sentences.

TO SET OFF NONRESTRICTIVE MODIFIERS AND APPOSITIVES

A nonrestrictive modifier is a phrase or clause that adds extra information not essential to the central meaning of the sentence in which it appears.

My mother, *who lives in Colorado,* visited me yesterday.

In this sentence, the clause *who lives in Colorado* contains extra information but does not affect the central meaning of the sentence. It does not tell *which* mother or *what* mother; it does not restrict the meaning of the word it modifies. Therefore, it is nonrestrictive and is set off by commas.

A restrictive modifier limits or restricts the meaning of the word it modifies, and it is therefore essential to the central meaning of the sentence.

The couple *who lived next door* have gone away.

In this sentence, the clause *who lived next door* contains essential information and does affect the central meaning of the sentence. It tells which couple went away; it restricts the meaning of the word it modifies. Therefore it is restrictive, and it is not set off.

In each of the following pairs of sentences a phrase or clause is used first as a nonrestrictive modifier and then as a restrictive modifier. Comparison of these sentences will help you to understand the difference between the two kinds of modifiers.

Nonrestrictive: My father, *wearing an old gray sweater,* met me at the airport.

Restrictive: The man *wearing an old gray sweater* is my father. (The modifier tells *which* man.)

Nonrestrictive: John W. Podner, *who owns this building,* is a rich banker.

Restrictive: The person *who owns this building* should make repairs.
(The modifier tells which person.)

Nonrestrictive: The Lincoln Memorial, *which is a famous tourist attraction,* is an impressive shrine.

Restrictive: Any building *which is a famous tourist attraction* must be protected from vandals.
(The modifier tells what building.)

Much the same distinction can be made between two other uses of dependent clauses. If a dependent clause restricts the action of the main clause—if it contains new information about why or when or where or under what conditions the action will take place—it is restrictive. Consider the following sentences:

Nonrestrictive: I shall go to the concert, *although I have very little money.*
(I shall go, no matter what.)

Restrictive: I shall go to the concert *if Jack will lend me $20.*
(Perhaps I shall go, perhaps not.)

Nonrestrictive: I shall not go to the concert, *whether you go or not.*
(I am not going.)

Restrictive: I shall not go to the concert *unless you go.*
(Perhaps I shall go, perhaps not.)

Nonrestrictive: I shall leave the concert at midnight, *when the clock strikes twelve.*
(This is old information; the word *midnight* gave it first.)

Restrictive: I shall leave the concert *when the clock strikes twelve.*
(This is new information in the sentence.)

Appositives are punctuated much like modifiers and most appositives are nonrestrictive:

George Washington, *our first President,* refused a third term.
George Orwell, *a famous writer,* wrote two satirical novels.
The Student Union, *a meeting place for all students,* is in the center of the campus.

But some appositives are obviously restrictive:

The word *moreover* is always a conjunctive adverb.
(Which word?)

My Aunt *Molly* is coming to visit.
(Which aunt?)

The reason for the difference in punctuation between the following two sentences is obvious:

My eldest brother, George, is the most brilliant of my brothers. (I can have only one eldest brother.)

My brother George is the most brilliant of my brothers. (Which brother?)

TO SET OFF SENTENCE MODIFIERS

Some words and phrases modify whole clauses or sentences. These sentence modifiers are ordinarily set off by commas. Conjunctive adverbs, for instance, ordinarily modify the whole clause in which they appear:

Young doctors, *moreover,* must expect low incomes when they are first beginning practice.

It is true, *nevertheless,* that population will ultimately increase more rapidly than the food supply.

My family, *however,* refused to attend my wedding.

Some phrases, similarly, modify whole clauses:

Art students, *on the other hand,* must spend much money on supplies.

My father, *as a matter of fact,* lost thousands of dollars in 1984.

The government agreed, *of course,* to compensate the owners of the condemned land.

One special kind of verbal phrase is always a sentence modifier: this is the absolute construction, one which modifies no special word in the sentence yet cannot stand alone. The following sentences contain absolute constructions:

Other things being equal, a large family costs more to feed and clothe than does a small one.

We shall, *weather permitting,* climb the mountain tomorrow.

He stood in front of the building, *his eyes lifted to the lighted window.*

Absolute constructions are always set off from the rest of the sentence in which they appear.

TO SET OFF CONTRASTED SENTENCE ELEMENTS

Contrasted elements, ordinarily negative phrases inserted for clarification or emphasis, are set off:

Dr. Samuels is a general practitioner, *not a psychiatrist.*

Only college students, *not high school students,* may use this swimming pool.

TO SET OFF INTRODUCTORY WORDS, CLAUSES, AND PHRASES

Mild Interjections

Although expressions of strong emotion are usually written as separate sentences and punctuated with exclamation marks, expressions of mild emotion, as well as filler words and simple affirmations and negations, are set off by commas:

> *Wow,* it's a hot day.
> *No,* I cannot come with you.
> *Yes,* they are going water-skiing.
> *Well,* I think I have finished the job.

Introductory Clauses

A dependent clause used as a modifier and put at the beginning of a sentence is ordinarily set off:

> *When I left the house,* she was crying.
> *Because his wife was ill and needed care,* he stole the money.
> *As Johnson limped slowly off the field,* the crowd applauded.

Introductory Verbal Phrases

Any introductory phrase containing a verbal is set off from the sentence that follows:

> *Realizing his danger,* George roped himself to the rock.
> *After feeding the pigs,* Sara churned the butter.
> *To understand this equation,* you must know calculus.

Introductory prepositional phrases, however, are not ordinarily set off unless they contain many words.

> *In the spring* we moved to Dallas.
>
> *After a very cold winter in the northern part of Nebraska,* we moved to Dallas.

TO SET OFF INTERRUPTING WORDS AND PHRASES

Some kinds of words and phrases are always set off because they interrupt the smooth flow of sentences. These words and phrases are (1) the second and third parts of dates and addresses, (2) names of people addressed, (3) phrases identifying speakers in direct quotation, and (4) echo questions.

Dates and Addresses

If a date or address contains only one item of information, such as the day of the week, the day of the month, or a street address, it is not set off from the rest of the sentence:

I met her on *Wednesday* and married her on *Friday.*
The meeting was held on *September 2* at *Hot Springs.*
My parents live at *2021 Ohio Avenue.*

But any additional parts of dates or addresses are set off by commas:

I met her on Wednesday, *September 23,* and married her on Friday, *September 25.*

The meeting was held on September 2, *1986,* at Hot Springs, *Arkansas.*

My parents live at 2021 Ohio Avenue, *Sherman Oaks, California 91403.* (Use no comma before a ZIP code.)

Names of People Addressed

The name of a person addressed, either by the writer or by a quoted speaker, is set off. So are titles and terms of scorn or endearment used in place of names.

Can you explain, *Sergeant Hageman,* why you deserted your post?

If you don't like the way I drive, *George,* drive the car yourself.

I admit my actions were strange, *Judge,* but I can explain everything.

You are, *my friend,* a true gourmet.

Speakers in Direct Quotation

A phrase identifying a speaker is always set off from the quotation itself.

"Mother," *asked the little girl,* "may I go swimming?"
Her mother replied, "Yes, but stay in the shallow water."
"Thank you very much," *said the little girl.*

Notice, however, that the name of the speaker is not set off if the quotation is indirect:

The little girl asked her mother for permission to go swimming.

The mother granted permission but told her daughter to stay in the shallow water.

The girl said that she was grateful.

Echo Questions

The echo questions that appear frequently in speech, though less frequently in writing, are always set off:

You know, *don't you,* that smoking is harmful to your health.

You don't work here, *do you?*

He was an astronaut, *wasn't he,* during the early days of the space program.

REVIEW 9b

EXERCISE 1

Insert the necessary commas in the following sentences. Some sentences require no commas. Then compare your answers with those in the back of the book.

1. Gladstone's Restaurant a favorite of fish lovers is located on Ocean Avenue.
2. The colonial houses on Ocean Avenue were built in the early nineteenth century.
3. My pet dog seeking affection jumped on the guest's lap.
4. Edna St. Vincent Millay my favorite poet led a fascinating life.
5. My best friend Alexandra Ross invented an automatic back scratcher.
6. Alexandra's youngest sister Amanda is studying to be a dentist.
7. Professor James our favorite lecturer was educated in Canada.
8. The play *Julius Caesar* is studied by most high school students.
9. My friend Oscar a native Texan is a talented inventor.
10. Sylvia Plath's only novel *The Bell Jar* is a favorite among young readers.
11. We plan to have pizza our favorite food more often.
12. America's first secretary of the treasury Alexander Hamilton was a hero at the Battle of Yorktown.
13. The library's most valuable book a first edition of *Leaves of Grass* was stolen last April.
14. Walt Whitman an American poet is the author of *Leaves of Grass.*
15. Services were held on Tuesday for James Watson inventor of the hand grenade.

EXERCISE 2

Insert the necessary commas in the following sentences. Some sentences require no commas. Then compare your answers with those in the back of the book.

1. The car that you just passed is a police car.
2. Women who have had sales experience should consider selling life insurance.

3. My blue Ford which is now 6 years old has been driven over a hundred thousand miles.
4. The singer who is now appearing at Club 611 was once a Broadway star.
5. The singer who was praised by the critics was a great disappointment to us.
6. Our youngest dog who recently had six puppies is an AKC champion.
7. This is the stereo system that I expect to buy.
8. Tenants who are behind in their rent are subject to eviction.
9. Our favorite professor who was born in England has decided to enter private industry.
10. The mountains that can be seen in the distance are in Vermont.
11. London's local buses which are usually double-decked are painted bright red.
12. Employees who work hard will be quickly promoted.
13. My older grandmother who is nearly 75 will visit us in June.
14. Joseph Wambaugh who spent 14 years with the Los Angeles Police Department is a best-selling novelist.
15. Ten-year-old Rover who is as playful as a puppy is really an old dog.
16. Our high school principal who speaks with a Boston accent is a former football coach.
17. Every question that appeared on the examination was both tricky and silly.
18. My employer who is often angry is difficult to work for.
19. The tree that was blown over by the high winds was over 100 years old.
20. Some computer jobs which were once plentiful are now difficult to obtain.

EXERCISE 3

Insert the necessary commas in the following sentences. Some sentences require no commas. Then compare your answers with those in the back of the book.

1. Carson McCuller's first novel is I believe one of the best I have ever read.
2. The director told us that our performance was worthy of an award.
3. He told us however that we must work hard for each performance.

4. The senator stood before the cheering crowd his eyes glazed with tears of happiness.
5. That you will be a success in life is certain.
6. I feel that NBC not CBS offers the most comprehensive news coverage.
7. Generally speaking this is one of the quietest neighborhoods in our city.
8. The repayment of your student loan you should remember is of utmost importance in the years ahead.
9. My appointment is with an ophthalmologist not a dermatologist.
10. However important preparing for this examination seems you must not tax your physical and mental well-being.
11. Mayor Bradley not Mayor Williams will give the welcoming speech.
12. This is I regret to say the last month that we will be offering bonus coupons.
13. Paris, Texas not the Paris in France is Grandfather's birthplace.
14. Grandmother we are sure enjoyed the party we gave in her honor.
15. I am interested in a position with a good salary not a job paying a minimum wage.
16. This summer vacation if anyone is interested in hearing my opinion should be spent hiking in the White Mountains.
17. You should have ended the sentence with a period not an exclamation mark.
18. Your progress report I am sad to say shows little improvement in your work habits.
19. We all agreed that the mayor was altogether too incompetent to seek a second term.
20. We agreed all things considered that the party had been a success.

EXERCISE 4

Insert the necessary commas in the following sentences. Some sentences require no commas. Then compare your answers with those in the back of the book.

1. Realizing that he was hopelessly lost Michael called for help.
2. Not long after the polls closed my opponent conceded.

3. In the spring the swallows returned.
4. Firing his own son was the most difficult task that my boss faced.
5. Because most of her opponents were away on vacation Louise proclaimed herself a probable winner.
6. Hoping to be rescued they kept a fire going all night long.
7. When the sun rose the next morning they were rescued by the Coast Guard.
8. In the locker we found the stolen money.
9. To illustrate my theory I have prepared a few diagrams.
10. Because she was bored by the long plane ride Violet vowed never to make the trip again.
11. In October Melville left for a long voyage to Tahiti.
12. After more than two months at sea Melville sighted land.
13. Dropping their saws and axes the lumberjacks ran for safety.
14. Keeping up with the latest gossip was Roger's greatest joy in life.
15. To become a psychologist was Lauren's greatest hope.
16. Yes the doctor will see you now.
17. When I first saw her I thought that she was the new dean.
18. Well I don't believe my administration has made many mistakes.
19. Thinking that no one was patrolling Joe parked in front of a fire hydrant on Saturday.
20. No you cannot borrow my car.

EXERCISE 5

Insert the necessary commas in the following sentences. Some sentences require no commas. Then compare your answers with those in the back of the book.

1. On September 17 1985 I enrolled at Ohio University Athens Ohio.
2. We flew from Los Angeles to London in the fall of 1985.
3. We all agreed that 1985 had been an exciting year in world politics.
4. Baseball star Jackie Robinson was born in Cairo Georgia in 1919.

5. On February 12 1809 Abe Lincoln was born in a backwoods cabin three miles south of Hodgenville Hardin County Kentucky.
6. Stowe Vermont and Vail Colorado are both popular ski resorts.
7. July 20 1969 was the date that the first person stepped on the moon.
8. Write me at 1515 Galloway Drive Agoura California 91301.
9. The year 1984 was an important one for Olympic athletes.
10. Let me explain your astrological chart Ms. Feathers.
11. Please my friend write me in care of John Doe 8 Arlington Street Boston Massachusetts 02116.
12. Robin are you sure that your mother was born in Miami Florida?
13. "Now ladies and gentlemen let us give a warm welcome to Nebraska's own Johnny Carson."
14. The third of June was the date that we moved from Miami Beach to New York City.
15. "Greetings everyone" shouted the master of ceremonies. "Welcome to Las Vegas Nevada."
16. "No I can't talk with you" said the stubborn old miner.
17. The old miner said that he would talk to no one.
18. Well I have decided to leave Frankfort Germany and move to Omaha Nebraska.
19. The tourist guide remarked that we would be visiting several French churches.
20. "I am going to major in business administration" she said "and minor in psychology."

EXERCISE 6

Insert the necessary commas in the following sentences. Some sentences require no commas. Then compare your answers with those in the back of the book.

1. The motion picture *Easy Rider* was most critics agree Jack Nicholson's first important film.
2. Tell us Alice is Jack Nicholson your favorite film star?

3. Joan Wilson once wrote love lyrics not short stories.
4. You have heard I am sure that smoking is not permitted in this market.
5. Ted Knight who once lived in our city is now a well-known television personality.
6. Women who are anxious to take a yoga class should call the YWCA.
7. Those who enjoy Polynesian food should try the Tiki Hut restaurant in New York City.
8. "Next summer" she stated "we are going to stay home and save our money."
9. Now my dear friends I have the honor of announcing the winner of the door prize.
10. John's latest address is 22 Clinton Place St. Louis Missouri 63108.
11. To meet a famous rock star was Allison's fondest wish.
12. You are aware therefore that you may be fired if your work doesn't improve.
13. Our neighbors never appreciated Buck our pet St. Bernard.
14. Uncle Ben is the kind of man who never takes his family responsibilities seriously.
15. When we heard the news of the accident we called every hospital in the city.

EXERCISE 7

Insert the necessary commas in the following sentences. Some sentences require no commas. Then compare your answers with those in the back of the book.

1. My youngest aunt who was once an astronaut now teaches geophysics and lives in Fort Worth Texas.
2. Sally Ride our first woman in space attended Stanford University not UCLA.
3. Realizing the importance of her mission the young CIA agent booked passage on a freighter leaving at dawn weather permitting.

4. We plan to move to Athens Georgia and attend the university although we will have to pay out-of-state tuition.
5. Because I was very late for my appointment Dr. Jamison my psychoanalyst lectured me sternly.
6. The company cafeteria the meeting place for us employees was I assure you an ideal place to hold the union meeting.
7. All employees who have not given their home phone numbers to the strike organizers should call the union office by Wednesday, June 12.
8. "Judge Wilson" said the bailiff "the jurors are going to be housed at the Hilton Hotel not the Grand Palace."
9. To learn French better I enrolled in the American College of Paris 65 Rue Voltaire Paris France.
10. The conference was held on January 14 1985 in Baltimore Maryland and you must agree was extremely instructive.
11. "You must know Officer Purdy that I was not exceeding the speed limit" said Mr. Baker my driving instructor.
12. Mr. Baker's wife who is a candidate for the city council was I believe once a television actress.
13. To live a hardy life in the Canadian wilderness running a trading post was all that Ed and Eva ever wanted from life.
14. The American explorer who first established an outpost in Little America was named Admiral Richard Byrd a hero to many Americans during the 1930's.
15. Will's latest novel a supernatural thriller was written during his vacation in Bar Harbor Maine.

REVIEW 9ab

Using Editing Skills

EXERCISE 1

Insert the necessary commas in the following piece of writing. There are five places where commas are needed. Then compare your answers with those in the back of the book.

On August 2 1985, I was hired as an assistant chef at Duffy's Tavern a popular restaurant in Omaha, Nebraska. The previous summer I had worked as a fry cook at McDonalds, and so Mr. Duffy felt that I was qualified to work in his busy kitchen. My job, a fairly difficult one as it turned out, was making soups salads, and desserts. When I first arrived at the restaurant, Walt Turner the head chef greeted me warmly and told me to relax. He explained my duties, introduced me to the waiters, and gave me a tour of the kitchen.

EXERCISE 2

Insert the necessary commas in the following piece of writing. There are five places where commas are needed. Then compare your answers with those in the back of the book.

The town of Dodge City, Kansas was once ashamed of its early reputation as a wicked brawling cattle center. In later years, however, it came to realize that its violent history had become the material of legend and romance. The city's business community, consequently reconstructed a whole block of nineteenth-century saloons, a livery stable, a Wells Fargo bank, and several general stores. These buildings were fronted by a wooden boardwalk of the kind that used to protect the early citizens of Dodge City from the mud and manure of the street. But now the saloons serve only soft drinks, the livery stable houses no horses, the bank sells postcards and stamps, and the only guns sold in the stores are harmless plastic toys. Although history has become show business both the eager visitors and the enterprising merchants enjoy the famous town's amusement area. Tourists who love Americana will love Dodge City once the home of the legendary Wyatt Earp.

EXERCISE 3

Insert the necessary commas in the following piece of writing. There are five places where commas are needed. Then compare your answers with those in the back of the book.

Our family's favorite vacation spot is Diamond Lake Maryland, a place we have visited for the last ten summers. We rent a rustic lakeshore cabin and enjoy a complete change of pace. My dad, who works in a high-pressure brokerage firm loves to relax in this quiet peaceful setting. He spends the month of July fishing, reading, and playing solitaire. My mother enjoys being away from the telephone, television, and daily paper. "If World War III breaks out," she quips "why should we be the first to know?" Students who spend the year studying and taking examinations need a relaxing place like our lakeside hideaway to recover from months of pressure. This is why I love our annual summer vacation. On the other hand, my brother hates Diamond Lake but that's another story.

EXERCISE 4

Insert the necessary commas in the following piece of writing. There are five places where commas are needed. Then compare your answers with those in the back of the book.

The play opened in New York City on October 2 1933, and ran for more than five years. Because it was a comedy that found humor in the trials and hardships of the Great Depression audiences laughed, applauded, and cheered as the plot unfolded. Even persons who were near bankruptcy were willing to pay a few dollars to forget their troubles for an evening. When the play closed on February 12, 1938 it had been seen by almost 1 million people. *Variety,* the newspaper of show business reported that it had been almost as successful as *Tobacco Road* and *Life with Father* two other very well known plays of the period.

10

How to Use Other Punctuation

ALTHOUGH COMMAS ARE THE MARKS OF PUNCTUATION most commonly used to separate and set off parts of sentences, other marks are required to show separations and enclosures that have greater force or particular meaning. And three special marks of terminal punctuation are used to indicate not only the end of sentences but also whether the sentences are questions, exclamations, or statements.

END PUNCTUATION

A question mark, an exclamation mark, or a period is used at the end of every complete sentence.

How to Use Question Marks

1. End every direct question with a question mark:

   How can we solve the problem?
   She asked, "What is the problem?"

2. Do not use a question mark after an indirect question:

   I asked how we could solve the problem.
   She asked what the problem was.

3. Do not use a question mark to emphasize irony or sarcasm:

   Juvenile: My brilliant (?) friend got lost in the subway.

How to Use Exclamation Marks

1. End an expression of every strong feeling with an exclamation mark:

   Help! Murder! Police!
   Let me alone!

2. Use exclamation marks sparingly in college writing. To achieve emphasis, professional writers use carefully chosen words rather than extreme punctuation.

How to Use Periods

1. End a complete statement or command with a period:

   I have completed twelve years of school.
   Go to the corner and turn right.

2. Use a period after some abbreviations:

   Ms., Mr., Mrs., Dr., M.D., D.D.S., Ph.D., Jr.

   Notice, however, that most abbreviations composed of initial letters of names of organizations are written without periods:

   FBI, UCLA, MIT, CBS, NBC, IRS, NATO

   Notice, too, that many abbreviations, such as those for nations, states, and cities, are almost never used in the text of formal writing.

3. Use three periods to indicate omission of words in a quotation (four periods to indicate the omission of the end of a statement):

   He said, "I enjoy the color . . . and excitement of these paintings."
   "The play is an exciting melodrama. . . ."

INTERNAL PUNCTUATION

Unlike commas, which have many different uses, other marks of internal punctuation are used to indicate special meanings or particular grammatical relationships in sentences.

How to Use Semicolons

1. Use a semicolon to separate two independent clauses not linked by a coordinating conjunction *(and, but, for, or, nor, yet, so):*

   During the recession, sales of durable goods declined; during the same period, however, sales of food, tobacco, and liquor increased.
   Both of Marion's brothers are dentists; Marion herself has decided to become a doctor.

Remember that conjunctive adverbs, like *consequently, furthermore, however, moreover, nevertheless, then,* and *therefore,* are not coordinating conjunctions and do not establish grammatical relationships between clauses. Therefore two independent clauses linked only by a conjunctive adverb should be separated by a semicolon (or written as two sentences):

He ate irregularly, drank to excess, and kept late hours; however, his health seemed unaffected.

The investigation disclosed widespread corruption; therefore, the mayor and the council were forced to resign.

2. Use a semicolon before a coordinating conjunction only if the sentence is very long and contains a number of other punctuation marks:

Rain and snow fall to the earth, where much runs away on the surface; but roots below ground and the dense nerve system of grasses and the preservative cover of forest floors detain the runoff, so that much sky moisture goes underground to storage, even through rock.

—PAUL HORGAN

3. Do not use a semicolon to separate a phrase or a dependent clause from the rest of the sentence.

4. Use two or more semicolons to separate complicated items in a series:

The company was represented by Joan Davis, Vice-President, Manufacturing Division; Henry Armstrong, General Sales Manager; and Lynn Brogan, Treasurer and Controller.

How to Use Colons

1. Use a colon at the end of a complete sentence to introduce a list, an explanation, or a formal quotation:

To repair this truck, we need the following parts: radiator hoses, a head gasket, and a new radiator.

This amplifier is not worth repairing: the required replacement parts would cost more than a new amplifier.

In opening the press conference, the President read the following statement: "After consultation with the Secretary of State, I have directed. . . ."

How to Use Parentheses

1. Use parentheses to set off words, phrases, and even whole sentences that add to the clearness or completeness of a text without changing its meaning:

Queen Elizabeth (1533–1603) used her personal prestige to rule a nation divided by religious and political differences.

As his fame spread (patients came to him from Europe, Asia, and Africa), Dr. Wentworth was forced to reduce the number of hours he spent in teaching.

Parentheses are ordinarily used only when commas would be inadequate or misleading.

2. Use parentheses to enclose figures or numbers marking items in a series:

The new contract provided for (1) payment of higher piece rates, (2) expansion of locker rooms and rest rooms, and (3) establishment of a seniority system.

3. Do not confuse parentheses with brackets [ ], which are ordinarily used only for editorial comments or explanations inserted into quoted material.

How to Use Dashes

1. Use dashes to set off parenthetical phrases and clauses. They establish a greater separation than commas do, and they make the enclosed material somewhat more prominent than parentheses do:

Three prominent citizens—Edward Wilkins, Joan Marsh, and Roberta Hawkins—were elected to the board.
(This punctuation makes it clear that *three* citizens, not *six*, were elected.)
After three minutes—they seemed an eternity—the doctor returned to the waiting room.

Professional writers employ dashes and parentheses sparingly, using them to set off parenthetical material only when commas would be inadequate or misleading.

2. Use a dash to show a sharp break or turn in thought:

He caught thirteen fish—and a bad cold.
"I can explain—at least, I hope I can."

3. Use a dash before a summarizing phrase or clause that follows a listing:

Cream, butter, cheese, and pork—these are the foods that I cannot eat while I am on my special diet.
He was promptly obedient, absolutely loyal, and a little stupid—a good dog in every way.

4. Use a dash instead of a colon to introduce a list or explanation whenever the greater formality of the colon seems inappropriate:

It made me ill to watch her eat her lunch—a cucumber sandwich, a soft drink, and a large mound of ice cream, chocolate sauce, nuts, and whipped cream.
As a student of cosmetology, Clarence had one great handicap—he hated women.

Do not, however, attempt to substitute the dash for all other marks of punctuation. One of the most common faults of inexperienced or careless writers is excessive use of dashes, a practice which results in disjointed, incoherent expression.

How to Use Quotation Marks

1. Use quotation marks to enclose the exact words of a speaker or writer:

   She said, "I can handle the Morrison account myself."
   According to Francis Bacon, "Reading maketh a full man, conference a ready man, and writing an exact man."

2. Do not use quotation marks in indirect quotation:

   She said that he would handle the Morrison account himself.
   Francis Bacon believed that practice in writing taught precision in thinking.

3. Use quotation marks to set off words or phrases used with special or limited meanings:

   In the oil fields, a "Christmas tree" is a cluster of pipes and valves.
   Cuvier believed that the geological record could be explained only by assuming that the earth had experienced "catastrophes" greater than any recorded in human history.

   But do not use quotation marks to set off words for which you want to apologize (he was a "loser"). Ordinarily, if a word is worth using, it needs no excuse; if the word is inappropriate, quotation marks do not excuse it.

4. Use quotation marks to indicate the titles of newspaper columns, chapters of books, short stories, articles, essays, and short poems. (Italics are used to indicate titles of books or plays and names of magazines and newspapers.)

   Eudora Welty wrote "The Demonstrators," which first appeared in *The New Yorker.*
   Tomorrow we shall discuss the poem "Ode on Melancholy," which appears on p. 521 of our anthology, *A College Reader.*
   His column, "The Conning Tower," appeared in the *New York World.*

5. Use single quotation marks to indicate a quotation within a quotation:

   Today the Associated Press reported, "Speaking before the Air Technology Conference, Henry Robinson said, 'We will put a human being on Mars before 1994.' "

How to Use Italics

1. Use italics (a single underline in typewritten or handwritten manuscript) to indicate titles of books or plays and names of magazines and newspapers.

2. Use italics to refer to letters, numbers, and words:

   On this typewriter the *e's* and the *6's* need to be cleaned.
   The words *principle* and *principal* are frequently confused.

3. Use italics to indicate foreign words and phrases:

   The detective's motto was *chercher la femme* [search for the woman].
   The Joneses were the worst kind of *nouveaux riches* [people who have recently become rich].

4. Use italics to indicate names of ships and spacecraft.

   The U.S. submarine *Skate* collided with the Japanese fishing vessel *Togomoru* during a thick fog off Golden Gate.
   Sally Ride was a member of the *Challenger* crew.

5. Use italics when they are required for special emphasis:

   He *says* he will do something, but he doesn't mean it.
   Take this medicine *before* meals, not after.

This mechanical kind of emphasis, like the use of exclamation marks, should appear very sparingly in ordinary writing. It is more common in textbooks, where italics are used as a teaching aid, than in books written for a general audience.

REVIEW 10

EXERCISE 1

Insert the necessary end punctuation in the following sentences. Then compare your answers with those in the back of the book.

1. Look at that '65 Mustang
2. The police asked whose car that was
3. Work begins when the sun rises
4. My physics professor, a UCLA Ph D, came from Washington, DC, last fall.
5. "Can we tolerate another four years of this administration No!"
6. Mr and Mrs North moved from New York City, NY, last month.
7. Mr Jones and Dr Smith were married on April 1, 1980, in Macon, Georgia
8. Turn around and put your hands up

9. Alfred Allen, Jr is being investigated by the FBI
10. William Stark, MD, reports on science and medicine for NBC

EXERCISE 2

Insert the necessary semicolons in the following sentences. All required commas have been provided. Some sentences do not require semicolons. Then compare your answers with those in the back of the book.

1. We entered the cabin and found the captives tied to an old brass bed.
2. The hurricane struck with savage fury the little town of Topsfield was nearly destroyed.
3. I enjoyed the movie in fact, it was one of my all-time favorites.
4. He has studied Italian for the last eight months and will find it helpful when he visits Rome this summer.
5. Our company has a mill in Lima, Ohio a warehouse in Augusta, Maine and a sales office in London, England.
6. Mark Twain was born in Florida, Missouri then the family moved to the riverside town of Hannibal.
7. The Mississippi is higher than usual as a result, several homes along its banks have been evacuated.
8. A person with a degree in computer sciences has a higher status in society than a librarian.
9. The film was directed by Mike Nichols, the famous American film maker, but the movie critics from coast to coast attacked it.
10. I love coffee and tea however, the caffeine in them keeps me awake at night.
11. My friend has bought a new sports car it was made in Japan.
12. We packed food, beverages, sleeping bags, ground covers, and tents, but we still were not sure that we would be comfortable.
13. Dictionaries do not always agree for instance, they differ on the word *emulate.*
14. The scholars who have won the awards are Lillie Marshall, Cornell Ken Lewis, Yale and Leslie King, Stanford.

15. We arrived at the box office early, found our third-row seats, and waited for the concert to begin.

EXERCISE 3

Insert the necessary colons in the following sentences. All required other punctuation has been provided. Then compare your answers with those in the back of the book.

1. The police officer began with a stern warning "You must evacuate the area immediately!"
2. There is one area of writing you must work on the clear topic sentence.
3. Here are the ingredients you will need for your recipe tomato sauce, pasta, cheese, and meat.
4. Have you read the article, "Watergate An Abuse of Power"?
5. Poetry communicates it is a lyrical expression of personal feelings.
6. These are the comedians I most admire Eddie Murphy, David Letterman, and Richard Pryor.
7. The most important advice I can give a young actor is this be as natural and honest as you possibly can.
8. The following adage should be remembered always "Neatness is not next to godliness."
9. My main educational goal can be summed up in a single phrase preparation for a good-paying job.
10. Your problem is simple to analyze you are a hopeless neurotic.
11. Remember this walk four steps, turn left, and walk toward the cabin.
12. I have made this difficult decision I shall marry Jennifer.
13. I have just finished reading *Bob Hope King of Comedy.*
14. We bought the following picnic supplies paper plates and cups, hot dogs and buns, and wine and beer.
15. Her response was short and sweet "I wouldn't marry you if my life depended on it!"

EXERCISE 4

Insert the necessary parentheses in the following sentences. Then compare your answers with those in the back of the book.

1. This particular issue of that magazine September, 1902 is extremely rare and valuable.
2. The committee decided to 1 adopt the suggested budget, 2 set a date for the next meeting, and 3 adjourn.
3. Our new house it is actually a log cabin is just a few yards from Walden Pond.
4. I never guessed would you have? that the President would decide to resign.
5. Edith Wharton 1862–1937 was one of America's best-loved writers.
6. He loved football college football, actually and seldom missed any home games.
7. The Hundred Years' War 1337–1453 was fought between England and France.
8. We have received some requests there were actually two for you to play the accordian and sing a few songs.
9. England's white cliffs of Dover they are really white! are the subject of many songs and poems.
10. The life of outlaw Billy the Kid 1859–1881 was brief but exciting.
11. He ordered another beer he had already drunk one too many before he drove back toward the ranch.
12. Jennifer was talking about herself she is always her favorite subject when I walked into the room.
13. My elementary school career it is only a faded memory to me was spent in Miami, Florida.
14. Mark Twain Samuel Clemens is the author of *The Innocents Abroad.*
15. When you go to bed, remember 1 to lock the door, 2 to put out the cat, and 3 to turn off the lights.

EXERCISE 5

Insert the necessary dashes in the following sentences. Some sentences do not require dashes. Then compare your answers with those in the back of the book.

1. We have a little problem where do we find our next meal?
2. We had but one option left to leave the building and make a run for it.
3. Patience, understanding, and faith these are the qualities I most admire in you.
4. I think no, I am positive that you must go to the police.
5. My three uncles Ben, Don, and Julian are successful accountants.
6. Albums, cigarette butts, unpaid bills, and magazines were scattered on the living room floor.
7. Poe's "The Raven," Mike's favorite poem, concerns the death of a young woman.
8. This is our most serious problem will we ever find a buyer for all this junk?
9. If you do succeed and try hard! send me a telegram.
10. The meeting between the two rivals who had thrown dishes at each other only two days before was warm and friendly.
11. Two of my very best friends Andrea and Joan will attend the high school reunion.
12. There is but one more stupid mistake you can make marry John in June!
13. Speed, agility, endurance, and balance these are the qualities a gymnast must possess.
14. My friend do you remember Harry Edwards? arrived at the party dressed as a gorilla.
15. My three favorite films *Star Wars, Star Trek,* and *2001* are now showing at a science fiction convention.

EXERCISE 6

Insert the necessary quotation marks in each of the following sentences. Some sentences do not require quotation marks. Then compare your answers with those in the back of the book.

1. You will find Elizabeth Bishop's poems The Armadillo and Five Flights Up in your anthology.
2. Carla said that she had no one to blame but herself.
3. In baseball terminology a frozen rope is a hard-hit line drive.
4. You can be sure that I shall never forget the time we spent together in the state that proclaims itself The Land of Enchantment.
5. We were warned that the fire would head our way if the wind changed.
6. Did you read the article The Law and You in *Newsweek?*
7. As a lover of nature, you will appreciate Thoreau's essay called Brute Neighbors.
8. President Roosevelt warned Americans by stating, The only thing we have to fear is fear itself.
9. You must never call me at this hour again, she shouted.
10. The person at the complaint desk said merely, Well, that's life.
11. Flannery O'Connor's story Parker's Back features a character named Obadiah Elihue Parker.
12. We asked the professor what she meant by the term manifest destiny.
13. We all wondered if the winter weather would ever go away.
14. My country, may she always be right, Stephen Decatur said, but right or wrong, my country.
15. The professor asked, Which poet said, It is better to have loved and lost than never to have loved at all?

EXERCISE 7

Underline for the necessary italics in the following sentences. Then compare your answers with those in the back of the book.

1. There is a fine article on Paul McCartney in the May 10 issue of Rolling Stone.
2. The pilot landed the Yukon Clipper on the rough water of Hudson Bay.
3. In England, neither is pronounced nyther.
4. She enjoys the short stories she reads in The New Yorker.
5. Both the Times and the Herald printed photos of the President boarding Air Force One.
6. The word accommodate is spelled with two c's and two m's.
7. After his illness, Grandfather seemed to lose his joie de vivre.
8. Among my favorite plays are Shakespeare's Hamlet, Othello, and Macbeth.
9. Peter claims to have had amnesia, but I don't believe him.
10. The talk show was interesting, but at times it reminded me of a Playboy interview.
11. I read in TV Guide a fine article on the social implications of several long-running soap operas.
12. On board the Queen Elizabeth II, we met a former astronaut who had flown on the Apollo XI mission.
13. The Latin in pace requiescat translates as "Rest in peace."
14. The lecture was enlightening, but the speaker's use of the word syzygy confused me.
15. My two favorite books are Catcher in the Rye and The Group.

EXERCISE 8

Insert the necessary marks of punctuation in the following sentences. Necessary commas have been provided. Then compare your answers with those in the back of the book.

1. The Reverend John Cox 1901–1985 was the author of a book titled The Paths of Glory.
2. We met at the airport in Atlanta then we drove south to Tallahassee, Florida.
3. Here is my direction for writing an effective resume be well-organized, brief, and neat.
4. Patrick Henry concluded his fiery address by shouting, I know not what course others may take, but give me liberty or give me death.
5. What did my lawyer mean when he said that my argument was a non sequitur
6. Edgar Allan Poe 1809–1849 is the author of some of my favorite short poems in fact, Ulalume is the one I love the best.
7. A pen, several sharpened pencils, a notebook, and an eraser these items can be found on my desk.
8. The violence in this motion picture it is shocking even to today's movie goer is what I liked least about the film version of Shirley Jackson's story, The Lottery.
9. As he was dying, Thomas Murphy is supposed to have said, I leave you knowing that I have done the very best I could however, I wish I had a few more years to complete some of my projects.
10. Each year people from all over the world visit Thomas Murphy's tomb it is said that Murphy's ghost still inhabits the estate.
11. I do not believe in ghosts nevertheless, I find stories about them fascinating.
12. During his coaching days, Jim Daley taught many players who later played college football Pete Davis, Paul Lunt, and Chet Dobson.
13. Last year I read three Toni Morrison novels Tar Baby, Sula, and Song of Solomon.
14. John Paul Jones said, I have not yet begun to fight.

15. Intelligence, personality, and a sense of humor these are the qualities that you most lack.
16. You must proofread your copy more carefully, Jim, said the editor, for you never cross your t's or dot your i's.
17. Ben Bunker, book critic for The River City Outlook, says that Anne Tyler's novel Earthly Possessions is one of his favorites.
18. Earthquakes I never get used to them occur often in Turkey in fact, last year that country recorded three major tremors.
19. I wonder what the senator meant, asked John, when he said, All's well that ends well.
20. In the textbook Words and Meanings, the author asserts that the word companion is of French origin.

REVIEW 9, 10

Using Editing Skills

EXERCISE 1

Insert the necessary marks of punctuation in the following selection. Use no more periods. Then compare your answers with those in the back of the book.

Benjamin Chandler Bentley the first American to scale the jagged treacherous peak of Tibet's Mount Hallal was the only son of a wealthy Boston banker. After a rebellious boyhood he was once expelled from the exclusive Durgin Park School for setting fire to the headmaster's house young Bentley entered Harvard graduating with the class of 1912. His father a stern practical Yankee expected his son to join the family firm Benjamin however had more adventurous plans. He had spent the summer of 1911 in Europe and had been introduced to the fascination of mountain climbing by Francois Dupin a skilled climber and the author of The Higher Life. Banking the world of high finance and Boston social life held no appeal to a youth of 22 one who had recently read of Mount Hallal and longed to climb its precipitous face.

Benjamin avoided his father for several days then Mr. Bentley summoned the recent Harvard graduate to his office and offered him the post of junior partner. No Father Benjamin said standing before the elder Bentley's great oak desk I shall never be satisfied until I conquer Hallal.

On August 12 1916 after more than three years of studying the route of ascent conditioning himself to the hardships of such a climb and assembling a team of hardy experienced climbers Bentley planted a tiny American flag on Hallal's summit. Courage endurance and pride in his own destiny these are the qualities that shaped the accomplishment of Benjamin Chandler Bentley.

EXERCISE 2

Insert the necessary marks of punctuation in the following selection. Use no more periods. Then compare your answers with those in the back of the book.

It has been said that the person who achieves fame in a field for which he or she has not been trained is one of history's chosen few. Lewis Carroll few people now know his real name was indeed such a person. Charles Lutwidge Dodgson 1832–1898 a lecturer in mathematics at Oxford and the author of several treatises on higher mathematics and symbolic logic is best remembered today as a writer of children's books not as a scholar and scientist. Dodgson was a shy retiring man in the presence of adults he was his happiest when he was with children for he knew loved and understood their world of imagination. Assuming the nom de plume Lewis Carroll he wrote Alice in Wonderland in 1865. Alice's adventures they were vastly popular with adults as well as children were an immediate success and Dodgson found himself a national celebrity at the age of 33. Writing in the Literary Observer on December 16 1865 one enthusiastic reviewer concluded his remarks with the following statement Charm whimsy subtle satire and richness of imagination those are the reasons that the book will be read and loved for years to come.

Six years after the success of his first book Dodgson wrote another story called Alice Through the Looking Glass in which his heroine has a series of adventures on a giant chessboard. Dodgson also wrote brilliant humorous verse his best-known work of this kind is a short poem called Jabberwocky.

On the event of his death in 1898 one admirer wrote the following lines It is true that Dodgson is dead. But Alice will live on as long as there are the young and the young at heart.

11

How to Write Notes, Examinations, and Papers

IN COLLEGE AND IN THE CAREER for which you are preparing yourself, you will find that you spend much of your time writing. You will begin by producing essays, quizzes, and short laboratory reports. You will go on to write term papers, examinations, and extended technical and business reports. All this work will be preparation for serious professional responsibilities in later life: the writing of legal briefs and arguments, medical case histories and articles, scientific and engineering reports, or business memoranda and correspondence.

You probably will not become a novelist or poet. Few college students do. Unlike many professional writers, you will not write primarily to give people pleasure, to make them laugh or cry, to inspire or amuse them. But you will write to give other people facts and ideas, to persuade them to buy or sell, to inform or persuade them. This is the kind of writing you will do in college; this is the writing you will do after your graduation.

Most of the writing you do in your courses will be in rather formal English. Only in writing to friends, in making notes for your own use, or in preparing brief reports for student groups will you use a more informal presentation. After college, much of your writing will also be formal.

NOTES

Many college classes are conducted as lectures, in which the college instructor explains, interprets, and supplements the material contained in textbooks and in suggested reference works. Class meetings are more infrequent than those in high school, and there are fewer recitations, fewer attempts to assist you in organizing and retaining the most important material of the course. Quizzes and examinations are given less frequently, but when they are given, they are usually longer and more difficult.

In order to learn and master the large amount of information and the large number of new ideas presented in college courses, you must learn to take useful notes on what you read and hear. The very act of taking them will help you to learn, and reviewing them will help you to remember.

A good textbook sometimes provides you with aids very similar to notes. The organization of the book is made clear by chapter headings, and the organization of the chapters is indicated by subheadings, which are usually displayed in boldfaced type. Important generalizations and rules may be printed in italics or set off in some other distinctive way. Many textbooks provide a summary at the end of each chapter, bringing together in a paragraph or two the most important ideas that have been discussed. All of these devices are useful to you when you come to review what you have read.

If you own a book which contains few or none of these aids, you can provide them for yourself. After you have read a chapter or section, you can underline the statements or generalizations which seem to be the most important. Or you can write brief statements on the top, bottom, or sides of the pages. You may, as some students do, type a short summary and attach it at the end of the chapter. Remember that you want to underline and emphasize only the most important material; you defeat your purpose if you underline almost everything.

You will not, of course, write in library books. Then, instead, you will take notes on what you have read. But your procedure will be similar in that you will try to find the most important ideas, the main heads, and display them prominently. Under these heads you will write the most important subordinate ideas and what seem to be the most important facts and pieces of supporting evidence. In this way, if you have read carefully, you will have written enough to aid you in recalling most of what was important.

You will do much the same thing when you take notes on lectures. You will find that good lecturers usually indicate clearly what they are going to cover and that they usually place heavy stress on what they believe to be most important. Sometimes they tell you that it is important and why it is important. At other times they indicate its importance by repeating the same words, or by restating ideas in different words. Sometimes they indicate the importance of statements by changes of pace or by a lowering or raising of voice.

Taking good lecture notes is a skill you must work to acquire. Like many students, you will find that your first notes may be too bulky, too disorganized. Sometimes you will find that you have failed to grasp the organization of a lecture.

Most students find that their notes are most useful when they are made in rough outline form. Then they are short, and the most important ideas are prominently displayed. But the form of your notes is comparatively unimportant; choose the form that you like best and that you find most useful. Notes are like diaries: you write them for your own use, and you can suit yourself.

QUIZZES AND EXAMINATIONS

Quizzes and examinations are of two kinds: *objective* examinations and *essay* examinations. Objective examinations are commonly used to test your knowledge of facts and of principles. In objective examinations you are asked to demonstrate this knowledge by making a series of decisions. Thus you may be asked in each question to decide whether a statement is true or false. Or you may be given four or five statements and asked to choose the one which is false or the one which is true. Or the question may be set in any other of a large number of different forms. Always, however, it asks you to make a decision or a series of decisions concerning material which is given to you.

Like objective examinations, essay examinations test your knowledge of facts and principles. But essay examinations ask that *you* supply the information and that you organize and express it in a particular way. You may be asked merely to list facts, dates, or formulas, or you may be asked to state a principle or rule and show its operation under particular circumstances.

The most common fault of students who have difficulty with essay examinations is that they fail to read the instructions carefully. Consequently, some of them omit whole questions; others, offered a choice among several questions, attempt to answer all. The same faults of reading appear in the answers to individual questions: students who have been asked to list facts write extended essays; students who have been asked to define take definitions for granted; students who have been asked to discuss a topic submit a sketchy outline.

When you begin an essay examination, consequently, your first job is not to begin writing but to begin reading carefully. Make careful note of how many questions you are asked to answer, and decide how much time you will give to each. Sometimes the examination suggests how much time should be given to each question; sometimes it states how much weight will be given to a question by the grader. This information is for your assistance; use it in planning your time.

Before you begin to answer a question, read it carefully. Too many students waste time answering questions that never were asked. Thus a student who has been asked merely to list the first ten amendments to the Constitution of the United States will write an extended essay on freedom of assembly; a student who has been asked to describe the workings of the internal combustion engine will write a brief history of the Ford Motor Company. Sometimes, of course, the student is trying ineffectually to hide ignorance of the proper answer, but more often he or she is merely demonstrating a failure to read and understand the question.

Note carefully the form of answer requested. If you are asked "to list," list. If asked "to define" or "to discuss," define or discuss. Sometimes you are given an hour to write a full answer; sometimes you are allowed only 15 or 20 minutes and asked "to discuss briefly." Nothing is gained if you ignore or fail to read these directions.

The language of an examination answer should be simple, straightforward standard English. It should present your information clearly without being either flowery or undignified. If you want to say that William Shakespeare, who was born in 1564, died in 1616, say just that. Don't write that "William Shakespeare, the immortal bard, first saw the light of day in the year of Our Lord 1564 and passed to his eternal rest in 1616." This kind of silly, pretentious writing will merely annoy your reader. On the other hand, don't write that "Old Will popped into the world in 1564, wrote a lot of plays, and bought the ranch in

1616." This kind of language may be all right in playful conversation among friends, but it has no place in an examination.

A good essay answer is a good little composition. It is unified because it sticks strictly to the question. It is coherent because it has the same logical organization that you expect to find in a well-written paper. It is effective because it presents ideas clearly and illustrates them with accurate, well-chosen data. Training in writing good compositions, therefore, is training in writing good examination answers.

As in all your writing, in answering an examination question you must have something to say. No amount of skill in writing can cover complete ignorance. Training in composition cannot substitute for the study of chemistry or anthropology. But it can enable you to make the most effective use of what you know, to state it clearly and emphatically in language appropriate to the subject and to the situation.

PAPERS

In college and in your business or professional life after graduation you will write a number of papers and reports. They will be very different from one another in length and in the forms they assume. Thus a home economics or engineering report is unlike a history research paper or a technical article. Each has its own conventions of organization and presentation.

All of these papers and reports are alike, however, in demanding a clear, logical presentation of facts and ideas. All of them, except for differences in technical terminology, use the same standard English. All of them, with only minor variations, observe the same conventions of sentence and paragraph construction, usage, punctuation, capitalization, and spelling. Consequently a student who can write any one of them well can easily turn to the writing of any of the others.

The best training for the writing of longer college and professional papers begins with the writing and revising of many shorter papers. In writing a short paper you face most of the problems you must solve in the preparation of a longer one. And, at the beginning, you find that you learn the conventions of college writing most quickly and most easily if you begin with short essays on limited and manageable subjects.

These short essays are the themes which you write in a college English class. They are practice exercises for the college student, just as scales are practice exercises for the beginning musician. The skill you develop in writing themes is one you will use in writing examinations and papers, in preparing reports and speeches, and in pursuing a business or professional career.

12

How to Plan and Write Essays

"I CAN TELL A FRAGMENT from a run-together sentence, spot an incorrectly used verb, spell *rhythm* and *occurred,* and recognize an effective paragraph. But I have trouble writing an interesting, well-developed essay."

This is the lament of far too many college students who find that years of instruction in sentence structure and usage have not prepared them for the writing of essays, papers, and examinations required in college courses. Although such study is valuable in helping you to edit and to recognize and revise faults in your manuscripts, it is not designed to help you to plan and write papers.

Learning to write short essays in a composition class will help you both in your later college courses and afterward. Short essays can be challenging because writing them results in a measurable growth of skill and confidence. So accept the challenge and train yourself to plan and write interesting, concise, and coherent essays. The following suggestions are designed to help you realize your goal.

THE PREWRITING STAGE

You are interesting, and your ideas can be interesting. Your experiences, your feelings, and many of your ideas are unique.

In selecting a topic to write about, you should usually be able to relate it to yourself—to how you feel, to why you feel as you do, or to experiences you have had. Of course, the personal viewpoint won't apply to the writing of a strictly technical explanation of molecular orientation in permanent magnets or the function of the internal combustion engine.

Although you may be assigned one topic or given a free choice of subject, frequently you will be given a list of topics from which to choose. You may, for instance, be asked to choose one of the "Suggestions for Writing and Discussion" given at the end of an essay in the first half of this book. Here are questions you should ask yourself as you make your choice:

1. "How much do I know about the topic? Will I be able to write about it with some knowledge and competence?" Running out of facts and ideas in the middle of a short theme is as embarrassing, though not so dangerous, as running out of gas in the middle of a freeway or parkway.

   Be certain that you can stick to the topic if you choose it. If, for instance, you are asked to describe a summer job, don't write an essay on why you dislike playing golf or why you dislike family picnics.

2. "How interested am I in this topic?" Choose, if you can, a subject in which you have a real interest or for which you have real enthusiasm. The resulting essay will certainly be better than a halfhearted treatment of a subject that bores you. It is possible, of course, that none of the assigned topics will interest you. Then, certainly, you will have to try to overcome or disguise your lack of interest, if only while you are writing.

Limiting the Topic

An essay is "a brief exercise or composition" and the key word in this definition is *brief.* Frequently you may be asked to plan and write an essay of fewer than 400 words in a 45- or 50-minute class. Such an essay may be only a fraction of the length of the shortest articles appearing in national magazines.

Therefore you will have to limit your subject. Instead of writing about "college experience," you will have to describe something like your first meeting with your roommate, your first college class, or your first final examination. Instead of writing about "freedom," you will have to limit yourself to a discussion of a particular kind of freedom: perhaps the freedom to bear arms (and even this subject is very big).

You cannot, obviously, write anything meaningful about "my favorite sport" in 400 words. Perhaps skiing is your favorite, the one you know best. As you think about it, you should decide to write a short composition on only one aspect of a big subject; such a paper might have a title like one of these:

"Safety Precautions for Cross-Country Skiing"
"The Longest Ski Run in America"
"My Only Skiing Lesson"
"How I Broke My Leg the First Time"

Collecting Information

After you have chosen and limited your subject, you will want to collect the information and ideas that may be used in your paper. But where do you go to collect information and ideas? What sources are available to you? Here are four of them. (1) Your most immediate source is your own *personal experience.* As you recall the events of your life, the experience you have had, and your reactions and impressions, you have the basis for the writing of many essays. This source of material is so precious and valuable for poets and novelists that many of them keep diaries or journals to record events, feelings, and emotions that may later be incorporated into literature. Many college students, for that matter, find that keeping a daily journal, written rapidly and even carelessly, helps to record not only personally important memories but also feelings and experiences that can be used in other forms of writing. (2) A second method of collecting information and ideas is the use of *interviews* in which you seek answers by asking questions of knowledgeable people. Interviewing is the formalization of what all of us do when we ask for directions in a strange town, for other peoples' opinions of restaurants and motion pictures, or for instructions on how to tune an engine or prepare a gourmet dinner. (3) Yet another method is careful *observation,* a process in which you become a camera and tape recorder, capturing the essence of a place or an activity—its sounds, sights, smells, and "feel." This is the technique that many journalists use in preparing feature stories and is sometimes called "saturation reporting." You can practice this method by sitting quietly at a busy corner on a college campus, at a table in a crowded cafeteria, or at a vantage point near the reference desk in a library and describing every event, transaction, or activity that your flying pencil can record. (4) Finally, you can use the information and opinions available in *newspapers, magazines,* and *books,* all of which you will find in the college library. These are rich sources for any writer doing research. Be careful, however, to collect only facts and ideas, not the exact words of other writers. Also, be prepared to give credit to the source of any information or idea you have taken from printed material, and be sure to use quotation marks whenever you use another author's exact words.

Getting Started

After you have collected some information from memory, interviews, observation, or library research, you can begin to search for relationships and significance in the material you have collected. As you do that you may come to recognize the truth stated and restated by many writers:

"I never really know what I want to say until I have said it." Many writers, consequently, use one or more of the following methods for exploring, arranging, and testing what they know about a subject.

One common method, often said to have been originated by advertising agencies, is called *brainstorming.* In some business and educational organizations, it may involve small groups of people who meet and discuss anything suggested as an answer to a question or a solution to a problem. Some of the suggestions may be ridiculous or trivial, but others may produce important new approaches to the subject or solutions to problems.

You may operate by yourself much like such a group by sitting in front of a writing pad or typewriter and listing—quite without regard for form or correctness—anything that comes to mind about the subject under consideration. You have already done some information gathering, but now you are using free association and playing with what is known. If you are hoping to write a short essay, 10 or 15 minutes of brainstorming will give you an unorganized list that may suggest a number of ways of organizing your paper. Let us say, for example, that you plan to write a paper on cigarette smoking. Your list, which may run for several pages, may begin like this:

dirty habit
scattered ashes
smelly ashtrays
wonderful after a meal
good way to relax
expensive habit—price constantly rising
damages clothes, rugs, seat covers
social activity—exchanging lights
something to do with hands
way to delay unpleasant work
looks sophisticated
cancer, heart disease, yellow teeth, bad breath and so on.

Such a list clearly makes no connections, but reading it immediately suggests some. This brainstormer knows some of the pleasures of smoking; on the other hand, the list records many of the dangers of smoking and the final paper may deal with one or both.

Another way of manipulating information—very similar to brainstorming—is called *free writing.* To do this, sit down, clear your desk, take out some paper, and begin to write. This kind of writing is "free" because it is done without planning or organization. It is also free because it is done rapidly, without concern for sentence structure, consistency, or word choice. Consequently, it may be disjointed, repetitious and ungrammatical. But it also may produce ideas, associations and phrasings that you can later use in a planned paper.

Free writing differs from brainstorming because it produces a continuous text, not merely a list. Because it is the product of free association, it will tend better to reveal connections—sometimes emotional, sometimes logical—among the materials it records. About 15 minutes of free writing may produce many suggestions for the organization and even the thesis of the paper you plan to write. Again, if you are planning to write about smoking, the first few minutes of your free writing may produce something like this:

> I have always enjoyed smoking and I remember fondly long conversations over coffee and cigarettes, times spent in animated conversation when the air was blue with smoke, the fun of drying off after a swim and lighting a cigarette. And, of course, as a one-time heavy smoker, I remember the last cigarette before I put out the light at night and the first one before breakfast. But I remember too waking up with a mouth that tasted bitter and felt furry—with a cough that sounded like a barking dog. . . .

Notice how this sample differs from the brainstorming list. Many of the same actions are remembered but here they are grouped by emotional associations and so suggest one kind of organization. This is, of course, only one kind of grouping: later in a free-writing exercise, you may go naturally from cause to effect, from minor burns to major fires, from early approval of smoking to later condemnation of it. You will produce a text which suggests many kinds of organization for a paper.

Both brainstorming and free writing depend upon rapid free association of facts and ideas. Other methods for recalling and imposing some basic organization and information are called *clustering,* or *mapping.* These methods are much the same as the haphazard recall of brainstorming—but they suggest that you scatter your notes on a piece of paper, frequently putting related ideas near one another, separated clearly from antithetical or quite different materials. Then, if you are inclined to think graphically, you can circle your most important ideas and show their connection or opposition with solid lines, dotted lines or even lines of different colors. There is no single prescribed method for clustering or mapping, just as there is no formula for creating nonrepresentational art. But for people who like to make meaningful use of some schemes and diagrams, clustering may be helpful and profitable.

Selecting a Thesis

After you have chosen, limited, and investigated your subject, you must determine clearly what you want to say about it. You must, in other words, define your purpose in writing. You must select your *thesis,* the controlling idea that will guide you in the choice and organization of details.

The controlling idea can ordinarily be expressed in a single sentence. This sentence may never appear in your essay, or it may become a part of your beginning or ending. But once it has been formulated, it will guide you in planning and writing your paper. It will express the single most important idea of your paper; it will be the point toward which you are driving.

If, for instance, you are going to write an essay about your reasons for quitting smoking, you may choose one of these sentences as a statement of your thesis: (1) *I gave up smoking to save money and to impress my parents and friends with my willpower.* (2) *I quit smoking when I realized it was harmful to my self-esteem, my health, and my social life.* If you choose the first thesis, your essay will necessarily concentrate on your desire to save money and impress others. If you choose the second, your essay will concentrate on the problems that smoking caused you and how your decision not to smoke affected your life. Perhaps a few of the same details may appear in either paper, but their importance, their organization, and their effect will be different.

Making an Outline

After you have chosen a subject, limited it, explored it, and decided on a thesis, you are ready to plan your paper. Just as an experienced contractor needs a blueprint before beginning to build a house, so you need a plan before beginning to write. The plan is ordinarily some kind of outline.

In the preparation of long papers or speeches, you may choose—or you may be required—to prepare a detailed, formal outline. In planning a short paper, however, you need to prepare only a brief topic outline. Both kinds of outlines have one common purpose: to help you make a logical division of your material and arrange it in the most effective order. Thus an outline for an essay on your reasons for stopping smoking could read like this:

Why I Quit Smoking

Thesis: I quit smoking because I realized it was harmful to my self-esteem, to my health, and to my social life.

I. Problems caused by smoking
   A. Loss of self-esteem caused by addiction
   B. Health hazards: immediate and future
   C. Effects on social life
      1. Personal unattractiveness: yellow teeth, bad breath
      2. Social annoyances: smoke, ashes, burns
II. Advantages of not smoking
   A. Pride produced by achievement
   B. Improvement of health
      1. Immediate gain in health and stamina
      2. Possible avoidance of serious diseases
   C. Improvement of social life
      1. Personal cosmetic improvement
         a. Whiter teeth
         b. Better breath
      2. Removal of annoyances to others

In a long paper, every heading of an outline may be developed in one or more paragraphs; in a short paper, a main head may be treated in a single paragraph.

THE WRITING AND EDITING STAGE

Whenever possible, you should prepare at least two drafts of a manuscript. This procedure ordinarily results in a clearer, more effective, and more graceful essay.

Under some circumstances, of course, you will find that you can prepare only one draft. When you are writing answers to essay examinations, for instance, or writing in-class papers in a limited time, your first draft is the one you must submit. Such situations place a premium on your ability to plan and write acceptable first drafts that are logical, clear, and correct. In doing this, you will find hasty outlining indispensable.

Writing the First Draft

When time permits, you should write a first draft, a manuscript that you will later revise carefully. Even in this first attempt, however, you may prefer to work slowly, paying careful attention to the style and mechanics of your sentences, carefully building your paragraphs. Or, like many writers, you may prefer to write rapidly, not pausing to review sentence construction or spelling, but attempting to cover the subject completely. If you work in this way, don't worry about writing an effective introduction or establishing smooth transitions; leave these for the revision. Merely follow your outline, writing in as much detail as possible, taking every advantage of the momentum—even the enthusiasm—of rapid writing.

Writing the Final Draft

After you have completed your first draft, attempt to put yourself in the position of a reader or critic. Read your manuscript first to be sure that it is complete and logical. Did you follow your outline, and does its development in your paper seem clear? Did you include all the information and details that the reader will need to understand your essay? Is your thesis clearly stated or implied?

Now read the paper again to see if it contains too much. Eliminate unnecessary repetitions and irrelevant details. Frequently you may find that your paper will be improved if you throw away or condense your first few paragraphs. Frequently you may find that your paper runs on too long, and that you can write a briefer, stronger conclusion. The beginnings and endings of papers need special attention and may be very much improved by revision.

Finally, check your work for careless or habitual errors of usage, punctuation, and sentence structure. Use your dictionary to check possible mispellings. Watch particularly for errors that have been marked on other papers. Anyone can err, but the best students profit from past errors.

Your first draft may now be a mess of crossed out words, circles, and arrows. If so, it probably has been improved. Now read it again—preferably aloud—so that your ear may detect awkwardnesses and mistakes that your eye missed.

Now you are ready to write or type a final draft. Following your instructor's requirements for acceptable manuscripts, write legibly or type carefully. After you have finished, proofread your paper for omissions or copying errors. If you must make a minor correction, make it as neatly as possible. If you must make a major revision or must correct many errors, recopy the page or the whole essay.

All this work can be difficult and time-consuming. But it is worth doing; remember that hard writing makes good reading.

13

How to Write Good Paragraphs

A PARAGRAPH, LIKE A SENTENCE, is a unit of thought. A complete paragraph may be only one sentence that has been indented; in much the same way a sentence may be only one word: *Stop!* or *Go!* Ordinarily, however, a paragraph is a group of related sentences, just as a sentence is ordinarily a group of related words.

A paragraph may describe a particular scene or person, tell of a particular action or sequence of actions, make a comparison or contrast, explain a phenomenon or an idea, establish a relationship between two or more phenomena or ideas, or develop an argument. Its form and organization, in short, will be determined by the writer's purpose. But all good paragraphs have certain common characteristics.

UNITY

The unity of some narrative paragraphs may be merely the unity of continuous or simultaneous action. What has happened is told in scenes, and each paragraph ends as the action shifts or as the writer's focus of attention is changed. To try to tell a long story in one paragraph would be like trying to film a motion picture with a continuously running camera—no cuts, no fades, no laps, no close-ups, and no editing.

Much of what applies to the narrative paragraph is true of the paragraph of description, which may be compared to a single snapshot. Thus you may take a picture of New York from the air or from the harbor or from the top of the World Trade Center; you may shoot scenes from the bottom of Wall Street, from a corner of Times Square, or from the platform of a subway station. From the air you may photograph the whole city, from the subway platform only two faces. Each picture is a paragraph, a particular view or a particular part of your subject.

The unity of a paragraph of explanation or argument is that of the single controlling idea. Thus you may devote a paragraph to explaining that the average age of students in your class is 18 years and 10 months. Is this "average" a mean or a median? Are all the students about the same age, or does this generalization hide the fact that the class contains a 12-year-old genius and a 65-year-old retired business executive? Is the average age of the men the same as that of the women? These are all questions that can be answered in the one paragraph, for all are developments or explanations of the single controlling idea.

Clearly your paragraph loses its unity if you describe the intelligence of the women, the strength of the men, or the dullness of classwork. These are unrelated ideas, and they are better left out or reserved for other paragraphs.

Most skillful writers produce paragraphs that contain a statement of the controlling idea. This *topic sentence* may appear at the beginning, at the end, or even in the middle of the paragraph. Occasionally, of course, it may not appear at all, perhaps because it is so clearly implied that it can be inferred easily by any reader.

CONSISTENCY

Even if a paragraph has unity, sticks to its subject, and rejects all irrelevancy, it may fail for lack of consistent development. It will fail obviously if it is self-contradictory. Do not, for instance, say that Jane is the most successful salesperson and then two sentences later say that someone else is even more successful. Do not say that a machine is economical and efficient, only to end your paragraph by saying that the machine is too expensive to be practical.

Be consistent in other ways. If you are analyzing a process, choose a person and a point of view. If, more specifically, you are explaining how to purchase a home computer, you may use any of these possible beginnings:

> To purchase a home computer, I would . . .
> To purchase a home computer, you should . . .
> To purchase a home computer, one should . . .
> To purchase a home computer, we should . . .

But once you have made your beginning, stick to the conditions you have set for yourself. Otherwise, you may produce something as ridiculous as this:

> To purchase a home computer, *one* should first determine how much money *you* want to spend. *I* may decide to spend about $1500, and then *we* know that an expensive word processor cannot be included in the equipment. *One* must settle for what *they* can afford if *we* are to stay within *your* budget.

ORDER

Arrange the facts and ideas in a paragraph. Don't expect them to come tumbling out of your mind and fall into perfect order, for such a result is no more likely than having a load of bricks fall out of a dump truck and arrange themselves into a wall. Walls must be built—and so must paragraphs.

Even telling a story requires some planning. If you don't know what you want to say, you can become hopelessly confusing.

> When I first got to the campus (I forgot to say that my father brought me), I met him. That is, I met him after I had a cup of coffee with Mary. I needed that coffee, too, because I hadn't had any breakfast. You see, when I got up that morning. . . .

But most short narratives are comparatively easy to organize if you select essential details, begin at the beginning, and move steadily to the end.

If you are describing a city, a campus, a building, or a room, make your description move in a way that the reader can understand and follow. Relate all the parts with a single comparison (the streets of Washington, D.C., have frequently been compared to the spokes of a wheel) or to a single prominent detail (the city hall, a college bell tower, an entrance hall, or a large fireplace). Remember that your description should be like a good design or painting: it should have a center of balance and interest, and it should not leave the reader's attention restless and wandering.

If you are attempting to explain or persuade, there are many ways in which you can order your material. If you plan merely to list details or examples, list them in some clear order. You may go from the oldest to the newest, from the most familiar to the least familiar, from the least important to the most important. Certainly you want to avoid unintentional anticlimax. Even in a single sentence it is ridiculous to write, "Wilkins was a wicked man; he neglected his children, beat his wife, murdered his mother, and sometimes forgot to feed the cats."

There are many ways in which you can develop your ideas. You can use an extended analogy, a series of comparisons, a striking example, a convincing number of facts and details, a reasoned argument, or an appeal to recognized authorities. The way you choose will depend upon your material and your attitude. Your success will depend upon your willingness to plan and construct a paragraph that has order and purpose.

COHERENCE

If your paragraph has unity, consistency, and order, it will necessarily have a kind of innate coherence. It may be compared to a stone wall that has been planned so carefully and constructed so skillfully that it needs no mortar. If, on the other hand, your paragraph lacks unity, consistency, and order, you will not be able to hold it together, just as no mason can use mortar to make a sound wall if he lacks a plan, a foundation, and good bricks.

You can, however, strengthen a basically good paragraph by showing how it was planned and constructed. Sometimes you can number divisions or examples of your thought explicitly as *first, second,* and *third.* You can repeat key words or phrases and maintain clear continuity by skillful management of pronouns. You can signal the direction of your thought by the use of transitional words *(however, moreover, nevertheless)* and phrases *(on the other hand, in fact, of course).* Although excessive use of such transitional words and phrases can be awkward and stilted, practice will teach you to link your sentences closely and gracefully.

Answers for Part One

Exercises for "Dad" (pp. 4–6)

Words

1. *uncanny:* mysterious, eery.
2. *heady:* exciting, stimulating.
3. *fedora:* soft felt hat.
4. *buttress:* support, prop up.
5. *incumbent:* officeholder.
6. *ostentatiously:* pretentiously, dramatically.
7. *deteriorate:* grow worse.

Form and Content

1. Although at first it appears to be a sketch of the father, it is actually about both father and son. The author characterizes his dad by showing the different influences the dad had on the son.
2. Part 1 deals with the early father-son relationship. Sentence 1 of paragraph 9 is a transitional sentence. Part 2 concerns the father-son relationship once the son has become a man.
3. Paragraph 2 comments on the father-son relationship in a general, impersonal way. It establishes the author's thesis: the relationship changes over time.
4. In paragraph 9 there is a rather touching reference as the author shakes hands with the opposing football captain; paragraph 15 refers to the final firm handshake. Both references are effectively placed and worded. Both are underplayed yet emotionally provocative.
5. Paragraph 6: the boy hears the word "instinct," but thinks his father is talking about smell. Paragraph 8: this is a play on the old expression, "I'll never forget what's her name."

Exercises for "Competition" (pp. 7–11)

Words

1. *estrangement:* alienation.
2. *chintz:* a bright-colored cotton fabric.

3. *omnipotent:* all-powerful.
4. *nucleus:* core, small group.
5. *nadir:* lowest possible point.
6. *commensurate:* proportionate, corresponding.
7. *persona:* made-up personality, assumed role.
8. *bizarrely:* strangely, eccentrically.
9. *sibling:* sister or brother.
10. *talisman:* charm, fetish.

Form and Content

1. The author, her sister, and her mother. Her grandfather is also significant.
2. The photo accentuates the reference to "estrangement" in paragraph 1: "leaning away with big spaces in between." The three women "didn't touch much."
3. The author contrasts her mother's adolescent plainness with her aunt's ravishing beauty (par. 4). Then Friday contrasts her own adolescent plainness with her sister Susie's beauty.
4. She poured nail polish on Susie's white evening dress and threw Susie's wallet down a sewer, but she was deeply ashamed.
5. The author's grandfather. Friday's mother did not train her daughters to be competitive, to express the emotions of rivalry. Because she did not teach them to win, they did not know how to lose.

Exercises for "Doc Marlowe" (pp. 12–16)

Words

1. *harangue:* speak loudly.
2. *soused:* drenched.
3. *suavely:* smoothly, politely.
4. *sciatica:* neuralgia, pain of hip or thigh.
5. *colic:* abnormal pain.
6. *tremulously:* shakily, tremblingly.
7. *lariat:* lasso, rope.
8. *decrepit:* worn-out, damaged by age.

Form and Content

1. Thurber comments on both the positive and negative aspects of Doc's life and actions. Doc was a liar and a cheat, but he also cured people and was exciting to be around.
2. He is treating standard medical terms lightly; however, Doc's treatments really work.
3. A medicine show was a troupe of traveling entertainers accompanied by a person who sold such products as "cure-all medicines" and hair restorers; General George Custer is usually pictured with long, wavy, blond hair.
4. In the final scene, Doc, now a dying man, gives the author a quarter with heads on both sides; it is the same coin that Doc cheated the boy with at the soda fountain.
5. The author's tone in paragraph 11 is hostile and angry. Such words as "swindler," "mad," and "furious" highlight his feelings; abruptly, the last paragraph is touching and tender. Thurber realizes that he has learned a valuable lesson from the life and death of Doc Marlowe.

Exercises for "The Teacher as Dragon" (pp. 17–20)

Words

1. *baleful:* menacing, threatening.
2. *countenance:* face, visage.
3. *porcine:* pig-like, swinish.
4. *indelible:* lasting, indestructible.
5. *uncannily:* strangely, weirdly.
6. *vixen:* ill-tempered woman.
7. *grandiose:* imposing, impressive.
8. *dawdles:* loiters, wastes time.
9. *cajole:* coax, persuade.
10. *impervious:* invulnerable, impenetrable.

Form and Content

1. In the fourth sentence of paragraph 16.
2. The negative words are *stout, ham-like, trunkish, yellow, calcified, savage, baleful, sparce, thick-lensed, beady* and *porcine.*
3. Paragraph four is a transitional paragraph between physical description and an explanation of the frustrations of teaching. Although the author can understand why some teachers become dragons, she resolves never to be one herself.
4. Villegas establishes the difficulties of teaching composition and criticizing student work.
5. The dragon teacher became disillusioned about and disenchanted with students' inability to think and communicate.

Exercises for "Loving County, Texas" (pp. 22–24)

Words

1. *hummocky:* marked by small swells or hillocks.
2. *berserk:* destructively angry or violent.
3. *sparse:* thin, widely diffused.
4. *lashings:* whippings, beatings.
5. *disaffected:* disillusioned, "turned-off."
6. *heritage:* legacy, inheritance.
7. *eerie:* strange, mysterious.
8. *aborted:* destroyed, miscarried.
9. *exotic:* foreign.
10. *tediums:* boredoms, drearinesses.

Form and Content

1. The population of Las Vegas is much more heterogeneous (racially, ethnically, culturally), transient and mobile, disparate in income and education, with access to wide varieties of sports, amusements, and dissipations.
2. Because their present is less exciting and adventurous.
3. Because Kansas City, a bustling and thriving Midwest American city, could seem exotic (foreign) only to a naive rural American who had seen few places outside his own little town.
4. *a great dry-docked ocean:* A dry dock is a structure that will hold a ship and from which all water can be removed so that the ship's hull can be repaired, cleaned, or painted. To dry dock a whole

ocean is a hyperbolic and startling metaphor; *like a blue chenille bedspread bleached by the seasons in the sun:* a simile that exactly describes the sky.

5. This sentence: "Outside the industrial sprawl of the prairie's mini-cities—on the occasional ranches or oil leases or in the flawed little country towns—the great curse is boredom."

Exercises for "The Crooked Wood" (pp. 25–27)

Words

1. *whimsical:* eccentric, odd.
2. *elixir:* essential requirement, cure-all.
3. *mandrake:* a European plant with narcotic properties and forked roots that sometimes are thought to resemble the human figure.
4. *translucence:* permitting passage of light, but not permitting a clear view, semitransparency.
5. *analogies:* similarities or resemblances.
6. *aspiring:* desiring something high or good.
7. *vulnerable:* liable to attack or injury, assailable.
8. *empiricist:* one who only believes in the results of observation, experience, or experiment.
9. *sentient:* feeling, capable of feeling.
10. *finite:* limited, bounded, not infinite.

Form and Content

1. These assurances are given the reader to make somewhat more believable the rather fantastic argument that makes the aspen grove both sentient and conscious.
2. No. He grants that some wood may be needed for shelter or fuel. And even after his experience with the aspen grove, he qualifies his vow never to chop a living tree with the phrase, "unless the need were urgent."
3. The only evidence the author offers is that after a time "you become aware" of the trees as a conscious presence.
4. These first two "scientific" paragraphs, like the author's later claims to being a skeptic, a doubter, and an empiricist, help to make more nearly credible his account of coming to be aware of the trees as sentient, conscious beings.
5. Most readers will recognize that these three "evidences" fall short of indicating a probability, let alone of establishing a rather fantastic proposition. Knowing that, the author makes a humorous near apology for his idea at the end of paragraph 3. Yet he pursues the idea further in the next three paragraphs.

Exercises for "In the Neighborhood" (pp. 28–31)

Words

1. *Boutique:* a small retail store selling fashionable merchandise.
2. *quotidian:* daily, everyday.
3. *nattering:* idle chatter, irritated noises.
4. *pram:* baby carriage, perambulator.
5. *paranoia:* psychological disorder characterized by suspicion and delusions of persecution.
6. *fervid:* fervent, impassioned.
7. *babushka:* a scarf made or folded into a triangle.

8. *kiosk:* a booth or retail stand.
9. *exuberantly:* joyfully, spiritedly.
10. *diction:* word choice, manner of speech.

Form and Content

1. What the author calls "boutiquification" (his own word) is sometimes called "gentrification." Houses and stores in older neighborhoods are remodeled and rented for higher prices, usually to more affluent tenants.
2. The community of people in your neighborhood, as distinct from either your professional and job associates or your immediate family and close friends.
3. *Central Casting* is, of course, the Hollywood name for an agency supplying a wide variety of actors for small, usually unimportant roles in motion pictures. The author is saying that the variety of characters in his neighborhood is so great as to suggest that they are supplied by such an agency.
4. When rents were increased, Joe's laundromat moved away and was replaced by a store selling wooden toys and instruction in woodcarving. Much the same thing could be expected to happen to other small, narrowly margined businesses that cannot afford higher rents.
5. The neighbors seem both better educated and more affluent than the "characters," and they are described in much less personal detail than the shopkeepers.

Exercises for "The Uses of Sidewalks" (pp. 32–36)

Words

1. *replete:* abounding, fully stocked.
2. *vantage:* place of opportunity, place for observation.
3. *ritual:* repeated in identical or prescribed form.
4. *crescendo:* greatest increase in activity.
5. *wary:* cautious, watchful.
6. *bravura:* brilliance, daring.
7. *frenetic:* excited, frantic.
8. *tenor:* settled course or manner.
9. *animated:* lively, full of life.
10. *innately:* naturally, inherently.

Form and Content

1. They are *dribble, heading, being made, emerge, hover, stopping, appeared, having dropped, bringing, crisscross, hurry, exchange, stands, folded, planted, looking, nod, glance, look, smile, means.*
2. The first sentence of the essay and the second sentence of the last paragraph.
3. Because the participants and their actions are various and not obviously coordinated.
4. Changes of time: morning (par.3), midday (par.4), late afternoon (par.5), and early evening (par.6).
5. They serve two purposes: (1) each sums up its paragraph in a short generalization, and (2) each is a dramatic change in sentence length and rhythm.

Exercises for "Living with Jellinek's Disease" (pp. 38–40)

Words

1. *subtle:* crafty, cunning.

2. *insidious:* treacherous, wily.
3. *ravaging:* destructive, ruinous.
4. *railed:* cursed, cried scornfully.
5. *prodromal:* premonitory sign of disease.
6. *hallmark:* official stamp of genuineness.
7. *morass:* trap.
8. *predisposed:* susceptible to.
9. *ingestion:* swallowing, drinking.
10. *resonates:* vibrates, resounds.

Form and Content
1. She insists that *alcoholism* is an illness and, therefore, should not be labeled with an "ism" as theories, styles, and doctrines are. Because it is a disease that can be treated and arrested, it should be called by a more appropriate name.
2. Her father died of Jellinek's disease, and she suffers from it.
3. The opening paragraphs play up the characteristics of this new-sounding disease as well as the statistics and personal anguish associated with it. The Jellinek references capture the reader's attention: how can such a common illness have such a strange, unfamiliar name? She hates the word *alcoholism* and is conditioning the reader to accept a new term.
4. She offers "hard" information concerning physical responses to drinking.
5. Paragraph 17 contains the author's thesis. Because she first introduces Jellinek's disease and doesn't reveal its other name until well into her essay, it is appropriate that the controlling idea be placed at the conclusion of the essay.

Exercises for "Grant and Lee" (pp. 41–44)

Words
1. *poignant:* keen, striking.
2. *pronounced:* strongly marked, extreme.
3. *sanctified:* made holy, consecrated.
4. *sinewy:* strong, tough.
5. *tenacity:* persistence, ability to hold fast.

Form and Content
1. An aristocracy would have a disinterested group of leaders with a strong sense of obligation to the community—people who would set an example for others.
2. The privileged class of the confederacy ordinarily inherited its property and wealth; in the Western country each man had to win privileges and wealth for himself.
3. No. He clearly admires both men, and he is interested in differences and similarities, not superiorities or inferiorities.
4. Both the first and last paragraphs refer to the historic importance of the meeting of the two men at Appomattox Court House.
5. Paragraphs 3–12 explain the differences between the two men; paragraphs 13–16 describe their similarities.

Exercises for "On Being a Mess" (pp. 45–47)

Words
1. *syndrome:* a set of symptoms.

2. *one-upmanship:* a technique of getting the better of another person.
3. *scoured:* washed and scrubbed.
4. *protean:* changeable, having different forms.
5. *omnivorous:* indiscriminate in eating habits, all-consuming.
6. *chide:* scold, criticize.
7. *metamorphosed:* changed, transformed.
8. *wreak:* to exact or vent in anger or vengeance.
9. *ingenious:* clever, inventive.
10. *meticulous:* extremely and painstakingly precise.
11. *delusions:* false beliefs.

Form and Content

1. Being a mess on a good day, being a mess on a bad day, and myths to justify messiness.
2. In order to strengthen her classification of messiness, she gives the word *mess* the status of a proper noun throughout her essay; thus it appears with a capital *M.*
3. Ames created a scapegoat—the protean monster—who is to blame for many of the actions resulting from her messiness: the "it" that complicates her life; eats shoes, keys, and bills; and cannot be controlled because it constantly changes form.
4. We are classified as messes and have devised the following myths to justify our condition: (1) we are not slobs because our mess is clean; (2) we are messes because we are intellectuals: we contemplate lofty ideas and have little time for such dull, routine work as being neat and orderly; (3) we are messes because our mothers drove us to it with their constant carping on cleanliness; (4) we are messes because our apartments are too small and our closets too full of important memorabilia, objects we would never think of throwing away.
5. Here Ames is paraphrasing the well-known expression made famous by the late cartoonist Walt Kelly: "We have met the enemy and they are us." We, the messes of the world, are the enemy, not a crazed gorilla.

Exercises for "The Plot Against People" (pp. 48–50)

Words

1. *inanimate:* lifeless.
2. *cunning:* craftiness, guile.
3. *idle:* not engaged in work, unoccupied.
4. *plausible:* believable.
5. *inherent:* inborn, intrinsic.
6. *infuriate:* to make furious, very angry.
7. *conciliatory:* tending to placate, appease.
8. *incredibly:* unbelievably.
9. *attained:* achieved, gained.
10. *baffled:* confused, perplexed.

Form and Content

1. *Personification,* a writing device in which an inanimate object is given human qualities, is used consistently by Russell Baker. For instance, the automobile possesses "cunning," a washing

machine has "human enemies," keys "burrow," purses "travel" and "hide."
2. Paragraph 6 completes the "breaking down" phase and paragraph 7 introduces the "lost" phase. The transition is made with the line "They get lost."
3. Baker's "science" references are, of course, playful and pseudoserious. He uses these references to make his observations pretentiously comic.
4. Paragraph 1.
5. Baker, throughout his essay, uses words and expressions that make his thesis seem far more important than it really is. He gives common objects a life-death significance.

Exercises for "Coon Hunt" (pp. 52–56)

Words
1. *disconsolately:* cheerlessly, gloomily.
2. *affinity:* liking, attraction.
3. *allure:* attraction, enticement.
4. *plied:* worked persistently.
5. *stealth:* secret movement.
6. *impenetrable:* incapable of being entered, dense.
7. *contretemps:* an embarrassing, awkward occurrence.
8. *lethargically:* apathetically, lazily.
9. *rime:* frost.
10. *tangent:* change of direction.

Form and Content
1. A "drummer" is an American expression meaning traveling salesman; a "way train" makes many stops, a local as compared to an express. The dog, therefore, is making the best of an uncomfortable situation. The similes are: "like a child being allowed to see"; "howling as though possessed"; "crazy as a loon."
2. White is amused by his fellow hunters. He is with them, but he is not one of them.
3. One has a smashed-in face, one a terrible cold, and one recently broken ribs.
4. White's fellow hunters are rural New Englanders (White was living in Maine at the time he wrote this narrative) and display a kind of country humor in what they say and how they say it.
5. Both White and the puppy are really observers rather than participants. They are on their first coon hunt and neither is particularly suited to the occasion. White tells us what happens, describes the various episodes that make up a coon hunt, and is able to relate to the events more vividly through the experience of the young dog.

Exercises for "Champion of the World" (pp. 57–59)

Words
1. *apprehensive:* anxious, uneasy.
2. *contender:* a rival who challenges the champion.
3. *assent:* agreement, concurrence.
4. *accusations:* charges, indictments.
5. *hewers:* choppers, cutters.
6. *ambrosia:* a drink of the gods, giving immortality (in mythology).

Form and Content

1. "Cracker": a poor white Southerner.
   "String-along song": a radio commercial for the Gillette Safety Razor Company, the fight's sponsor.
   "master's voice": the trademark of R.C.A., a dog listening to an old time victrola.
   "Brown Bomber": a nickname for Joe Louis.
   "Carnera": one-time heavyweight champion Primo Carnera.
2. The author employs standard English; the crowd uses a black country dialect; the radio (the commentator and referee) uses boxing jargon, including "champeen" for champion.
3. The three paragraphs interrupt the blow-by-blow narrative of the commentator: "Louis is going down" completes paragraph 15 and "he's off the ropes" begins paragraph 19. Here the author "freezes" the action to make comments on the plight of the American black and to gain a sense of drama as Joe Louis goes from probable loser to winner and still champion of the world.
4. "as a black sky"; the tide "poured out of the door"; the sound grows "into a baby roar."
5. Although Louis' people were "the strongest in the world," they still lived in fear of being "caught on a lonely country road."

Exercises for "Duel at Red River" (pp. 60–63)

Words

1. *vouchsafed:* assured, guaranteed.
2. *chafed:* angered, irritated.
3. *statute:* law.
4. *scrupulously:* carefully, meticulously.
5. *affronts:* insults.
6. *monarchist:* one who prefers government by a king.
7. *sanguine:* cheerful, hopeful.
8. *repaired:* went, retired.
9. *frock:* double-breasted, knee length.
10. *furrow:* long, narrow gash.

Form and Content

1. These are the first personal details about Jackson's personality and character. They reveal a talkative, opinionated, knowledgeable, humorous American, one who is fiercely anti-British.
2. There was a law against dueling.
3. He was an excellent snap shot. Jackson would give Dickinson the first shot; then, if he were still standing, he would shoot to kill.
4. Jackson appeared relaxed, friendly. One would not have suspected that he soon would take part in a duel. He was self-confident and unexcitable.
5. Part 1 constitutes necessary background information; it gives the reader a glimpse into lives of the duelists, especially Andrew Jackson's. It is a prelude to Part 2, the actual duel itself.

Exercises for "38 Who Saw Murder Didn't Call the Police" (pp. 64–67)

Words

1. *borough:* one of five political divisions of New York City.

2. *recitation:* oral report, response.
3. *Tudor:* a style of English architecture.
4. *deliberation:* careful consideration.
5. *solemn:* serious, grave.

Form and Content

1. The opening paragraphs arouse the reader's interest by offering the shocking details of the murder, as well as the equally shocking reactions of those who saw what happened and did nothing about it. The "good people" reference is ironic; it helps to focus on the witnesses who, because they failed to call the police, were not good people at all. Finally, the adjectives serve to establish the setting as a conservative, respectable neighborhood, not an urban locale where such a murder might not be so uncommon.
2. It ends with paragraph 18. Paragraphs 19–31 deal with the aftermath of the murder.
3. The quotations all express weak reasons for inaction, for not wanting to become involved.
4. (A) simple and matter-of-fact.
5. Presented in simple, easy to understand news style, the essay poses a major moral question: when should one become involved in the personal affairs of others? When does someone else's business become everyone's business?

Exercises for "Heels on Wheels" (pp. 69–72)

Words

1. *admonition:* caution, advice.
2. *forbearance:* patient endurance, sufferance.
3. *gladiator:* [the qualities of] one who fights to the death to entertain the public.
4. *scofflaws:* habitual law violators.
5. *conjecture:* guess, tentative opinion.

Form and Content

1. By overstatement, hyperbole.
2. The light-hearted lawlessness of Massachusetts drivers.
3. That even the most respectable of Massachusetts people may be cheerfully outrageous drivers.
4. Lack of adequate law enforcement.
5. The evidence in paragraph 12 is statistical, the product of research; the rest of the essay is anecdotal.

Exercises for "Driving for Dear Life" (pp. 73–76)

Words

1. *crests:* reaches the top.
2. *culmination:* climactic event.
3. *maniacal:* crazy, mad.
4. *slalom:* zigzag.
5. *instantaneous:* immediate, quick.

Form and Content

1. "old-boy network": a friend-to-friend system of fraternal helpfulness.

"white-knuckle express": terrifying, fearsome ride.
"hardball": serious, earnest game.
"macho types": super-masculine he-men.
"Third World": undeveloped countries, those aligned with neither East nor West.

2. He uses vigorous, dramatic language and places the reader in the driver's seat along with the student driver. The reader is there on the scene without knowing quite what is happening.
3. Speaking in an upbeat, colorful manner, Scott, an ex-race car champion and a Yale Ph.D., adds total credibility to the author's essay. Wurmstedt describes what is going on, but Scott is the total authority. What he says gives the reader important insights and information.
4. "the driver lunges," "jams down hard," "he jerks the wheel," "car twists savagely," "driver guns his motor," "sweat on the driver's palms," "tires scream," "heads and stomachs spin," etc.
5. The author closes with an anecdote that is directly relevant to what Scott's students learn. It shows how a graduate must be suspicious and must act instantaneously, even if his suspicions are unfounded.

Exercises for "On-the-Job Training" (pp. 77–80)

Words

1. *whims:* sudden urges or desires.
2. *queasy:* squeamish, uneasy.
3. *unbridled:* unchecked, unrestrained.
4. *trauma: shock.*
5. *gall:* irritation, exasperation.
6. *flux:* constant change.

Form and Content

1. In the opening paragraph, the author sounds like a very reasonable man, one who is genuinely happy and excited that his wife has "launched a new career." The last paragraph has a quite different tone. If his family life is to remain intact, it will take luck. He hopes for the best. Paragraphs 2 and 20 both contain references to the plumber. His wife's pre-working duty was to wait at home for the plumber; now the duty belongs to the author.
2. Paragraphs 3–8 record the author's gradually changing attitudes, his new household duties, and his reactions to his wife's outside-the-home responsibilities.
3. Paragraph 9 begins with a *but,* and reveals his open hostility to his new role as well as to his wife's. His response to a series of questions is that he is "hurt" by what is happening to his married life.
4. Paragraphs 14–20 alternate between a series of frantic questions (pars. 15–16) and the physical and mental anguish the author is feeling: he has stomach aches, his stress level is rising, he is scared, he feels his masculinity is being stripped away. The only thing left is his hope that their relationship can withstand the stress.
5. He painfully admits (par. 18) that he is not so tolerent and liberated as he earlier thought he was. His male image has been threatened. He has not wanted to admit this fact, but in this paragraph he says, "I have said it."

Exercises for "It's Getting Hard to Ride the Gravy Boat" (pp. 81–83)

Words

1. *categorically:* unequivocally, without qualification.

Answers for Part One

2. *satiated:* gratified, surfeited.
3. *delectable:* delightful, delicious.
4. *sylphs:* slender, graceful young women.
5. *galling:* exasperating, irritating.

Form and Content

1. Examples are phrases like "with infinite sorrow," "physical disaster," "probably a wreck," and "live out the night."
2. The sentence of paragraph 3 that begins: "But what any rational person would like to know . . . ?"
3. "the sight is heartbreaking" and "all but inundated."
4. Devotion to fitness is more "serious" than merely losing weight; it is a total program for "well-being."
5. Playful, humorous irony.

Exercises for "Farewell to Fitness" (pp. 85–87)

Words

1. *pectoral:* pertaining to chest or breast.
2. *hamstring:* tendons behind the knee.
3. *isometrics:* exercises characterized by balanced tension or pressure.
4. *obnoxious:* disagreeable, offensive.
5. *narcissist:* self-admirer, self lover.

Form and Content

1. Schwarzenegger is known for his muscular body, developed through a program of weight lifting and other exercises; Welles, in addition to being a famous film actor and director, is known for his gourmet tastes and obese figure. Royko sees Welles as admirable and Schwarzenegger as a symbol of an unpleasantly strenuous life.
2. The opening paragraph and paragraph 22 deal directly with Royko's personal experience. Much of the rest of the essay is humorous exaggeration of his observation of others.
3. Other long lists are found in paragraphs 7, 8, and 23.
4. The modifiers in paragraph 22 are in the phrases "their magnificent bellies" and "smile happily." The verbals that make exercise unattractive are "sprawled," "hanging," "wheezing," "moaning," "writhing," and "throwing up."
5. "Unpatriotic" is an exaggerated protestation of guilt; the "Me Generation" is a humorous allusion to Tom Wolfe's name for the people of the 1970s.

Exercises for "Who Cares about the Renaissance?" (pp. 88–90)

Words

1. *Renaissance:* the great revival of art, learning, and literature in Europe during the 14th, 15th, and 16th centuries.
2. *elicited:* brought forth, evoked.
3. *lugubrious:* mournful, doleful.

4. *lurid:* vivid, sensational.
5. *abysmal:* depressed, very bad.
6. *aberrations:* deviants, abnormalities.
7. *pragmatic:* practical, realistic.
8. *relegated:* sent or consigned to an inferior or obscure place or condition.
9. *esoteric:* profound, understood by few.
10. *sterile:* barren, fruitless.

Form and Content

1. The lack of employment opportunities.
2. Although loaded against the author, the question asks for your own opinion.
3. A knowledgeable student could cite many engineers, scientists, and businessmen who have also been collectors, students, or even practitioners of fine arts.
4. This question calls for your own opinion.
5. This question, similarly, calls for both a philosophical and aesthetic judgment.

Exercises for "Strike Out Little League" (pp. 91–93)

Words

1. *sustained:* continued, maintained.
2. *farce:* absurdity, ridiculous situation.
3. *incompetent:* lacking ability, unfit.
4. *retards:* slows, hinders.
5. *alternatives:* other choices.

Form and Content

1. The author begins his first paragraph by saying that he doesn't know what the three organizers of Little League baseball had in mind. Then, at the end of the essay he writes, "For the life of me, I can't figure out what they had in mind."
2. Challengeable assumptions: that a mother or father must go to every game (par. 3); that Little League participants have a concentration span of no more than five seconds (par. 4); that Little Leagues have no value in teaching baseball fundamentals.
3. They offer possible alternatives to present practice and protect the author from the charge that his criticism is merely negative.
4. The numbers show that the author has done some research and has more than a mere observer's knowledge of his subject.
5. The negative statements come full circle (back to the three first organizers of Little League mentioned in the first paragraph) and at the same time absolve the organizers of evil or malicious intentions.

Exercises for "A Comeback for Commitment" (pp. 94–96)

Words

1. *mogul:* very rich, powerful person.
2. *lip-service:* marked by insincere payment of respect.
3. *tortuous:* complex.
4. *cynicism:* distrust, embittered emotions.

Answers for Part One

5. *pseudonamed:* nicknamed.
6. *zealotry:* fanaticism.
7. *hedonism:* the pursuit of pleasure.
8. *hostility:* anger, antagonism.
9. *mobile:* moving from one level to another.
10. *elation:* joyous, satisfied feeling.

Form and Content

1. *altar-opting:* combination.
   pseudonamed: modified form of pseudonym.
   myselfism: combination.
2. The author's expression is the most informal of these three, and because it is more specific than the two suggested substitutions, it tells more about the conversationalists.
3. Commonly, alliteration is the repetition of sounds at the beginning of stressed words in a phrase or statement. The most obvious alliteration in paragraph 4 is in the first sentence: "commitment ran more to causes than coupling."
4. A paradox is a seemingly self-contradictory statement. In paragraph 7 the paradox is, "the newest wrinkle is the oldest."
5. Pronoun: *this* in paragraph 6. Coordinating conjunction: *So* in paragraph 7.

Answers for Part Two

1a. Exercise 1

1. a
2. b
3. a
4. a
5. b
6. a
7. b
8. b
9. b
10. b
11. b
12. a
13. a
14. a
15. b
16. b
17. a
18. b
19. b
20. a

1a. Exercise 2

1. a
2. a
3. a
4. b
5. a
6. a
7. b
8. b
9. b
10. a
11. b
12. b
13. b
14. a
15. b
16. b
17. b
18. a
19. a
20. a

1a. Exercise 3

1. candidate
2. becoming
3. laboratory
4. destroy
5. criticism
6. occurrence
7. sophomore
8. let's
9. paid
10. tries
11. A lot
12. dining
13. disastrous
14. interesting
15. government
16. speech
17. hindrance
18. exaggerated
19. familiar
20. professor

1a. Exercise 4

1. successful
2. knowledge
3. library

1b. Exercise 1

1. dessert
2. accept
3. peace

1b. Exercise 2

1. morale
2. weather
3. quiet

Answers for Part Two

4. dependent
5. studying
6. excellent
7. necessary
8. separate
9. weird
10. safety
11. writing
12. surprise
13. preceding
14. accommodate
15. cemetery
16. existence
17. superintendent
18. villain
19. quizzes
20. athlete

4. lead
5. capital
6. choose
7. It's
8. advise
9. desert
10. its
11. It's, lose
12. led, capitol
13. Except, advice
14. its, hear
15. chose, desert
16. fourth, lead
17. here, have
18. advice, clothes
19. break, course
20. all ready, due

4. loose
5. too
6. personal
7. whose
8. than
9. past
10. Their
11. plain, they're
12. whether, you're
13. right, stationery
14. Who's, than
15. women, passed
16. piece, plain
17. your, personal
18. quite, where
19. morale, past
20. through, two

1b. Exercise 3

1. compliment
2. an
3. advice
4. all ready
5. affect
6. principal
7. an
8. capitol
9. principal
10. compliment
11. effect
12. an
13. desert
14. past
15. whose
16. principle
17. due
18. stationery
19. woman
20. affect

2a. Exercise 1

1. Spanish
2. Derby
3. Day
4. Dad
5. Ohio River, West
6. American
7. October
8. Social Security Act
9. Chief, Police
10. Salvation Army
11. Grand Canyon, Arizona, Phoenix
12. Monday, Lakers, Knicks
13. Mother, Mercury, Cougar
14. Professor, Shakespearean
15. Democratic
16. Dad's
17. The American Way, Death
18. We, New Year's Eve
19. Mammoth Falls, Mount Everett
20. Father, Mother

2a. Exercise 2

1. high school, Roman
2. physics
3. Missouri, River
4. Army, Catholic
5. Iowa, Avenue
6. dance
7. father
8. college
9. Air Force, Captain
10. American, science fiction
11. French, German, Spanish
12. High School
13. Well, Mayor, governor
14. Senator, Belgium
15. Polish
16. professor, Hebrew
17. American
18. Railroad, Creek
19. Day, colonel, Light
20. Public Library, Buddhism

2a. Exercise 3

1. Uncle
2. September
3. Saturday
4. French
5. Hall
6. Thanksgiving
7. Dad

2b. Exercise 1

1. Jenny's
2. children's
3. men's
4. staff's
5. manager's
6. Someone's
7. Audrey's
8. mayor's
9. nobody's
10. reporters'
11. managers'
12. waiters'
13. one's
14. soldiers'
15. women's

2b. Exercise 2

1. can't
2. shouldn't
3. they're
4. o'clock
5. he's
6. It's
7. Don't
8. doesn't
9. shouldn't
10. I'll
11. '66
12. Won't
13. we'll
14. Haven't
15. We'll

2b. Exercise 3

1. i's, t's
2. 1960's
3. 3's
4. g's, m's
5. er's, ah's
6. 9's, 10's
7. A's, B's
8. 1970's
9. r's, a's
10. 2's

2b. Exercise 4

1. Women's, can't
2. They're, it's, weren't
3. Charles', Cindy's
4. Frank's, Richard's, it's
5. they'd, *Gulliver's*
6. brother's, can't
7. senator's, he'd, o'clock
8. Wanda's, Harriet's, Boris'
9. Let's, r's
10. waitresses', aren't, Donald's
11. It's, Holmes', let's
12. weeks', Henry's, year's
13. else's, Wilsons'
14. women's, Everett's
15. Let's, Sam's
16. Didn't, Roberta's
17. Jeff's, o'clock
18. Harris', aren't
19. friend's, nice's, neat's, for sure's
20. Curt's, Kennedy's, Mets', '71

Answers for Part Two

3a. Exercise 1

1. Aspen, town, Rocky Mountains
2. vote, electorate, father
3. Basketball, sport, stamina, intelligence
4. uncle, sheriff, county
5. fall, states, part, Canada
6. vacation, Sussex, Cornwall
7. boxer, bell, round
8. mountain, village, farmland
9. television, newscast
10. bandits, demands, tones

3b. Exercise 1

1. whom, you
2. We, who
3. Someone, us
4. Which, you
5. who
6. Anyone, she
7. they
8. Everyone
9. I, which
10. Nobody, anybody

3c. Exercise 1

1. regret, annoyed
2. is, tell, went
3. cheered, warmed
4. thought, deserved
5. must repeat
6. have been reported
7. arrived, had finished
8. Pass, pour
9. had been walking, arrived
10. are required

3d. Exercise 1

1. dense, dark, lonely
2. old, sick, poor
3. Three, muscular, young
4. German, formal, polite
5. Many, poor, final
6. flat, stale, foreign
7. much, new
8. beautiful, unprofitable
9. English, handsome
10. chief, despicable

3e. Exercise 1

1. properly, slowly, carefully
2. very, much, too
3. always, clearly, rapidly
4. poorly, well
5. tomorrow
6. truly, accidentally
7. angrily, rather
8. surely, thoughtlessly
9. easily
10. usually

3f. Exercise 1

1. in
2. at, of
3. about
4. behind
5. between
6. outside, beyond
7. in, during
8. After, for
9. after, with
10. At, in

3g. Exercise 1

1. so
2. either . . . or
3. although
4. yet
5. Not only . . . but . . . also
6. so that
7. Either . . . or
8. for
9. that
10. neither . . . nor

3h. Exercise 1

1. however
2. therefore
3. Thus
4. Unfortunately
5. moreover
6. furthermore
7. hence
8. consequently
9. consequently
10. nevertheless

4a. Exercise 1

1. library *buys*
2. I *attend*
3. tree *fell*
4. mother *sells*
5. fancy *turns*
6. mayor *owns*
7. men *found*
8. father *built*
9. jury *returned*
10. everybody *voted*
11. man *leads*
12. chef *wrote*
13. women *are*
14. men *sat*
15. development *revealed*

4a. Exercise 2

1. cadets *were beginning*
2. all *had been told*
3. captain *is standing*
4. Edward *must have known*
5. authors *have predicted*
6. we *shall have been married*
7. engineer *is preparing*
8. person *has been traveling*
9. artistry *can be seen*
10. person *can be paid*
11. carpenter *should have been paid*
12. he *awoke*
13. painting *might have been done*

14. they *may have been plotting*
15. member *has been hoping*

4a. Exercise 3

1. we *have been watching*
2. father, mother *are leaving, will arrive*
3. cats, dogs *ruined, soiled*
4. corporation *may be*
5. clothes, shoes, hats *had been purchased*
6. Tom, Dick, Harry *go, cheer*
7. she *will begin, work, be*
8. statue *dominates, dwarfs*
9. I *attend, take, study*
10. clerk, bailiff *assist, record, maintain*
11. teacher, lawyer, actor *must speak, avoid*
12. restaurant *is*
13. canals, bridges, buildings *make*
14. patrolman *has been walking, has checked*
15. trophies, medals, citations, *are standing, displayed, hung*

4b. Exercise 1

1. *in the middle, of the next block*
2. *Behind the podium, of the faculty*
3. *In this election, of the candidates*
4. *under the door, through the keyhole*
5. *about her adventures, in the South Seas*
6. *of the best dishes, on the menu*
7. *Without any doubt, from this state*
8. *At the end, of the play, on the stage*
9. *across the river, into the forest*
10. *of the people, by the people, for the people*
11. *to the park, into the zoo*
12. *of the economic theory, of statistics*
13. *During the recession, in the management, of the corporation*
14. *in a house, by the side, of the road*
15. *Above the pond, under the cliff, for our horses*

4b. Exercise 2

1. *to visit Paris*
2. *Whistling a happy tune*
3. *Learning modern Greek*
4. *him to be the speaker*

5. *to be admired*
6. *breaking*
7. *running*
8. *to spend many hours*
9. *helping the prime minister*
10. *Dancing the samba*
11. *To understand this contract, to read German*
12. *to go home immediately*
13. *her singing and dancing*
14. *leading the white horse*
15. *Visiting European friends*

4b. Exercise 3

1. *to join us*
2. *studying unusual foreign languages*
3. *Eating shellfish*
4. *committing suicide*
5. *Keeping a budget*
6. *To sing popular songs well*
7. *visiting you*
8. *To spend that much money*
9. *stealing watermelons*
10. *cheating the local merchants*

4b. Exercise 4

1. *in the picture*
2. *to see*
3. *Wearing a black dress*
4. *watering his lawn*
5. *to do*
6. *written rapidly*
7. *Crossing the finish line*
8. *whispered very softly*
9. *chewing my slipper*
10. *wearing a surgical gown*

4b. Exercise 5

1. *to do*
2. *into the room*
3. *on the stage*
4. *to criticize the work*
5. *to work every day*
6. *under the bridge*
7. *into the saloon*
8. *to find*
9. *in the rain*
10. *before the football game*

4c. Exercise 1

1. *she was dressed in a white robe*
2. *we finally came to the river*
3. *I am the woman*
4. *he will tell us*
5. *he went home*
6. *he walked*
7. *I doubt it*
8. *I came*
9. *he refused to accept charity*
10. *I want to find an electrician*
11. *I ran to meet her*
12. *We need a car*
13. *Ralph wandered off into the forest*
14. *She left the theater after the first act*
15. *we hired her*

Answers for Part Two

4c. Exercise 2

1. *who is extraordinarily intelligent*
2. *that I saw*
3. *who lives in North Dakota*
4. *which took place in 1932*
5. *whom you saw*
6. *which move about only at night*
7. *that she did*
8. *that had many important duties*
9. *who has a large income*
10. *which receives heavy rainfall near the coast*

4c. Exercise 3

1. *since she was elected mayor*
2. *Before he goes*
3. *while he was President*
4. *that you could come to dinner*
5. *If he does not complete the assignment*
6. *Although he was an engineer*
7. *when the clock strikes midnight*
8. *if he were a very old man*
9. *because you enjoy solving problems*
10. *although it has had a good record*

4c. Exercise 4

1. *that she would succeed*
2. *What he wants*
3. *that the contract could not be enforced*
4. *that he would serve*
5. *That you can make an omelette without breaking any eggs*
6. *that she would be a millionaire*
7. *that the church can survive this financial crisis*
8. *how you did it*
9. *that I shall lose my mind*
10. *What you are doing*

5a. Exercise 1

1. (3)
2. (5)
3. (2)
4. (5)
5. (2)
6. (4)
7. (4)
8. (3)
9. (2)
10. (5)

5a. Exercise 2

1. (1)
2. (5)
3. (3)
4. (1)
5. (4)
6. (3)
7. (5)
8. (5)
9. (2)
10. (2)

5a. Exercise 3

1. (2)
2. (3)
3. (8)
4. (10)

5a. Exercise 4

1. (4)
2. (7)
3. (9)
4. (10)

5b. Exercise 1

1. (1)
2. (3)
3. (1)
4. (5)
5. (2)
6. (5)
7. (3)
8. (2)
9. (1)
10. (2)

5b. Exercise 2

1. (2)
2. (3)
3. (4)
4. (3)
5. (1)
6. (5)
7. (2)
8. (3)
9. (5)
10. (4)

5b. Exercise 3

1. (2)
2. (4)
3. (7)
4. (9)
5. (10)

5b. Exercise 4

1. (1)
2. (3)
3. (6)
4. (8)
5. (10)

5ab. Exercise 1

Our summer vacation was nearly over. My youngest sister, Jenny, and I were traveling the last leg of our journey, a lonely stretch of highway between Middleton and Victor's Ferry. *The latter being our hometown.* A steady rain, which had begun to fall around noon, was now pouring, making the road dangerous and visibility poor. Jenny, always a cautious driver, reduced speed and stayed in the right lane. In the distance we could barely make out a sign announcing that Victor's Ferry was only four miles away. *Suddenly the engine began to sputter, then it let out a noisy cough and died.* We pushed it to the side of the road, locked the doors securely, and waited for the storm to pass over. In a few minutes the rain stopped, and the sun came out. Jennifer then tried to start the car. To our surprise, it purred smoothly. Once on the road again, we headed for home. *Singing a silly child's song as we rolled merrily along. Soon we arrived at our house, it felt good to unpack and tell the family about all the good times we had shared. Never mentioning the brief interlude with the coughing engine.*

5ab. Exercise 2

One of the greatest novels in English literature is Jane Austen's *Pride and Prejudice,* first published in 1813. Its heroine, Elizabeth Bennet, is both lively and intelligent, but unfortunately she is prejudiced against the hero at their first meeting. *Particularly by his proud and haughty manner.* Later her prejudice is increased by a false report of the hero's mistreatment of a young soldier. *Other plot developments also strengthen her dislike of the hero, consequently, she refuses his unexpected proposal of marriage. Speaking, as she does so, angrily and bitterly about his conduct.* Later, however, she learns that she has made at least one mistake. *The young soldier has lied, he is really a villain, as he later proves.* Elizabeth comes to regret her prejudice, and the hero eventually explains and apologizes for his proud speeches and actions. Jane Austen handles a complicated plot skillfully as she develops her novel and brings it to a happy ending.

6a. Exercise 1

1. were
2. is
3. are
4. was
5. is
6. was
7. is
8. stands
9. is
10. sing
11. was
12. was
13. were
14. are
15. has

6a. Exercise 2

1. were
2. was
3. are
4. is
5. want
6. have
7. has
8. Are
9. has
10. know
11. come
12. is
13. was
14. was
15. is

6b. Exercise 1

1. its
2. This
3. have their
4. their
5. their
6. this
7. he or she
8. her head
9. his or her
10. they
11. his
12. her
13. himself or herself

6b. Exercise 2

1. its
2. his
3. his
4. her
5. his or her
6. her
7. his
8. his
9. his
10. his or her
11. their
12. her
13. his or her

14. its
15. his

14. her
15. these

6ab. Exercise 1

1. (1)
2. (3)
3. (4)
4. (5)
5. (5)

6ab. Exercise 2

1. (3)
2. (3)
3. (1)
4. (3)
5. (1)

7a. Exercise 1

1. My father is a geologist, but I am not interested in geology.
2. Until they had exhausted themselves, the hounds chased the foxes.
3. The sports page says that tonight's game has been postponed.
4. Jim called Jeff and said, "I won the prize."
5. I didn't call you because I was very angry and had mislaid your phone number.
6. Uncle Don has become disillusioned with professional football because the games have become too violent.
7. We do our weekly shopping at Hardin's Market, for its produce is always fresh.
8. Janis wept for an hour after she told Holly the sad news.
9. The clumsy waiter was very much embarrassed after he dropped the hot soup on the customer's new white suit.
10. I have received only one letter from Judy, and the news is depressing.
11. Finland has long, cold, depressing winters.
12. Tom went home, found the key in the car, and returned the car to me.
13. My mother occasionally reads a detective novel or does a crossword puzzle, but, as a rule, she considers such activities a waste of time.
14. Pamela said, "Mother, you are gaining too much weight."
15. The opera star smiled at Uncle Ted and gave him an autograph, actions that thrilled him immensely.

7a. Exercise 2

1. Alfred enjoyed his tour of Germany, even though he could not understand the German language.
2. We were all amused when Stephanie made a dramatic entrance and then tripped over the dog.
3. The next day Ralph told his brother, "Your books are still in the car."
4. Pamela says that she is unable to live in the dormitory because the dining hall serves too few fruits and vegetables.
5. We were delighted when Father showed us the outdoor spa that he had recently built.
6. Stephen says that his father died at the age of 30.
7. Because she has always wanted to be a chemist, Elizabeth has been studying chemistry for five years.

8. Veteran travelers say that New Zealand has the most varied scenery of any country in the world.
9. All of the graduate students gave Professor Scott a set of The New Oxford English Dictionary, a gift which left her speechless.
10. Because he knew how careless the salesmen were, the sales manager refused to let them lend the automobiles to customers.
11. The vice-president asked the plant manager, "Do you know how expensive your new plan will be?"
12. Whenever you see a new gopher hole, poison the gopher.
13. I went to the payroll office and announced that I was quitting.
14. Immediately after we heard his roar, the lion charged at us.
15. While he was climbing the mountain, Mr. Miller had a mild heart attack that frightened him very much.

7a. Exercise 3

1. I agree that she is talented, but it is difficult to make a living as an artist.
2. We visited Mexico during the summer, for we love that country's food and culture.
3. We are told that the price of gas will be higher than it was last year.
4. I seldom watch television, for usually the shows are either violent or silly.
5. If the children refuse to eat, cut up the raw vegetables and make a soup.
6. Because my friend has always wanted to be a photographer, he is taking courses in photography.
7. The almanac says that this winter will be unusually cold.
8. The plumber we hired worked for two hours, but the faucet continued to drip.
9. I am studying engineering, for I have always wanted to be an engineer.
10. He went to the police station and reported that someone had stolen his truck.
11. The opening chapter of this novel describes life in Victorian England.
12. Uncle Jim said to his son, "My hair is turning gray."
13. Dust the antique statues after you take them off the shelves.
14. Paris restaurants serve the world's finest food.
15. Frowning, the judge spoke to my father.

7a. Exercise 4

Incorrect sentences: 2, 5, 6, 7, 9, 12, 13, 14, 15

7b. Exercise 1

Illogically written sentences: 1, 3, 4, 6, 7, 8, 9, 11, 13, 14

7b. Exercise 2

Illogically written sentences: 1, 3, 4, 6, 7, 8, 9, 11, 13, 15

7b. Exercise 3

1. When we were standing at the curb, a crosstown bus splashed us with water.
2. When one is applying for a new job, neatness and courtesy are essential.
3. From a breeder, we bought a purebread Irish setter that was thoroughly trained.
4. Several times during their senior year at the university, Don asked Martha to marry him.
5. Looking north, one can see the old O'Hara plantation in the distance.
6. After I saved the company several thousand dollars, the boss gave me a generous raise in pay.
7. On Monday, the manager said we would reevaluate our advertising campaign.
8. From a professional musician, I bought a valuable antique guitar with steel strings.
9. The treasure hunters searched for the chest full of Spanish gold pieces that was buried somewhere on the little island.
10. As she finished her foreign policy address, the applause of the crowd pleased the senator.
11. To understand some modern poetry, one must study each word carefully.
12. From a friendly neighbor, I borrowed a gas-powered mower that was rusty and in need of repair.
13. After I filled out my application form, the personnel director asked me to come to his office.
14. When I graduated from college, my parents bought me a late model used car.
15. My brother wanted to borrow only $50.

7b. Exercise 4

1. Our relatives from Crawfordsville, Indiana, are visiting our house.
2. I have to rewrite only the last chapter of my book.
3. The study group that I am now attending meets on Monday evenings.
4. After I jogged for several miles, the cool glass of orange juice gave me welcome relief from the heat.
5. To register to vote, one must give a permanent home address.
6. While I was addressing the alumni association, my raincoat and umbrella were stolen.
7. Upon hearing the news of the mayor's defeat, the people in the reception hall cheered loudly.
8. To receive the scholarship, one needs a high grade-point average.
9. Even after I met Mayor Kelley, my attitude toward him remained cautious and noncommittal.
10. If all goes well, we want to visit Niagara Falls in July.
11. Shortly before noon, we had prepared almost the entire Thanksgiving meal.
12. Using a bow and arrow, the hunter killed the grizzly bear that attacked him.
13. He was sitting in front of the ski lodge wearing a bandage on his head and a leg cast that had just been put on by the orthopedist.
14. People who run marathons are occasionally injured.
15. While Nancy was visiting London, the rich collections of the British Museum occupied most of her time.

7c. Exercise 1

Sentences with faulty parallelism: 1, 2, 3, 4, 6, 7, 8, 9, 11, 12, 13

7c. Exercise 2

Sentences with faulty parallelism: 3, 4, 6, 8, 11, 12, 13, 14

Answers for Part Two

7c. Exercise 3

1. He could not decide whether he wanted to play professional baseball, become a teacher, or join the U.S. Marine Corps.
2. A good driver is alert, skillful, and careful.
3. The old witch's teeth looked as long and sharp as those of a wolf.
4. Mayor Dellworth is a woman of legislative ability who always speaks her mind.
5. The acceptance speech was tedious, rambling, and not readily understandable.
6. We were told to report to the army base because we had been placed on a 24-hour alert.
7. The house built by my grandfather and designed by my father was recently destroyed by fire.
8. My employer is not only kind but also generous.
9. My brother has always enjoyed writing essays, short stories, one-act plays, and newspaper articles.
10. I wrote Uncle Ted to ask for a loan and to see if he could write me a letter of recommendation.
11. Tell the other climbers to walk in single file, to listen to instructions from the trail leader, and to be aware of falling rocks.
12. Cousin Sue enjoyed going to movies and writing long love poems.
13. The wide receiver ran at top speed, leaped in the air, caught the ball in the end zone, and then did a little victory dance.
14. The nurse told me to rest and not to get nervous about my many problems.
15. Yosemite has beautiful scenery, clean campsites, friendly rangers, and half-tame bears.

7c. Exercise 4

1. To get to Hollywood, an aspiring actress may travel by bus, train, plane, or private car.
2. The hourly wage of a plumber or a carpenter is larger than that of a high school teacher.
3. . . . (1) you keep the profits, (2) you work your own hours, and (3) you enjoy tax advantages.
4. The hobbies I really love are woodworking and stamp collecting.
5. You can repair the tire either in the driveway or in the garage.
6. He wanted a full-time job rather than unemployment insurance.
7. Your instructions are clear and timely and have given me many valuable ideas.
8. The movie was long, confusing, boring, and overacted.
9. My business failure not only was a financial disaster but also caused damage to my ego.
10. She has worked as a dance instructor, tennis coach, and bank teller.
11. That television movie was exciting and dramatic and had an involved plot.
12. The commencement speaker concluded her address with a personal anecdote and then wished the graduates success and prosperity.
13. They were shocked when they discovered that one tire was flat and that the jack was missing.
14. During the summer, I learned to groom horses, to exercise them, and to pick winners.
15. I was told that I should report to the police department and that my license would be revoked.

7abc. Exercise 1

1. (4)
2. (4)
3. (4)

4. (5)
5. (3)
6. (1)
7. (2)
8. (3)
9. (1)
10. (3)

8a. Exercise 1

1. me
2. us
3. me
4. she
5. I
6. me
7. us
8. she
9. us
10. they
11. he
12. me
13. I
14. I
15. they

8a. Exercise 2

1. me
2. me
3. We
4. we
5. me
6. me
7. I
8. me
9. he
10. us
11. she
12. me
13. me
14. her
15. they

8a. Exercise 3

Incorrectly written sentences: 2, 5, 6, 7, 11, 12, 13

8a. Exercise 4

1. whoever
2. whom
3. whom
4. whom
5. whom
6. who
7. whoever
8. who
9. who
10. whoever

8b. Exercise 1

1. rises
2. eaten
3. frozen
4. swum
5. used
6. chosen
7. drunk
8. set
9. supposed
10. rung
11. broken
12. torn
13. thrown
14. came
15. used

8b. Exercise 2

1. bitten
2. broken
3. saw
4. chosen
5. drank
6. spoken
7. rung
8. stolen
9. known
10. run
11. swum
12. torn
13. taken
14. frozen
15. given

8b. Exercise 3

1. used
2. prejudiced
3. supposed
4. written
5. swum
6. burst
7. given
8. broken
9. threw
10. drowned
11. used
12. supposed
13. prejudiced
14. raise
15. used

8b. Exercise 4

1. lay
2. lie
3. lie
4. laid
5. laid
6. lay
7. lain
8. lying
9. lay
10. laid

8ab. Exercise 1

1. my youngest brother Bob and *me*
2. *used* to belong to
3. *whom* Lisa had known in college.
4. *We* adventurous souls
5. We *sat* down
6. She had *drunk*
7. Greg, Bob, and *I* decided
8. Bob and *me* beside him
9. Lisa *lying* ill in the bed
10. Lisa's feet were nearly *frozen*

8ab. Exercise 2

1. no one ever worked harder than *she.*
2. She *came* to be called
3. she frequently *used* to talk
4. with leaders of other civic groups and *me*
5. It was *I,*
6. She had *chosen* me,
7. She was herself *supposed* to send out
8. all of *us* prominent citizens

9a. Exercise 1

1.
2.
3. legibly,
4. session,
5. days,
6.
7. 1774,
8.
9. success,
10.
11.
12.
13. actor,

9a. Exercise 2

1. material, tired jokes,
2. den, rose garden,
3. French, Spanish,
4. brakes, . . . left,
5. loud,
6. trees, . . . billboards, . . . lines,
7. warm, sunny,
8. symphonies, quartets, concertos,
9.
10. gone, . . . visiting,
11. early, . . . breakfast, . . . horses,
12.
13. dirty, . . . harsh,

14. friends,
15. legislature,
16.
17. graduation,
18. success,
19. fans,
20.

14. drums, cymbals,
15.
16.
17. me, . . . number,
18. Oregon, Washington, Utah,
19. hot,
20.

9a. Exercise 3

1. us,
2. glove, . . . clothing, . . . books,
3. soon,
4. rainy, windy night,
5.
6. job,
7. engine, . . . pipe,
8. twelve, . . . dangerous,
9.
10. soon,
11. before,
12.
13.
14. painting, . . . brushes, . . . paints,
15.

9a. Exercise 4

1. crowd, . . . host,
2.
3.
4.
5. hostile,
6. candidates,
7. waxing,
8. free-for-all,
9. brushing,
10. after,
11. Mary,
12. silver-haired,
13. old,
14. overcrowded,
15. idealistic,

9a. Exercise 5

1. beauty,
2. Texas,
3. Odessa,
4. charming,
5. grades,
6. team,
7. *Rolling Stone,*

9b. Exercise 1

1. Restaurant, . . . lovers,
2.
3. dog, . . . affection,
4. Millay, . . . poet,
5. friend, Alexandra Ross,
6. sister, Amanda,
7. James, . . . lecturer,
8.
9. Oscar, . . . Texan,
10. novel, . . . *Jar,*
11. pizza, . . . food,
12. treasury, Alexander Hamilton,
13. book, . . . *Grass,*
14. Whitman, . . . poet,
15. Watson,

Answers for Part Two

9b. Exercise 2

1.
2.
3. Ford, . . . old,
4.
5.
6. dog, . . . puppies,
7.
8.
9. professor, . . . England,
10.
11. buses, . . . decked,
12.
13. grandmother, . . . 75,
14. Wambaugh, . . . Department,
15. Rover, . . . puppy,
16. principal, . . . accent,
17.
18. employer, . . . angry,
19.
20.

9b. Exercise 3

1. is, I believe,
2.
3. us, however,
4. crowd,
5.
6. NBC, not CBS,
7. speaking,
8. loan, . . . remember,
9. ophthalmologist,
10. seems,
11. Bradley, not Mayor Williams,
12. is, I regret to say,
13. Texas, . . . France,
14. Grandmother, we are sure,
15. salary,
16. vacation, . . . opinion,
17. period,
18. report, . . . say,
19.
20. agreed, all things considered,

9b. Exercise 4

1. lost,
2. closed,
3.
4.
5. vacation,
6. rescued,
7. morning,
8.
9. theory,
10. ride,
11.
12. sea,
13. axes,
14.
15.
16. Yes,
17. her,
18. Well,
19. patrolling,
20. No,

9b. Exercise 5

1. September 17, 1985, . . . University, Athens,
2.
3.
4. Cairo, Georgia,
5. February 12, 1809, . . . Hodgenville, Hardin County,
6. Stowe, Vermont, and Vail, Colorado,
7. July 20, 1969,
8. Drive, Agoura,
9.
10. chart,
11. Please, my friend, . . . Doe, 8 Arlington Street, Boston,
12. Robin, . . . Miami,
13. "Now, ladies and gentlemen, . . ."
14.
15. "Greetings, everyone," . . . Las Vegas,
16. "No, . . . you,"
17.
18. Well, . . . Frankfort, Germany, . . . Omaha,
19.
20. administration," she said,

9b. Exercise 6

1. was, most critics agree,
2. us, Ms. Faulkner,
3. lyrics,
4. heard, I am sure,
5. Knight, . . . city,
6.
7.
8. summer," she stated,
9. Now, my dear friends,
10. Place, St. Louis,
11.
12. aware, therefore,
13. Buck,
14.
15. accident,

9b. Exercise 7

1. aunt, . . . astronaut, . . . Fort Worth,
2. Ride, . . . space, . . . University,
3. mission, . . . dawn,
4. Athens, Georgia, . . . university,
5. appointment, Dr. Jamison, my psychoanalyst,
6. cafeteria, . . . employees, was, I assure you,
7.
8. "Judge Wilson," said the bailiff, . . . Hilton Hotel,
9. better, . . . Paris, 65 Rue Voltaire, Paris,
10. January 14, 1985, Baltimore, Maryland, and, you must agree,
11. know, Officer Purdy, . . . limit," said Mr. Baker,
12. wife, . . . council, was, I believe,
13.
14. Byrd,
15. novel, a supernatural thriller, . . . Bar Harbor,

9ab. Exercise 1

1. August 2,
2. Tavern,
3. soups,
4. Turner,
5. chef,

9ab. Exercise 2

1. Kansas,
2. wicked,
3. consequently,
4. business,
5. Dodge City,

9ab. Exercise 3

1. Diamond Lake,
2. firm,
3. quiet,
4. quips,
5. Diamond Lake,

9ab. Exercise 4

1. October 2,
2. Depression,
3. 1938,
4. business,
5. *Father,*

10. Exercise 1

1. Mustang!
2. was.
3. rises.
4. a UCLA Ph.D., came from Washington, D.C.,
5. administration?
6. Mr. and Mrs. North . . . City, N.Y.,
7. Mr. Jones and Dr. Smith . . . Georgia.
8. up!
9. Jr. . . . FBI.
10. M.D., . . . NBC.

Answers for Part Two

10. Exercise 2

1.
2. fury;
3. movie;
4.
5. Ohio; . . . Maine;
6. Missouri;
7. usual;
8.
9.
10. tea;
11. car;
12.
13. agree;
14. Cornell; Ken Lewis, Yale;
15.

10. Exercise 3

1. warning:
2. on:
3. recipe:
4. "Watergate:
5. communicates:
6. admire:
7. this:
8. always:
9. phrase:
10. analyze:
11. this:
12. decision:
13. Bob Hope:
14. supplies:
15. sweet:

10. Exercise 4

1. (September, 1902)
2. (1). . ., (2) . . ., and (3)
3. (it is actually a log cabin)
4. (would you have?)
5. (1862–1937)
6. (college football, actually)
7. (1337–1453)
8. (there were actually two)
9. (they are really white!)
10. (1859–1881)
11. (he had already drunk one too many)
12. (she is always her favorite subject)
13. (it is only a faded memory to me)
14. (Samuel Clemens)
15. (1) . . ., (2) . . ., and (3)

10. Exercise 5

1. problem—
2. left—
3. faith—
4. —no, I am positive—
5. —Ben, Don, and Julian—
6.
7.
8. problem—
9. —and try hard!—
10.
11. —Andrea and Joan—
12. make—
13. balance—
14. —do you remember Harry Edwards?—
15. —*Star Wars, Star Trek,* and *2001*—

10. Exercise 6

1. "The Armadillo" and "Five Flights Up"
2.
3. "a frozen rope"
4. "The Land of Enchantment."
5.
6. "The Law and You"
7. "Brute Neighbors."
8. "The . . . itself."

10. Exercise 7

1. *Rolling Stone*
2. *Yukon Clipper*
3. *neither . . . nyther*
4. *The New Yorker*
5. *Times . . . Herald . . . Air Force One.*
6. *accommodate* . . . *c*'s and *m*'s.
7. *joie de vivre.*
8. *Hamlet, Othello, and Macbeth.*

9. "You . . . again,"
10. "Well, that's life."
11. "Parker's Back"
12. "manifest destiny."
13.
14. "My . . . right," . . . "but . . . country."
15. "Which poet said, 'It . . . all'?"

9. *claims* [an optional reading]
10. *Playboy*
11. *TV Guide*
12. *Queen Elizabeth II, . . . Apollo XI*
13. *in pace requiescat*
14. *syzygy*
15. *Catcher in the Rye* and *The Group.*

10. Exercise 8

1. (1901–1985) . . . *The Paths of Glory*
2. Atlanta;
3. resume:
4. "I . . . death."
5. *non sequitur?*
6. (1809–1849) . . . poems; in fact, "Ulalume"
7. eraser—
8. (it . . . movie goer) . . . "The Lottery."
9. "I . . . could; . . . projects."
10. tomb;
11. ghosts;
12. football—[or football:]
13. novels: *Tar Baby, Sula,* and *Song of Solomon.*
14. "I . . . fight."
15. humor—
16. "You . . ., Jim, ". . ." for . . . *t*'s . . . *i*'s.
17. *The River City Outlook, . . . Earthly Possessions*
18. (I never get used to them) . . . Turkey;
19. "I . . . meant," asked John, "when he said, 'All's . . . well'?"
20. *Words and Meanings, . . . companion*

9, 10. Exercise 1

Benjamin Chandler Bentley the first American to scale the jagged treacherous peak of Tibet's Mount Hallal was the only son of a wealthy Boston banker. After a rebellious boyhood he was once expelled from the exclusive Durgin Park School for setting fire to the headmaster's house young Bentley entered Harvard graduating with the class of 1912. His father a stern practical Yankee expected his son to join the family firm Benjamin however had more adventurous plans. He had spent the summer of 1911 in Europe and had been introduced to the fascination of mountain climbing by Francois Dupin a skilled climber and the author of The Higher Life. Banking the world of high finance and Boston social life held no appeal to a youth of 22 one who had recently read of

Mount Hallal and longed to climb its precipitous face.

Benjamin avoided his father for several days then Mr. Bentley summoned the recent Harvard graduate to his office and offered him the post of junior partner. No Father Benjamin said standing before the elder Bentley's great oak desk I shall never be satisfied until I conquer Hallal.

On August 12 1916 after more than three years of studying the route of ascent conditioning himself to the hardships of such a climb and assembling a team of hardy experienced climbers Bentley planted a tiny American flag on Hallal's summit. Courage endurance and pride in his own destiny these are the qualities that shaped the accomplishment of Benjamin Chandler Bentley.

9, 10. Exercise 2

It has been said that the person who achieves fame in a field for which he or she has not been trained is one of history's chosen few. Lewis Carroll few people now know his real name was indeed such a person. Charles Lutwidge Dodgson 1832–1898 a lecturer in mathematics at Oxford and the author of several treatises on higher mathematics and symbolic logic is best remembered today as a writer of children's books not as a scholar and scientist. Dodgson was a shy retiring man in the presence of adults he was his happiest when he was with children for he knew loved and understood their world of imagination. Assuming the nom de plume Lewis Carroll he wrote Alice in Wonderland in 1865. Alice's adventures they were vastly popular with adults as well as children were an immediate success and Dodgson found himself a national celebrity at the age of 33. Writing in the Literary Observer on December 16 1865 one enthusiastic reviewer concluded his remarks with the following statement Charm whimsy subtle satire and richness of imagination those are the reasons that the book will be read and loved for years to come.

Six years after the success of his first book Dodgson wrote another story called Alice Through the Looking Glass in which his heroine has a series of adventures on a giant chessboard. Dodgson also wrote brilliant humorous verse his best-known work of this kind is a short poem called Jabberwocky.

On the event of his death in 1898 one admirer wrote the following lines It is true that Dodgson is dead. But Alice will live on as long as there are the young and the young at heart.